Making Sense of Homicide
A Student Textbook

Making Sense of Homicide: A Student Textbook
Adam Lynes, Elizabeth Yardley and Lucas Danos

ISBN 978-1-909976-86-3 (Paperback)
ISBN 978-1-909976-87-0 (Epub ebook)
ISBN 978-1-909976-88-7 (Adobe ebook)

Cover design © 2021 Waterside Press by www.gibgob.com

Main UK distributor Gardners Books, 1 Whittle Drive, Eastbourne, BN23 6QH. Tel: (+44) 01323 521777; sales@gardners.com; www.gardners.com

North American distribution Ingram Book Company, One Ingram Blvd, La Vergne, TN 37086, USA. Tel: (+1) 615 793 5000; inquiry@ingramcontent.com

Cataloguing In-Publication Data A catalogue record for this book can be obtained from the British Library.

Ebook *Making Sense of Homicide* is available as an ebook including via library models.

Published 2021 by
Waterside Press Ltd
Sherfield Gables
Sherfield on Loddon, Hook
Hampshire RG27 0JG.

Telephone +44(0)1256 882250
Online catalogue WatersidePress.co.uk
Email enquiries@watersidepress.co.uk

Making Sense of Homicide
A Student Textbook

Adam Lynes, Elizabeth Yardley
and Lucas Danos

With a *Special Contribution* by

Former Police Superintendent Ronald Winch

Foreword David Wilson

❈ WATERSIDE PRESS

Table of Contents

Publisher's note

The views and opinions in this book are those of the authors and not necessarily shared by the publisher. Readers should draw their own conclusions concerning the possibility of alternative views, accounts, descriptions or explanations.

About the authors

Adam Lynes is a Senior Lecturer in Criminology at Birmingham City University (BCU), where he has taught since 2012, covering topics such as criminological theory, homicide, and transnational organized and corporate crime. He has published research in such areas as serial murder, family annihilation, organized crime and knife crime, and is the author of *The Road to Murder: Why Driving is the Occupation of Choice for Britain's Serial Killers* (2017); co-author of *Serial Killers and the Phenomenon of Serial Murder: A Student Textbook* (2015) (with David Wilson and Elizabeth Yardley); and co-author (with Craig Kelly and Kevin Hoffin) of *Video Games, Crime and Next-Gen Deviance: Reorienting the Debate* (2020).

Elizabeth Yardley is Professor of Criminology at BCU. She has published extensively on such topics as homicide, domestic abuse, media portrayals of violence, and the use of technology in violent acts. She is co-author (with David Wilson and Adam Lynes) of *Serial Killers and the Phenomenon of Serial Murder: A Student Textbook* (2015). Elizabeth Yardley is passionate about making a difference to the lives of those affected by violence and challenging the myths and stereotypes that exist around crime.

Lucas Danos is a Lecturer in Criminology at BCU where he has taught since 2017. Passionate about learning and teaching, he has worked on modules across all BCU undergraduate Criminology courses. His work focuses on areas of homicide, stalking and the commodification of crime. Prior to joining BCU, he worked as a lawyer and then studied for his MA in Criminology.

Ronald Winch served for over 30 years with the Metropolitan Police Service and West Midlands Police. This included front-line Criminal Investigation Department (CID) work, as well as senior command roles in local policing, public order policing, firearms policing and as a Senior Investigating Officer (SIO) for major and complex crime, including covert (i.e. undercover) policing. He is now a Senior Teaching Fellow in Policing at BCU.

The author of the Foreword

David Wilson is one of the UK's best-known Criminologists from his work as a presenter of crime-related TV programmes. A former prison governor, he is a National Teaching Fellow and was the Founding Director of BCU's Centre for Applied Criminology, being based at BCU for many years and where he is now Emeritus Professor. His books include *Serial Killers: Hunting Britons and Their Victims 1960–2006* (2007); *A History of British Serial Killing* (2009); and *Mary Ann Cotton: Britain's First Female Serial Killer* (2017) later made into an ITV drama of the same name.

Acknowledgements

Adam Lynes

First and foremost I would like to thank Lore for her continual love and support, without which I would have given up a long time ago. Special thanks also go to the contributors to this textbook, who I know took time out of their (incredibly) busy schedules to make this possible. I would also like to thank my family for their unwavering encouragement, guidance, and who instilled in me the priceless value of knowledge. Special thanks also go to Emeritus Professor David Wilson for the Foreword. I would also like to take this opportunity to thank Bryan Gibson at Waterside Press, who saw the value of such a textbook long before it materialised.

Professor Elizabeth Yardley

I'd like to thank my colleagues and the students in the Department of Sociology and Criminology at BCU. Being surrounded by curious minds is a powerful driving force for projects like this one and we hope our contributions bring a few additional answers and even more critical questions to the table.

Lucas Danos

First and foremost, I would like to thank Professors David Wilson and Elizabeth Yardley for their continuous guidance and support throughout my academic journey. My special thanks also go to Dr Adam Lynes for conceptualising this textbook and giving me the opportunity to be part of it. I would also like to acknowledge my colleagues at BCU who have contributed to a welcoming and supportive working environment. Last but not least, I would like to thank my family for their love and constant encouragement in all my pursuits.

Ronald Winch

First and foremost, I would like to thank Kerri for her continual love and support, without which I could not have completed my part in this project. Special thanks also go to the contributors to the collection, who I know took time out of their (incredibly) busy schedules to make this possible and for their generosity in seeking my participation. Last but not least, I would like to thank my family for their unwavering encouragement, guidance, and who instilled in me the priceless value of seeking knowledge. Thank you to Emeritus Professor David Wilson for the Foreword.

Foreword

As I sit down to write this at the beginning of September 2020, the world is experiencing tumultuous times. Wild fires have ravaged both Australia and several western States of the USA; protest marches and civil unrest is proliferating, spurred on by the systematic racism of the American police; and around a million Muslims are being held captive by the Chinese government in 're-education camps.' Perhaps most pressing for much of the human race, the Covid-19 pandemic is ongoing with over 40,000 lives lost so far in the United Kingdom alone. It would seem that things will only get worse. We are on the cusp of a recession, on a level that we have not endured since the Great Depression and foodbanks across Britain are already creaking under the pressure of consistently rising child poverty. In the last week, the British Government has voted against increased regulation of social housing, despite recommendations made in the wake of the Grenfell tragedy and it would now seem that it is even prepared to break international law. Poignantly, the specific morning I am writing marks the nineteenth anniversary of the attacks on the World Trade Centre in 2001.

It may seem unusual to begin a foreword to a book with such a bleak—albeit incomplete—overview of contemporary realities. However, for me it is fitting for it displays perfectly the strength of this book, which seeks to highlight the ever-increasing need for criminology to closely, rigorously and critically interrogate the realities of homicide—the most extreme form of violence.

In opposition to the soothing, populist and stereotypical narratives of homicide which dominate mainstream discussion of the subject, this collection offers students and scholars alike a comprehensive and robust overview of contemporary homicide studies. Throughout the book, the contributors challenge orthodox accounts of contemporary violence whilst drawing upon much needed critical theoretical perspectives to explore various areas of the topic, centred within perspectives of zemiology, the political economy and critical understandings of violence from an ultra-realist perspective.

In opening this book the authors set the tone by asking, 'What is violence?' This is answered through an accessible yet nuanced discussion of the importance of both structural and symbolic forms of violence being at the fore of considerations when scholars construct their notions of homicide. This discussion then explores why some homicides are viewed as more deplorable than others. For instance, why do acts of serial murder garner wider condemnation and panic than corporate killings?

Having set a critical yet accessible opening, the writers follow on with chapters that set the foundations for a homicide textbook. They consider single murder and the theoretical perspectives on why people commit such crimes, and then serial, mass and spree killings are discussed, offering up-to-date theoretical perspectives. Increasingly relevant to what is happening in the world, the chapters that follow explore theoretical discussions of police killings and the death penalty. Continuing the deep dive into homicide related to the State, there is a chapter on genocide, which moves past the typical cases utilised—such as the abhorrent acts of violence in Rwanda and instead explores the those of reserve police Battalion 101 to show how 'ordinary men' can commit horrific acts as a collective. Following on from this is a chapter about corporate killings, which includes a section focusing on the Bhopal disaster, and brings to the fore how profit is often engrained in the causation of homicide, and which therefore also seeks to question why and how society consumes murder. The penultimate chapter of the book offers the reader an understanding of how the police in Britain investigate acts of homicide.

It is no small feat to offer such robust understandings of homicide, whilst taking the reader so fluidly between theoretical considerations and real-world applications. The book digs deeper than most student textbooks, displaying vividly and accessibly the sometimes-convoluted nature of homicide studies whilst offering new and expertly informed perspectives. Overall, this is a judicious and much needed collection at a time in which our existence is evermore enveloped by aspects of death, despair and homicide in all its various malignant forms.

Professor Emeritus David Wilson
11 September 2020

CHAPTER 1

What is Homicide?

'The Justifications of men who kill should always be heard with scepticism, said the monster.'

Patrick Ness, *A Monster Calls*

Introduction

The term homicide may appear, at least at first glance, a rather simplistic concept in which particular images and ideas spring to mind. For instance, as academics we often ask students in lectures to provide an example of what exactly constitutes homicide and, on almost all occasions, responses include such criminal acts as: serial murder, mass shooters, contract killers and occasionally domestic and confrontational homicide. It is important to note here that, when it comes to the concept of homicide, almost without exception serial killers are at the front and centre of students' awareness and, for some, one of the reasons why they enrolled on a Criminology degree. Similarly, there have been many debates and discussions around why our society is so interested in serial killers, but Wilson et al (2015) perhaps provides the most succinct yet resonate of rationales:

'The description "serial killer" has the power to fascinate and attract, as much as it shocks, repels and disgusts. We want to know more about the people whom we label in this way because they seem to operate outside of our moral universe — something which can be both frightening and exciting all at the same time.' (Ibid, p. 1)

One of the central aims of this book is to provide a thoughtful and considered analysis as to why we are so fascinated by serial murderers, whilst also shedding away some of the prevailing myths—often perpetuated by mainstream media—and to reveal the actuality of this incredibly rare form of crime. This examination into serial murder presents, as previously alluded to, only a slither of the complex landscape of homicide, and as such this book critically considers a range of homicides that are both well-known and underacknowledged.

Later in the book, in *Chapter 4* and *Chapter 8* we situate and frame society's fascination with serial murder through the lens of consumerism and commodification. But first we need to consider various other academic debates and discourses concerning why people commit acts of murder, including biological, sociological, and psychological explanations. With a more holistic understanding of the numerous approaches towards understanding why certain individuals kill, attention will then shift towards single, serial, spree and mass forms of homicide. The running theme across these chapters is that they are concerned with those forms of homicide carried out by an identifiable agent, or individual(s). *Chapter 6* and *Chapter 7* depart from this convention, and will explore those forms of homicide where an identifiable individual of responsibility or culpability is difficult to discern, including mass murder carried out at the hands of the State and those deaths caused in the pursuit of 'justice' and law and order. The final content specific chapter, *Chapter 10,* through the words of a practitioner, explores the real-world processes, procedures and challenges in the investigation of homicide in the UK. This textbook is designed to provide students with the necessary intellectual tools which will inform and enhance their academic understanding of homicide and criminology more generally.

Before we commence this exploration into these various forms of homicide, it is also important to consider the concept of violence, and how it assists in situating and framing the following chapters within wider criminological literature and theoretical frameworks. Similar to how students respond with regard to identifying types of homicide, most responses to the question 'What is violence?' involve various examples of inter-personal violence that consists of either beating, stabbing or shooting another person to death. While such responses appear, at least on the surface, as sensible and more importantly accurate, it again only reflects one facet of a much wider 'violence tapestry.'

> **Key Term: Violence**
> - Violence is often considered to be an essential component of most, if not all, acts of homicide.
> - Violence is often referred to as being behaviour involving physical force intended to hurt, damage, or kill someone or something.
> - With this in mind, most conceptualisations of violence consist of an identifiable agent inflicting harm to another individual or group (for instance, a husband killing his wife, acts of terrorism and someone who is paid to kill another individual).

Violence: A Critical Introduction

One of the central issues with the aforementioned terminology is that it alludes to a general trend amongst academics to neglect to consider the philosophy of violence. As noted by Ray (2011), the social context for 'both the performance and understanding of violence is of central importance' (p. 6). According to Bufacchi (2005) there are two ways of conceptualising violence. First, there is the often narrow 'minimalist conception' that focuses upon bodily harm through physical force (Glasser, 1998). Stanko's often cited definition of violence consists of 'any form of behaviour by an individual that intentionally threatens to or does cause physical, sexual or psychological harm to others or themselves' (2001, p. 316). This form of violence is often referred to as being direct violence, and according to Galtung (1969) represents only the tip of the 'iceberg of violence.' Its main characteristic is the fact that most of its effects are visible, for example, the physical results of violent confrontations.

Being the most popular and obvious with regards to mainstream media accounts, it is commonly thought that direct violence is the worst kind of violence, which according to Galtung is not true for precisely the reason that its visibility makes it easier to identify. It is important to note that this type of violence is the manifestation of something, not its origin, and it is in the beginning where it should be sought. Direct violence does not affect as many people as cultural and structural violence, which are the hidden part of the iceberg and will be covered next. Direct violence assists in framing the following chapters centring on various forms of homicide. Yet, as noted by Ray (2011), such a definition offers restrictive conceptualisation.

The second approach offers what Ray (Ibid, p. 8) observes as a 'comprehensive conception,' which attempts to capture forms of violence and subsequent harms not recognised by the former definitions. This latter approach, as noted by Felson (2009), attempts to capture those behaviours that do not necessarily produce harm that is 'not necessarily physical' (cited in ibid, p. 9) but that can also include social harm or a deprivation of resources. Such an approach broadens the notion of an individual agent inflicting physical harm onto a subject, and instead invokes Galtlung's (1969) concept of 'structural violence' — the deepest and most hidden component of the 'iceberg of violence.' Factors such as job insecurity, unemployment, cuts in public spending and dismantling of social welfare (to name but a few) cause social harm and can be considered violent in nature. As noted by Galtung (Ibid), structural violence is a means to describe social arrangements that place individuals in the way of harm. These arrangements are structural because they are entrenched in the political and economic organization of our social world; they are violent because they cause injury to people. It is important to stress here that neither culture nor individual agency is at fault; rather, historically given (and often economically driven) processes and forces conspire to constrain individual agency.

Žižek (2008) further explains that one should put an emphasis on this particular form of violence which 'refers to the violence inherent to the system itself: the violent consequences of the smooth functioning of the capitalist economic and political system' (in Oksala 2011, p. 475). As a consequence, he finds this form of violence in current economic capitalist structures of society that spurs 'exploitation, hunger and poverty, ecological decay, human misery, inadequate welfare systems and systemic inequality' (Ibid). Referring to the work of Kaul (2009), violence can be understood as 'not only the violence caused for economic reasons, but also [as] the violence caused by spurious economics' (Ibid, p. 299). Violence caused for economic reasons can evolve when, for example, people protest or riot against a scarcity of resources which subsequently poses threats to the security of the State. Conversely, violence caused by inherent economic structures is referring to the harm that is done to people who have to tolerate unjust structural inequalities of wages, income, resources, or opportunities. In neoliberal states, while promising growing productivity and improvement, such structural inequalities are created when the 'most vulnerable (low-skilled, manual or factory labour, women and children)' (Ibid) are deprived of opportunities, being unable to compete and hence suffer exclusion from society.

> **Key Term: Neo-Liberalism**
> - Neo-liberalism is the twentieth century resurgence of nineteenth century ideas associated with *laissez-faire* economic liberalism and free market capitalism.
> - The defining features of neo-liberalism include economic liberalisation policies such as privatisation, austerity, deregulation, free trade and reductions in government spending in order to increase the role of the private sector in the economy and society.

So too, given the increasing awareness of environmental issues, Soron (2007) has supported study of the structural violence of climate change. Similar to others forms of structural violence, such actions are not committed with malice and intent. Whilst the long-lasting impacts of climate change have been well-documented (Bonds, 2015; Hales, et al, 2014) we are witnessing immediate economic impacts of climate-related disasters. Interestingly, as noted by Bonds (2016) 'the bulk of these deaths will be experienced in the global South, among groups who contributed least to global warming but are also most vulnerable to its effects' (p. 10; see also Parr, 2014; Roberts and Parks, 2006). As noted by Soron (2007), the structural violence of climate change is created by the normal operation of global capitalism, in which corporate profits and economic growth have been prioritised over environmental well-being and justice (see also Klein, 2014; Lynch et al, 2013).

Whilst direct forms of violence such as inter-personal violence and the various forms of structural violence highlighted above represent both the tip and the most hidden part of Galtung's iceberg, cultural violence can be located within its centre. Cultural violence is a form of symbolic violence that is expressed in mainstream media, religion, ideology, language, art and education. Understanding the importance of symbolic violence is also key in understanding how we, as a society, struggle to conceptualise violence beyond physical manifestations. Žižek, building upon the work of Lacan and psychoanalysis, expands upon this notion of symbolic violence, stating that:

'…subjective violence is just the most visible portion of a triumvirate that also includes two objective kinds of violence. First, there is a "symbolic" violence embodied in language and its forms, what Heidegger would call "our house of being." As we shall see later, this violence is not only at work in the obvious—and extensively studied—cases of incitement and of the relations of social domination reproduced in our habitual speech forms: there is a more fundamental form of violence still that pertains to language as such, to its imposition of a certain universe of meaning.' (Žižek, 2008, p. 1)

Symbolic violence signifies the implicit, unacknowledged violence of capitalist intersubjective domination. For Lacan, who Žižek draws heavily from, the *symbolic* is a generally unconscious order of laws, regulations, internalised forms of oppression, and immersion into language (Lacan, 1997). Žižek utilises Lacan's conception of the symbolic to illustrate an implicit order of power and oppression that is beyond subjective (direct) forms of violence. As stated by Recuero (2015), while objective violence is easily perceived against a background of 'normality,' 'it is precisely in this background that symbolic violence stands, sustaining, through language, the current status quo' (p. 1).

To summarise, subjective violence is directly experienced intersubjectively, in relationships of dominance (So, for instance, being a victim to a physical assault). This is what we experience most overtly, therefore we have an inherent assumption that all violence is subjective in nature. Consequently, according to Žižek, we subjectivise forms of violence by attributing it to one person or one group, when really this person or group is being motivated by a much larger structure of violence. With reference to the work of Lacan and more specifically Žižek, it is suggested that we are unable to see beyond these rather myopic perceptions of violence committed by identifiable agents.

Key Term: Symbolic Violence
- The concept of symbolic power was first introduced by French sociologist Pierre Bourdieu (Bourdieu, 1979) to account for the tacit, almost unconscious modes of cultural/social domination occurring within the everyday social habits maintained over conscious subjects.
- Symbolic power accounts for discipline used against another to confirm that individual's placement in a social hierarchy, at times in individual relations but most basically through system institutions, in particular education.

As an extension, symbolic violence is the gentle, invisible, pervasive violence that is exercised through cognition and misrecognition, knowledge and sentiment, often with the unwitting consent or complicity of the dominated. Cultural violence also serves to provide justifications for individuals to destroy each other and to be rewarded for doing so. For example, while many may recoil at the thought of a serial murderer targeting and killing strangers, far fewer people may negatively respond to acts of violence in the name of country or religion. According to Galtung, often causes of direct violence are related to structural violence and justified by cultural violence. For example:

'Cultural violence makes direct and structural violence look, even feel, right — at least not wrong … One way cultural violence works is by changing the moral colour of an act from red/wrong to green/right or at least to yellow/acceptable; an example being "murder on behalf of the country as right, on behalf of oneself wrong." Another way is by making reality opaque, so that we do not see the violent act or fact, or at least not as violent.'
(Galtung, 1990, pp. 291–292)

Taking the above quote into consideration, cultural violence is the prevailing attitudes and beliefs that justify and legitimise both structural violence and various forms of direct violence, making it seem natural or unavoidable. For instance, history has repeatedly demonstrated that perceptions of superiority/inferiority based on class, race, sex, religion, and nationality are instilled in large swathes of the population, as a consequence other members of society are continually harmed by the exclusionary effects of structural violence and are routinely victims of perceived righteous or morally permissible forms of direct physical and psychological violence at the hands of others.

While this discussion concerning these various other forms of violence may appear extraneous for a book on homicide, it is important to note that Galtung (1969) stresses the entrenched inter-relationship between structural violence, cultural violence and direct forms of violence. Here Žižek refers to the work of Heidegger (in Wrathall, 2005), in which he argues that the essence of violence has nothing to do with ontic violence, suffering, war, destruction (to name but a few). Essential violence, according to Heidegger, is something that grounds or at least opens up the space for the explosions of ontic or physical violence itself. Thus, whenever people are denied access to resources, physical and psychological violence exists. This definition, in essence, removes the necessity for any intent to harm from an outcome to be considered violent. Moving forward with this re-orientation of violence, it is important to consider the words of Derrida, who states that,

'[C]ritique does not simply mean negative evaluation, legitimate rejection or condemnation of violence, but judgment, evaluation, examination that provides itself with the means to judge violence.' (2002, p. 265)

While this book is concerned with direct violence it will be useful to consider that these criminal actions—while indeed horrific—present only the exposed tip of Galtlung's iceberg. As you progress through the following chapters, keep in mind the various other forms of violence that may not be readily visible and which are hidden from view. Consider how the multitude of structural and cultural factors may have influenced, pressured or triggered such individuals, and how these same processes created vulnerabilities with regard to the victims.

In bringing this concise overview of structural and, to a degree, cultural violence to a close, it is important to reiterate that the inequalities and injustices caused by structural violence creates the space in which direct (or inter-personal) violence can manifest. As stated by Ray (2011), 'conditions of hunger, sickness and destitution are then "violence" and it is often from such structurally induced conditions that further violence emanates' (Ibid, p. 9). It is these forms of violence emanated from the structural level that will now take central attention.

Returning to direct forms of violence—the central component of most forms of homicide included in this text—it is important to highlight that such exemplars of violence can also manifest in different ways depending on motive and situational precipitators. In particular, inter-personal violence can often be separated into either expressive or instrumental acts of violence. Expressive forms of violence are often described as being those crimes motivated by factors other than material gain or money. So too, such actions are often triggered by emotional reactions that are disproportionate to the situational factors that elicit them, and such triggers may stimulate feelings of hurt or fear that are transformed into anger.

Expressive forms of violence can also include those crimes that are sexually-motivated, in which deviant sexual fantasises develop to the point at which they manifest in the form of violent, sadistic forms of sexual aggression including such acts as rape or sexually-motivated murder. It is important to stress that this form of motivation manifests in different ways across offenders. For example, the serial murderer Peter Sutcliffe (often referred to as the 'Yorkshire Ripper') did not have sexual intercourse with his victims but it is accepted that his crimes fit Brooks et al's (1988) description of serial murder in that they 'reflect[ed] sadistic sexual undertones' (cited in Castle and Hensley, 2002, p. 455). In comparison, the sexual nature of another serial murderer, Robert Black, were more overt, with reports noting that there were signs that his victims had been 'sexually assaulted' (Guardian, 2011).

In contrast, instrumental forms of violence are typically defined as being goal-oriented aggression or violence that occurs as a by-product of an individual attempting to achieve a superordinate goal. For instance, an individual who is paid in order to kill another person may not receive any internal satisfaction from that act, but it may be motivated by the prospect of a monetary reward.

It is important to note here that instrumental and expressive forms of violence do not necessarily operate or exist within a void. For example, actual crimes may be a combination of expressive and instrumental aggression. For instance, a bank robber, who is obviously after the cashier's money, may become angry at the cashier when he or she refuses to hand it over. So too, during the course of an offender's life, they may begin with either expressive or instrumental forms of violence and eventually evolve into the other. For instance, Peter Tobin, a British serial killer who was convicted of murdering three young women, started with instrumental violence before moving on to more expressive forms of offences. At the age of seven Tobin was sent to a reform school due to being difficult to control (Addley, 2009). On leaving reform school he is known to have spent some time at a young offender institution, and he was later charged with a series of robberies and burglaries ('Was Peter Tobin Bible John?,' *The Scotsman*, 2008). Whilst it would be a number of years before Tobin was charged with any sex-related offences and sexually-motivated murders, this gradual move from instrumental to more expressive forms of violence demonstrates how an individual can move between these two manifestations of violence for a variety of reasons including experience, contextual factors and perceived wants or needs.

To summarise this brief introduction to violence, it is important to keep in mind that the following sections and indeed chapters are mainly focused on what we consider to be direct forms of violence. Nevertheless, it is important to consider the words of Heidegger, Galtung and Žižek, in that the physical violence routinely displayed in the mainstream media is significantly influenced and a consequence of structural forms of violence, and that structural violence and direct violence are highly interdependent, including family violence, gender-based violence, hate crimes, racial violence, police violence, State violence, terrorism, and ultimately war.

With a more holistic understanding of the various forms of violence that can and do manifest, attention will now shift to conceptual understandings of homicide. Similar to this discussion around violence, it is important to recognise that homicide is also a contentious concept that is fraught with ambiguity and at times contradictions.

The Ambiguity of Homicide

Whilst defining homicide may appear at first glance a relatively smooth task, taking into account the sheer number of definitions and laws across the globe makes the task of a unified definition much more difficult. Here we enter the realms of the social construction of homicide, and how various cultures, laws, religions, histories and politics can shape how we perceive homicide. Before we go further it is important to summarise what exactly social constructionism is, and how such an epistemological perspective assists in explaining why there are various definitions for homicide across the globe.

Social constructionism posits the idea that knowledge is created and formed between individuals (Gergen, 1985; see also Elder-Vass, 2012). Social exchanges that take place at a routine level essentially form people's understandings of the world, and cause individuals to construct their historically and culturally relative notion of the 'truth' (Burr, 2003). So, as an example, many people in Britain during the 1960s shared a collective belief that young people were immoral and committing crimes, such as vandalism, in ever greater numbers due to events surrounding the 'mods' and 'rockers' conflict (Cohen, 2002). Due to these 'clashes' between these two youth cultures, many people came to the consensus that society was 'sick,' and that those under a certain age were prone to being immoral and cared little for the values held by society. In contrast, it is arguable that this shared belief was, in fact, the result of a combination of the media, government and various authoritative bodies such as the police (Cohen and Young, 1981) that fuelled daily interactions between people which recreated, reinforced and added to the discourse of fear towards young people. In turn, these interactions created the shared knowledge that crimes committed by young people were not only likely, but also something to be afraid of. With this classic example, made famous in the work of Cohen (2002), we can see how various societal actors and agencies can manifest and perpetuate a shared belief surrounding all manner of crime-related actions, including homicide, and as a consequence can become embedded in the Criminal Justice System.

According to the United Nations Office on Drugs and Crime (UNODC) (2013, p. 102), homicide is defined as 'unlawful death purposefully inflicted on a person by another person.' The definition provided by Eurostat (European Commission, 2010) is 'intentional killing of a person.' Despite the apparent clarity of the definitions, in practice, States have difficulties in unifying their definitions of what constitutes homicide. In England and Wales, homicide covers a range of situations where a person is killed, irrespective of the classification of killing as lawful or unlawful. For example, it includes premeditated and intentional killing, but also non-intentional killing, whereas not every country has such a comprehensive word in their lexicon. In other words, in some European countries the English terms 'homicide' and 'murder' are translated into the same word, although very much different concepts in English (Smit et al, 2012). It may seem intuitive to include the term 'intentional killing' in a book concerned with acts such as serial murder and mass killings, but this rather narrow definition excludes, e.g. killing in self-defence, killings in lawful legal interventions, those due to genuine accidents, negligence (but see manslaughter later in this chapter), or that are downgraded from murder where 'partial defences' (see later in this chapter) succeed and so reduce that offence to manslaughter. The point is that some forms of killing are omitted. This limits ability to gain an holistic sense of the landscape of homicide (UNODC, 2013).

The term 'intentional killing' is also conceptually dubious when we consider those homicides committed for reasons other than for monetary gain or revenge, for example. Let us take euthanasia as an example. Although legally possible in some countries, such as The Netherlands, Belgium and Luxembourg, in countries where euthanasia is considered unlawful it matches the term homicide, that of 'intentional killing of a person by another' (Smit et al, 2012). This example represents only a drop in the ocean with regard to the sheer multitude of scenarios, motivations and individuals (or lack thereof) involved in acts of homicide, and it extends far beyond a criminally-motivated offender killing an innocent victim.

Within the context of England and Wales, legislators and those who work within the Criminal Justice System have grappled (and continue to grapple) with these various discrepancies with relation to the act of 'homicide.' As a result, England and Wales currently has three distinct categories for homicide where the term covers offences of murder, manslaughter and infanticide.

Murder and manslaughter are common law offences (i.e. defined by case law, also sometimes called 'precedent,' rather than statute) in England, Wales and Northern Ireland (Scotland has no offence of manslaughter but does have a comparable crime of culpable homicide). The manslaughter category now includes the statutory offence of corporate manslaughter created by the Corporate Manslaughter and Corporate Homicide Act 2007, which came into force in April 2008. More generally, as well as manslaughter per se, this offence can by statute result from one of several 'partial defences' put forward by an accused person to murder (see later). The offence of infanticide was created by the Infanticide Act 1922 and refined by the Infanticide Act 1938 although this crime also existed historically at common law. There are also certain more specifically targeted criminal offences of causing death under road traffic laws, see

Chapter 8 (although this does not prevent a charge of murder or manslaughter where the facts so dictate, e.g. deliberately running down the victim).

Under the common law murder is defined as the unlawful killing of a reasonable person in being under the Queen's (or King's) peace with malice aforethought express or implied. One of the central tenets that distinguishes this offence from other acts of homicide is the nature of the *mens reus* (or 'guilty mind') that must exist on the part of the accused person on the facts of a given case. Murder was defined by English barrister, Attorney General, Chief Justice and politician Sir Edward Coke in the seventeenth century.

Key Term: Murder
'Murder is when a man of sound memory and of the age of discretion, unlawfully killeth within any county of the realm any reasonable creature *in rerum natura* under the King's peace, with malice aforethought either expressed by the party or implied by law, so as the party wounded, or hurt, etc. die of the wound or hurt, etc. within a year and a day of the same'

Edward Coke (1628-1644), *Institutes of the Lawes of England*

Let's briefly unpack Coke's definition for acts of murder. The *actus reus* of murder therefore requires the unlawful killing of any reasonable creature *in rerum natura* (in existence) under the Queen's peace. The *mens rea* of murder is 'malice aforethought,' which has been interpreted by the courts as meaning an intention to kill or intention to cause grievously bodily ('really serious') harm that results in the death of the victim or victims.

It is important to note that it is not necessary for a defendant to intend to kill a given victim. This is due to the doctrine of transferred malice, i.e. the legal rule that when intention to harm one individual inadvertently causes a different person to be hurt instead, the perpetrator's initial *mens rea* transfers to this (possibly quite unintended) other victim, with the same consequences so far as criminal liability is concerned. Furthermore, where a defendant does not intend the death of any particular victim, but simply intends to harm a random group of individuals, he or she will *prima facie* be liable due to the notion of *general malice* (in effect reckless disregard for the law in general and of the risks their actions pose to others).

With regard to 'any reasonable creature *in rerum natura*,' this element is most simply defined as any human being. A new born baby does not fulfil these requirements until it is living independent of its mother. Despite this, murder can occur if it is possible to show that the defendant intended to kill the mother and that they also intended that the child should die soon after being born.

Historically, perhaps one of the most significant weaknesses of the definition of murder was the temporal component of 'within a year and a day of the same.' This element was removed by the Law Reform (Year and a Day Rule) Act 1996. Formerly, if a victim survived for more than a year after an incident, and then died, the *actus reus* could not be considered the proximate cause of death. Advances in modern medicine and patient care, including stabilised states such as comas, which can last for more than a year before death, made this assumption no longer appropriate.

With regard to the punishment of those found guilty in court of murder, the sentence received in the UK is a *mandatory* life sentence. Where some confusion comes to the fray is the often mistaken belief that a life sentence actually means 'for the offender's natural life,' which is not correct (Appleton, 2010, p. 1). Most offenders sentenced to life imprisonment routinely qualify to be considered for release from prison after serving what if known as their 'tariff', a number of years set by the trial judge when the life sentence is imposed. This tariff may, in the worst of cases be 'whole life.' The available tariffs are set out in Schedule 21 to the Criminal Justice Act 2003. Where the tariff is less than whole life, murderers may leave the custodial environment once they have served their tariff if deemed by the authorities (the Parole Board makes its recommendation to the Justice Secretary) not to be a risk. However, with all life sentences, he or she may be recalled to prison at any time thereafter, e.g. if he or she engages, or is suspected to be at risk of engaging in, further violence. So from this perspective a life sentence does last for life.

With those given a whole life tariff, usually multiple murderers or who have committed offences of murder involving significant levels of brutality and malice, it is the case that they will likely die in prison. It has been reported that there have been around 100 such cases since the first introduction of the whole life order in 1983 (although a significant percentage of these prisoners have since died or had their sentences reduced on appeal). There are some 40 UK prisoners currently serving such a sentence. The independent Homicide

Review Advisory Group (Modernising Justice, 2018) has called for a review of the law of murder and, in particular, the whole life sentence (further details of the law and practice involved are conveniently set out in that report). This same group of experts also previously reported on public opinion concerning the penalty for murder including the operation of the mandatory life sentence (HomRag, 2011).

Infamous murderers such as Joanne Dennehy (a female spree killer), Michael Adebolajo (one of the murderers of Fusilier Lee Rigby) and Thomas Mair (the murderer of MP Jo Cox) are subject to whole-life tariffs and are unlikely ever to be released from prison. Nevertheless all those given these whole life tariffs even if it appears that they will 'never' be released, might be if an exception is made on compassionate grounds, e.g. if they are thought to be dying (this with the approval of the Justice Secretary). This requirement was a main reason why the European Court of Human Rights has declined to declare whole life sentences not to be a breach of human rights (Modernising Justice, 2018).

It is evident that the act of murder is distinct from other forms of homicide, with the differential being between levels of fault based on *mens rea* or by reason of a 'partial defence' to murder (see manslaughter below).

There are two fundamental types of manslaughter, along with further distinctions depending on the accused's defence and situational and/or contextual factors that resulted in the victim's death.

> **Key Terms: Voluntary and Involuntary Manslaughter**
> - **Voluntary manslaughter**—Whereby the defendant is found to have had the intent to kill or cause serious bodily harm to the victim. This type of conviction can only happen if the defendant successfully pleads one of three partial defences to a charge of murder: loss of self-control, reduced mental capacity or that he or she is the survivor of a suicide pact. Without one of these defences, the offence will be classified as murder.
> - **Involuntary manslaughter**—The defendant is found to be responsible for the homicide, but there is no clear intention to kill (e.g. based on motive), i.e. no *mens rea* for murder.

Voluntary manslaughter occurs when an individual kills with *mens rea*, but there is acceptable evidence of factual circumstances which reduce the defendant's culpability. The Homicide Act 1957 (as amended) provides two defences which may be raised to permit the court to find the accused guilty of voluntary manslaughter. The first is diminished responsibility (reduced mental capacity) where the accused must have suffered from an abnormality of mind at the time of the killing, which substantially impaired his or her mental responsibility for the homicide. Abnormality of mind was defined by Lord Parker, Lord Chief Justice, as a 'state of mind so different from that of ordinary human beings that the reasonable man would term it abnormal' (*R v Byrne*, 1960). Such a defence does not excuse the act, it only reduces the level of severity of the crime. It is important to note that the argument as to whether the abnormality substantially impaired the defendant's mental responsibility for the killing is a question of degree for the jury. It can also be compared with a plea of insanity (though these are rare) which connotes a more serious mental state and means that the offender will be wholly unfit to stand trial and will be detained in a secure special hospital such as Broadmoor or Rampton. Such hospitals also accommodate other mentally-ill offenders.

Second, loss of control is also a defence for the reduction of murder to voluntary manslaughter. Again, this defence does not operate to absolve the defendant of liability completely. This defence was introduced in response to concerns in relation to the former defence of provocation. That defence proved problematic and was subject to much consideration by the appeal courts. In particular, it was considered to have a gender bias in that it was too favourable to those who killed as a result of losing their temper (generally male defendants) but did not provide a tailored response to those who kill out of a fear of serious violence (often women experiencing domestic violence).

The Homicide Act 1957 also introduced the defence of 'suicide pact'. Parliament's intention was to show some compassion for those who had been involved in a such a pact but survived when the other party (or parties) to the pact died. This defence rests on 'a common agreement between two or more persons having for its object the death of all of them, whether or not each is to take his own life' (Section 4 Homicide Act 1957). Further, the accused must have had a 'settled intention of dying in pursuance of the pact.' This is to avoid people entering into a supposed pact with the disguised intention of committing murder.

With regard to sentencing for manslaughter, the maximum penalty is a *discretionary* life sentence. Graded punishments are outlined in definitive judicial guidance (Sentencing Council, 2018). Sentencing for manslaughter can be complex and the severity of punishment bestowed on someone guilty of this offence varies depending on the type of manslaughter involved, the level of culpability (voluntary manslaughter is generally perceived as more severe), whether the defendant poses a threat to the public, how best to rehabilitate the defendant and deter them from committing another crime, whether the defendant pleads guilty before the judge, and the circumstances and history of the defendant. These factors can in the case of manslaughter impact on whether they receive a life sentence, a prison term, a suspended prison sentence or even a community order or fine.

> **Key Term: Community Order**
> - This can be imposed on a defendant for offences that are serious but not so serious as to warrant custody. It means that the punishment will be carried out in the community instead of in a custodial environment.
> - A community order is made up of one or more 'requirements.' Such requirements may include, e.g. unpaid work, supervision, drug rehabilitation and/or alcohol treatment, mental health treatment, a curfew and attendance for those under the age of 25.

With regards to involuntary manslaughter, it is crucial that the facts demonstrate the *actus reus* for murder, but an absence of the *mens rea* of murder. Simply put, evidentially the defendant is responsible but no prescribed intention to kill can be established. Involuntary manslaughter covers a range of contexts and scenarios that may lead to an individual's death. In this section we will briefly examine unlawful act manslaughter, gross negligence manslaughter, and corporate manslaughter.

With regard to *unlawful act manslaughter*, there must be an intentional and unlawful act that must be objectively dangerous insofar as 'all sober and reasonable people would inevitably recognise must subject the other person to, at least the risk of some harm resulting therefrom' (*R v Church,* 1965). An example of this form of manslaughter can be seen in *R v Larkin* (1942), whereby the appellant brandished a razor, intending to frighten his mistress' lover. The mistress, who was drunk at the time, stumbled against the razor. It cut her throat and she later died. An unlawful act had been committed by the assault against the mistress. This was considered objectively dangerous to a sober and reasonable person. Another, more recent of example of unlawful act manslaughter is the death of Dean Haverley in 2016. Haverley, who was 48 at the time of his death, died as a result of a single punch thrown by 62-year-old Anthony Gardner whilst both men were at a pub. Gardner received an eight year prison sentence and at the trial Detective Inspector Stuart Blaik of Thames Valley Police said:

> 'The jury has concluded today that the single punch thrown by Anthony Gardner was not in self-defence as he claimed but was an unlawful act which caused the death of Dean Haverley [and] the CCTV clearly shows that this was not an act of self-defence but an act of cowardly violence which has resulted in Dean's death.' (BBC News, 2017)

As can be seen from this quote, *unlawful act manslaughter* covers those deaths that were an unintentional consequence of another unlawful act that, as demonstrated in the previous two examples, consist of varying degrees of physical violence. To summarise, whilst there is evidence of *mens rea* with regard to an unlawful act, this refers to the initial act, which whilst criminal was not motivated by the need or desire to kill another person (as in murder).

Gross negligence manslaughter is a form of involuntary manslaughter where the defendant is ostensibly acting lawfully. Involuntary manslaughter may arise where the defendant has caused death but neither intended to cause death nor intended to cause serious bodily harm and thus lacks the *mens rea* of murder. Whereas unlawful act manslaughter exists where the defendant commits an unlawful act which results in death, *gross negligence manslaughter* is not dependant on demonstrating an unlawful act has been committed. This form of manslaughter can be said to apply where the defendant commits a lawful act in such a way as to render the actions criminal. It also differs from unlawful act manslaughter in that it can be committed by omission or oversight. According to the Court of Criminal Appeal in *R v Bateman* (1925), gross negligence man-slaughter consists of the following components:

- The defendant owed a duty to the deceased to take care;
- The defendant breached this duty;
- The breach caused the death of the deceased;
- The defendant's negligence was gross, that is, it showed such a dis-regard for the life and safety of others as to amount to a crime and deserve punishment.

Higher penalties have been proposed for acts of gross negligence manslaugh-ter in light of events such as the Grenfell fire, in which 72 people lost their lives, and the deaths of 96 people at the 1989 Hillsborough football stadium. Despite this, there have been a number of successful prosecutions related to this form of manslaughter. In 2017 an engineer was sent to prison for three-and-a-half years when an electric gate he had installed fell on a client and killed her (Spillett, 2017). Only a month after the gate was installed, the client attempted to shut it by hand when it failed to close behind her. However, a stop device had not been fitted to prevent it sliding off the track. It fell on her and she sustained fatal injuries. A joint investigation by Norfolk Constabulary, Norfolk County Council's Trading Standards team and the Health and Safety Executive (HSE) found that the engineer had not provided the client with an instruction book or operating manual for the gate. In addition, a complete technical file, which demonstrated how the gate met the necessary safety standards, had not been produced as part of the installation. Generating the file was a legal requirement and would have identified the safety deficiencies in the installation.

In 2018, a husband and wife operating a bouncy castle that blew away in a high wind, leading to the death of a seven-year-old girl, were jailed for three years each for gross negligence manslaughter (Siddique, 2018). At the trial, the court was told that the couple had failed to anchor the inflatable to the ground securely and did not monitor the weather to ensure the castle was safe to use. At the trial, a meteorologist confirmed weather warnings were in place for the area and wind speeds and gusts increased throughout the day. The HSE said the maximum wind speed recorded was 66 kph and that the dome should not have been used in wind speeds above 38 kph.

Culpability factors have included negligent conduct motivated by the avoidance of cost or financial gain, both of which can be discerned from the above two examples of gross negligence manslaughter.

Importantly, we also need to mention here the still relatively new offence of corporate manslaughter which became law in 2008 when the Corporate Manslaughter and Corporate Homicide Act 2007 came into force. Section 1 of the 2007 Act provides that an organization is guilty of manslaughter, 'if the way in which its activities are managed or organized causes a person's death.' This new conceptualisation of homicide is designed to make companies accountable in criminal law where they fall far below what can be expected in the circumstances. The offence is often neglected in academic, legal and political discourse and many questions remain about the responsibility of company directors and crimes of the powerful more generally which are discussed when that offence is treated in greater detail in *Chapter 8*.

Conclusion

In bringing this introduction to various forms of homicide to a close, Brookman (2005) defines homicide as having a range of characteristics as opposed to a single definition. These include: the legal perspective from a different country's point of view; the type of homicide itself; the culprit; who the victim(s) is or are, social factors, political influence and involvement, environmental factors, political economy and the public's and media's responses. All of these factors are essential in order for us to grasp the complexity in defining such an act, and comprehend and appreciate the multi-faceted nature of homicide.

As you progress through this textbook and encounter many different forms of homicide it is important to remember that there are a large number of definitions, conceptualisations and theories of violence, and the actual act of a person killing another represents only a slither of what can be considered as harmful actions. So too, the concept of homicide is far from homogenous, open to political, economic and cultural influences that shape our understanding of such a phenomenon. With these important considerations in mind, the following chapters will now introduce both well-known and underacknowledged forms of homicide.

Questions to consider:
- What are the consequences of only considering violence through the perspective of just physical acts?
- How does structural violence influence the prevalence of physical violence?
- What role does cultural (symbolic) violence play in our understanding and perception of violent acts?
- To what extent do current definitions of homicide recognise these other forms of violence?
- Is *mens rea* an adequate concept to differentiate forms of homicide in the contemporary world?

References

Addley, E. (2009), 'How the police caught Peter Tobin,' *Guardian,* 16 December: http://www.theguardian.com/uk/2009/dec/16/peter-tobin-dinah-mcnicol-police

Appleton, C. (2010), *Life After Life Imprisonment*, Oxford: Clarendon.

BBC News (2017), 'Dean Haverley death: Man jailed for "single punch" killing,' 11 October: https://www.bbc.co.uk/news/uk-england-beds-bucks-herts-41584488

Bonds, E. (2015), 'Challenging Climate Change's New "Security Threat" Status,' *Peace Review: A Journal of Social Justice*, 27, pp. 209–216.

Bonds, E. (2016), 'Upending Climate Violence Research: Fossil Fuel Corporations and the Structural Violence of Climate Change,' *Human Ecology Review*, 22(1), pp. 1–22.

Bourdieu, P. (1979), 'Symbolic Power,' *Critique of Anthropology*, 4(13–14), pp. 77–85.

Brookman, F. (2005), *Understanding Homicide,* London: Sage.

Brooks, P. R., Devine, M. J., Green, T. J., Hart, B. L. and Moore, M. D. (1988), *Multiagency Investigation Team Manual*, Washington: Police Executive Research Forum.

Bufacchi, V. (2005), 'Two Concepts of Violence,' Political Studies Association, 3, pp. 193–204.

Burr, V. (2003), *An Introduction to Social Constructionism* (2nd edn.), London: Routledge.

Castle, T. and Hensley, C. (2002), 'Serial Killers With Military Experience: Applying Learning Theory to Serial Murder,' *International Journal of Offender Therapy and Comparative Criminology*, 46(4), pp. 453–465.

Clarkson, C. M. V. (1996), 'Kicking Corporate Bodies and Damning their Souls,' *Modern Law Review*, Blackwell, 59(4), pp. 557–572.

Cohen, S. (2002), *Folk Devils and Moral Panics: The Creation of the Mods and Rockers* (3rd edn.), Abingdon: Routledge.

Cohen, S. and Young, J. (1981), *The Manufacture of News: Deviance, Social Problems and the Mass Media* (2nd edn.), London: Constable.

Derrida, J. (2002), 'Force of Law: The Mystical Foundation of Authority,' in G. Anidjar (ed.), *Acts of Religion*, pp. 228–298, New York, NY: Routledge.

Elder-Vass, D. (2012), *The Reality of Social Construction*, Cambridge: Cambridge University Press.

European Commission (2010), *Europe in Figures-Eurostat Yearbook 2010*, Luxembourg: Publications Office of the European Union.

Felson, R. B. (2009), 'Violence, Crime and Violent Crime,' *International Journal of Conflict and Violence*, 3(1), pp. 23–39.

Galtung, J. (1969), 'Violence, Peace and Peace Research,' *Journal of Peace Research*, 6(3), pp. 167–191.

Galtung, J. (1990), 'Cultural Violence,' *Journal of Peace Research*, 27(3), pp. 291–305.

Gergen, K. (1985), 'The Social Constructionist Movement in Modern Psychology,' *American Psychologist*, 40(3), pp. 266–275.

Glasser, M. (1998), 'On Violence: A Preliminary Communication,' *International Journal of Psychoanalysis*, 79(5), pp. 887–902.

Guardian (2011), 'Child killer Robert Black's past revealed to Northern Ireland jury,' 7 October: http://www.theguardian.com/uk/2011/oct/07/child-killer-robert-black-trial

Hales, S., Kovats, S., Lloyd, S., and Campbell-Lendrum, D. (eds.) (2014), 'Quantitative risk assessment of the effects of climate change on selected causes of death, 2030s and 2050s,' Geneva: World Health Organization: www.who.int/globalchange/publications/quantitative-risk-assessment/en/

HomRAG (2011), *Public Opinion and the Penalty for Murder: Report of the Advisory Group On the Mandatory Sentence of Life Imprisonment for Murder*, Hook, Hampshire, Waterside Press.

Kaul, N (2011), 'How many zeroes are there in a trillion? On Economics, Neoliberalism, and Economic Justice,' *Open Democracy*: www.opendemocracy.net/openeconomy/nitasha-kaul/how-many-zeroes-are-there-in-trillion-on-economics-neoliberalism-and-econom

Klein, N. (2014), *This Changes Everything: Capitalism vs. The Climate*, New York: Simon & Schuster.

Lacan, J. (1997), *Ecrits: A Selection*, London: Routledge.

Lynch, M. J., Long, M. A., Barrett, K. L., and Stretesky, P. B. (2013), 'Is It a Crime to Produce Ecological Disorganization? Why Green Criminology and Political Economy Matter in the Analysis of Global Ecological Harms,' *British Journal of Criminology*, 53(6), pp. 997–1016.

Modernising Justice (2018), *The Case for a Review of the Law of Murder* (Foreword Sir Henry Brooke), Hook, Hampshire: Waterside Press.

Oksala, J. (2011), 'Violence and Neoliberal Governmentality,' *Constellations*, 18(3), pp. 474–486, Oxford, UK: Blackwell Publishing Ltd: http://onlinelibrary.wiley.com/doi/10.1111/j.1467-8675.2011.00646.x/full

Parr, A. (2014), *The Wrath of Capital: Neoliberalism and Climate Change Politics*, New York: Columbia University Press.

R v Church (1966), Court of Appeal (Criminal Division).

R v Larkin (1942), 29 Cr App R 18.

R v. Bateman (1925), 19 Cr App R 8.

Ray, L. (2011), *Violence and Society*, London: Sage.

Recuero, R. (2015), 'Social Media and Symbolic Violence,' *Social Media and Society*, 1(1), pp. 1–3.

Roberts, J. T., and Parks, B. C. (2006), *A Climate of Injustice: Global Inequality, North-South Politics, and Climate Policy*, Cambridge: MIT Press.

Sentencing Council (2018), *Manslaughter: Definitive Guidline*: https://www.sentencingcouncil.org.uk/wp-content/uploads/Manslaughter-definitive-guideline-Web.pdf

Siddique, H. (2018), 'Bouncy castle death: couple convicted of manslaughter,' *Guardian*, 9 May: https://www.theguardian.com/uk-news/2018/may/09/bouncy-castle-death-couple-convicted-of-manslaughter

Smit, P. R., De Jong, R., and Bijleveld C. C. J. H. (2012), 'Homicide Data in Europe: Definitions, Sources, and Statistics,' in A. C. M. Liem and W. Pridemore (eds.), *Handbook of European Homicide Research: Patterns, Explanations and Country Studies,* New York: Springer Science and Business Media.

Soron, D. (2007), 'Cruel weather: Natural disasters and structural violence,' *Transformations*, 14: https://www.transformationsjournal.org/journal/issue_14/article_01.shtml

Spillett, R. (2017), 'Workman who installed 40-stone iron security gate that fell and crushed grandmother, 56, to death in front of her granddaughter is jailed for three years for manslaughter by gross negligence,' *Daily Mail*: https://www.dailymail.co.uk/news/article-5034753/Workman-jailed-faulty-gate-killed-grandmother.html

Tombs, S. and Whyte, D. (2015a), 'Introduction to the Special Issue on "Crimes of the Powerful",' *Howard Journal of Criminal Justice*, 54(1), pp. 1–7.

Tombs, S. and Whyte, D. (2015b). 'Counterblast: Crime, Harm and the State-corporate Nexus,' *Howard Journal of Criminal Justice*, 54(1), pp. 91–95.

UNODC. (2013). 'Global Study on Homicide,' https://www.unodc.org/gsh/

'Was Peter Tobin Bible John?' (2008), *The Scotsman,* 6 December: http://www.scotsman.com/news/was-peter-tobin-bible-john-1-1302021

Wells, C. (2001), *Corporations and Criminal Responsibility* (2nd.edn.), Oxford: Oxford University Press.

Wilson, D. Yardley, E. and Lynes, A. (2015), *Serial Killers and the Phenomenon of Serial Murder: A Student Textbook*, Hook, Hampshire: Waterside Press.

Wrathall, M. (2005), *How to Read Heidegger*, London: Granta Books.

Žižek, S. (2008a), *The Sublime Object of Ideology*, London: Verso.

Žižek, S. (2008b), *Violence*, London: Profile Books.

CHAPTER 2

Single Homicide

'Murder is always a mistake. One should never do anything that one cannot talk about after dinner'

Oscar Wilde, *The Picture of Dorian Gray*

Introduction

Everywhere one might turn these days, it appears that there is an abundance of books, films, TV shows and true crime podcasts relating to violent crime or, in other words, crime that typically involves physically hurting or threatening to physically hurt someone. Among all offending behaviours that constitute violent crime such as assault, domestic violence, robbery, and hate crime, homicide appears to be the most intriguing. Humans do love a good puzzle and homicide cases set the ground for us to play the *armchair detective* (Bonn, 2014), examine the clues we are presented with, in order to find out who did it and solve the mystery — hopefully before the law enforcement authorities catch the perpetrator. It is an activity that involves an adrenaline rush, albeit in a controlled manner, in the context of the safety and comfort we are feeling in our livingrooms. There is no real risk involved. We are happy and willing to attentively explore murderous cases, whilst keeping a safe distance from them at the same time. We feel the need to maintain this distance because homicide is widely perceived to be the most serious form of violent crime, as it results in humans losing their lives and that is what the majority of us value most. Further to this, homicide has an immediate and tremendous impact not only on the victims, but also on their families and friends, individuals that social scientists tend to refer to as *secondary victims*.

The impact of homicide cases can further reach out to the wider community in which protagonists lived and operated, and is usually experienced through pervasive emotions of fear and insecurity. Once the carefully held-at-distance mediated representations of homicide become very much a physical reality, we indeed tend to put ourselves in the place of the victims, facing the alarming reality that certain factors which led to their victimisation are evident in our lives as well. Despite its devastating consequences, homicide is a relatively rare type of crime, which is exactly why most of us learn about it through media representations. *Chapter 1* of this textbook outlined what legislators and criminologists mean when they use the terms *homicide, murder* and *manslaughter*, all of which were defined with references to their socially constructed natures. This chapter takes as its main focus single homicide, meaning those homicide incidents which involve just one victim. This approach will help us differentiate this form of homicide from multiple homicide or multicide (spree, serial, mass killing) that typically involves two victims or more. It specifically aims to provide a descriptive overview of the things we know so far in relation to such homicides, thereby serving as a solid basis for subsequent chapters to build upon.

Existing trends and typologies will be explored, critically evaluating their usefulness. In this context, case studies will be utilised in order to reinforce key arguments and to further showcase the applicability of theoretical frameworks in real life situations. Finally, this chapter pays particular attention to the relationship between homicide and other criminal behaviours, specifically stalking, which seems to be on the rise at the time of writing.

Trends of Single Homicide

Considering the statistical picture of homicide enables the extensive analysis of identified patterns, comparisons across case studies, the careful evaluation of theoretical frameworks, and efficient policy planning. Homicide data, extracted from the Home Office Homicide Index, effectively helps us to gain a deeper understanding of the phenomenon and inform our responses to it. This is predominately the result of the detailed volume of information entailed. As Eisner (2017) outlines, homicide statistics typically include the characteristics of the offender and the victim, usually with specific references to their age, sex and social class (and possibly their race or ethnicity). They also contain valuable information in relation to the crime in its own right, such as the time and location, and the weapon that was used, as well as information regarding the court process, for instance conviction rates.

If we want to explore the landscape of homicide, we first need to outline its scale, to address the simple question 'How much homicide is there?' This should provide a solid basis upon which to subsequently consider its individual characteristics and patterns. According to the Office for National Statistics (2020) there were a total of 662 single homicide incidents in England and Wales during the year ending March 2019. What do these figures tell us about the scale of homicide though? To answer the question, we need to put the figure into context, and specifically consider the volume of offences in terms of resident population. We then see that the incidence rate for single homicide is considerably low, with approximately eleven homicides recorded per million population during the year ending March 2019. This helps us gain a much more balanced understanding of the phenomenon, and subsequently to critically evaluate media reports that tend to exaggerate its proportions. What should be further noted is that this numerical prevalence of homicide in England and Wales is often conceptualised in relation to the lower homicide numbers of Scotland and Northern Ireland. Homicide figures of the Scottish Government and the Police Service of Northern Ireland for the year ending March 2019 pale in comparison indeed, as there were only a total of 60 and 26 homicide cases recorded in Scotland and Northern Ireland respectively. But why is there such a considerable difference between these jurisdictions?

Brookman (2005) explains that England and Wales has chronically drawn the largest share of homicide due to its population being considerably higher than the population of Scotland and Northern Ireland. Things are quite different though when one considers these jurisdictions in terms of homicide rate. For example, approximately 11.2 homicides were recorded per million population in both 2018 and 2019 in Scotland, a number that is quite close to the above outlined figure for England and Wales. This simply means that people inhabiting these countries are essentially at the same risk of being killed. What should be further noted is that the current homicide rate in Scotland constitutes a significant drop. Scotland has chronically had a higher homicide rate than England and Wales, in certain years one-and-a-half or even two times higher (Brookman, 2005). The current statistical drop in Scotland is widely attributed to its Violence Reduction Unit (VRU) that was established back in 2005, with the aim of dealing with all forms of violent crime, essentially undertaking a public health approach towards that end. Drawing upon that success, a VRU was established in London in early 2019. Later in August of that year, funding was announced for 18 Police and Crime Commissioners in order to set up VRUs across England and Wales. The current rise in homicide rates clearly necessitates a more collective response, which is why police, local communities, and health and education agencies are asked to work together towards understanding the causes of violent crime and subsequently inform- ing their policy, in order to deal with the issue effectively (UK Government, 2019). In this context, the question that needs to be addressed is why homi- cide numbers in England and Wales appear to be on a steady rise during the past decade, specifically since year ending March 2008. This is explained in the next chapter that is predominately concerned with theoretical explanations of homicide. Preceding this analysis however, it is important that we now focus on certain types of homicide, in order to understand the nature of the phe- nomenon and to outline the methodological approaches social scientists have adopted in their attempt to make sense of it.

Types of Single Homicide

Typologies constitute well-established tools that social scientists employ, in order to classify human behaviour into neat categories, quickly make sense of case studies which fall under the outlined classifications, provide a point of refer- ence for academic discourse on particular subject areas, and facilitate relevant empirical research and crime measurement. Along these lines a divergent set of typologies in relation to the crime of homicide has been produced, focusing on a wide range of such criteria as legislation, age, sex, motivation, the relation- ship between the victim and the offender, and the context in which the killing took place. Simply put, one can examine homicide from a variety of different perspectives. It is important that we touch upon these typologies, in order to be able to critically evaluate their usefulness.

As outlined in *Chapter 1,* homicide is the broad term used to describe the killing of a human being, irrespective of its classification as lawful or unlawful. Examples of lawful homicide would be the killing of a human being during war combat or the implementation of a lawfully ordered death penalty (Brookman et al, 2017). According to existing legislation in England and Wales, murder, manslaughter and infanticide are the main criminally legal outcomes, and may be terms used to describe the same act when a killing is perceived to be unlawful (As mentioned in *Chapter 1* here are also certain special categories, not discussed in detail in this book, under road traffic law, such as causing death by dangerous driving: see *Chapter 8*). Looking at the statistical data, during the year ending March 2019 a total of 250 people were convicted of homicide (Homicide Index, 2020). Further considering its legal categories, we specifically see that 178 people were convicted of murder, 71 of manslaughter and only one of infanticide. As a matter of fact, during the past decade there have only been eleven convictions of infanticide, a clear indication of its extreme rarity in modern times. This particular typology has proven to be useful for social scientists to draw upon, essentially serving as a basis upon which to discuss homicide, evaluate conviction rates and conduct relevant research. Its scope is quite narrow though, as it specifically focuses upon legal codes, thereby neglecting key socio-demographic information that, when taken into account, help us shed light into the various aspects of this complex phenomenon.

Considering the age of the offender, for instance, can help us further distinguish homicide as adult or juvenile homicide, terms used to refer to killings committed by those over or under the age of 18, respectively. A considerable body of research has specifically focused on explaining juvenile homicide that accounts for approximately six per cent of all homicides in England and Wales (Rodway, Norrington-Moore, While, Hunt, Flynn and Swinson, 2011). Why is it important to place so much emphasis on this specific category of homicide though, considering its rarity? The answer to this question can be found in the meaning that we attach to conceptions of adolescence. Child-perpetrated homicide constitutes both a concern for society and a controversial issue, as it challenges well-established notions of childhood and innocence. The murder of James Bulger by two ten-year-old boys, Jon Venables and Robert Thompson, in 1993 was a defining moment for the Criminal Justice System, resulting in politicians and penal reformers re-theorising penal sensibilities and re-considering the morals and values that we attach to young offenders. The names of the victim and the perpetrators remain deeply rooted in public consciousness, still constituting a recurring theme in debates surrounding criminal responsibility, imprisonment and the rehabilitation of youth offenders in England and Wales. The impact of the case was profound, rightfully sparking academic interest. Further exploring the phenomenon of juvenile homicide, there appears to be consensus in terms of it being predominately perpetrated by male offenders, whose chief methods of killing involve either beating, or strangling, or stabbing their victims. Explored motivations are various and diverse in nature, including physical abuse, substance abuse, behavioural problems and mental health issues. It has also been outlined that an even number of male and female victims tend to be targeted by juvenile homicide offenders (Hammond and Ioannou, 2015).

According to the Homicide Index (2020), a total of only ten young people, all male, under the age of 16 were convicted of homicide in the year ending March 2018. Consistent with data of previous years, the biggest volume of recorded convictions belongs to those in the 16–24 age group (89 convictions), followed by those aged 25-to-34-years-old (60 convictions), those aged 35-to-44-years-old (46 convictions), and finally those aged 45-to-54-years-old (30 convictions). And here lies a problem in terms of the statistical data in relation to juvenile offenders. Whilst academic literature and existing legislation refer to juvenile homicide offenders as those who are aged below 18-years-old, we see that statistical data tends to lump people together. Specifically, the 16-to-24 age group appears to be a problematic one, as it essentially encompasses both juvenile and adult homicide offenders, making it difficult for us to put the available information of 89 convictions into these theoretically established categories. Further, looking into the victims of homicide in terms of their age, we notice that the 16-to-24 age group is the second most vulnerable one with a total of 113 recorded victims for the year ending March 2019. How many of these victims were adults though? We are facing the same issue here, as before. The statistical data available does not help us draw firm conclusions with regards to the victimisation rates in terms of age. This is not to doubt the usefulness of the Homicide Index that still remains a source that provides continually updated and publicly available information, thereby ensuring public aware-ness and transparency in police crime recording methods. The argument that is put forward here is that there needs to be consistency between conceptual frameworks and crime measurement. Finally, it is worth noting that the 25-to-34 age group is the most vulnerable one with 136 recorded victims in the same time period. We see here that these two particular age groups constitute a peak both in terms of offending and victimisation. Age however is only a specific facet of our identities. There are other important factors that shape who we are and how we choose to act. For us to obtain a more thorough understanding of homicide, focus should be placed upon these factors as well.

This rationale pretty much explains why social scientists have examined homicide through the lens of sex, exploring the individual characteristics of male and female homicide offenders. The first thing that needs to be outlined at this point is that homicide is by and large a male phenomenon, with men chronically and persistently leading the way both in terms of offending and victimisation (Dobash and Dobash, 2015; Monckton-Smith, 2012). This simply means that offenders and victims of homicide are predominately male. To further put things into perspective, 250 suspects were convicted of homicide in the year ending March 2019, a staggering 229 of whom were men. This leaves us with only 21 female suspects being convicted. Considering the victims of homicide, data for the year ending March 2019 illustrates that the homicide rate for males was almost double that for females. Specifically, 64 per cent of homicide victims were male, as opposed to 36 per cent female (Homicide Index, 2019). What should be further noted is that men tend to kill both men and women, with *femicide* being a specific term used to refer to those cases where men kill women. The average age of male homicide offenders is 29. By contrast, women usually kill men that they are intimately connected with or their own children. The average female homicide offender is 25-to-40-years-old, has below average education, is unemployed, economically disadvantaged, has suffered domestic abuse, whereas substance misuse appears to be another risk factor (Brookman, 2005). Putting the pieces of the puzzle together in terms of the sex of homicide offenders, we can begin to explore more specific patterns. For instance, when men and women kill, how do they usually commit their crimes? According to Brookman (2005) both male and female homicide offenders tend to kill their victims by using a sharp instrument. Recent data for the year ending March 2019 confirms this observation, as approximately 39 per cent of recorded homicide cases involved one. Other frequent causes of death for male victims involved beating, whereas for female victims it is strangulation and asphyxiation.

Drawing upon existing typology we can further divide homicide in terms of motivation and to address the simple question why men and women kill. An abundance of different, unrelated motives have been proposed throughout the years, usually relating to the psyche of the offender and the victim-offender relationship (Dobash and Dobash, 2015). Homicide offenders can be linked to their victims in various ways: they can be friends, family members, or acquaintances. Of course, there might be no prior relationship at all, meaning that the offender and the victim can be strangers. The list provided here in terms of motives is not an exhaustive one. The focus is, rather, put on frequently cited and easily distinguishable motives for homicide. Specific categories emerge such as confrontational homicide, revenge homicide, sexual homicide, and mercy killings. The first two types of homicide discussed here, confrontational and revenge, are primarily related to male offenders, thereby falling under the overarching umbrella of masculine homicide. According to Polk (1994), *confrontational homicide* is a term used to refer to those incidents where a spontaneous confrontation results in the death of one of the combatants, irrespective of whether the offender or the victim was the first to resort to physical violence. This indicates how this type of homicide is usually unplanned, with the killing constituting an escalation of the spontaneous argument. It usually takes place amongst friends, acquaintances, and strangers. As a concept, it is primarily related to characteristics that are stereotypically attributed to men such as competition, aggression, selfishness and domination. This explains why the underlying theme in confrontational homicide cases is honour (Daly and Wilson, 1988), whereby men choose to respond to offensive remarks directed at them or their female partners by resorting to physical violence. By contrast, *revenge homicide* is a term used to describe those homicide cases where the offender chooses to use violence in order to harm the victim as a means of conflict resolution (Polk, 1994). This type of homicide is usually planned, rational, and therefore involves a greater element of risk, in the sense that its premeditated nature is more likely to result in the offender being convicted of murder. Revenge homicide usually takes place amongst friends and acquaintances, indicating that the offender and the victim have usually known each other for a considerable amount of time. Further focusing on the psyche of the offender, when sexual gratification is their primary motive, then the kill-ing can be classified as *sexual homicide*. Despite the absence of a universally accepted definition of the term, anger, sadism, control and personality disor-ders, such as psychopathy, appear to be common themes in sexual homicide cases (Kerr, Beech and Murphy, 2013). It is worth noting that these themes are usually identified in cases of sexual assault, which is why sexual homicide is widely perceived to be an escalation or an extreme form of this kind of crimi-nal behaviour. Given the intention to control the victim sexual homicide is usually premeditated and planned.

By contrast, *mercy killings* involve the deliberate action of ending a life as a means of relieving the pain and suffering of the victim. In this sense, the motive behind the killing can be seen as more altruistic. It usually takes place amongst family members and friends. *Euthanasia* is the more medical term used to describe the same act when a doctor kills a patient who suffers from a painful disease that cannot be cured (Jackson and Keown, 2012). The term derives from the Greek words *Eu* and *Thanatos*, which mean good and death, respectively. Remaining a highly controversial issue across the world, laws regu-lating euthanasia vary by country. Much like mercy killing, euthanasia is still illegal in the UK, meaning that individuals who help or encourage someone to die could face charges of murder or manslaughter according to the exact circumstances. In practice prosecuting authorities have been relatively tolerant where, e.g. terminally-ill relatives have been taken to specialist clinics abroad.

Having touched upon existing typologies in terms of motive, we have pro-vided a solid basis upon which to discuss explanations of homicide in the next chapter. What are the limitations of this approach however? What is problem-atic about aiming to understand homicide by solely focusing on the identified motivation? The first thing we need to be mindful of is that the list provided here is not exhaustive. Homicide can be committed by both men and women for other reasons, such as monetary gain and jealousy. The second thing we need to consider is that motives are not mutually exclusive within any list we may make, meaning that more than one motivation could be potentially iden-tified in a specific event.

Finally, we should keep in mind that existing information of particular cases might not be adequate enough to shed light on the motivation of the offender. The Homicide Index indeed acknowledges the unspecified circumstances of certain homicide cases, when it is deemed impossible to identify the reasons behind the killing. This explains why homicide has been explored beyond the narrow scope of psychological motivation. Homicide can indeed be further conceived in terms of the context in which the event took place. We can therefore now discuss domestic homicide and homicide in the streets. The Homicide Index (2019) specifically refers to residential homicide and homicide committed in public spaces. Residential homicide takes place in houses and residential homes, including spaces like gardens, garages and corridors.

Data for the year ending March 2019 reveal that 43 per cent of all male homicide victims and the vast majority (77 per cent) of female victims died in a domestic setting, which explains why this specific form of homicide has sparked academic interest. Brookman (2005) explains how domestic abuse and control are two key themes when examining domestic homicide. When men kill women in a domestic setting, homicide is often conceptualised as an escalation of abuse on their part. The act of killing usually takes place when men feel that they are losing control over their abused victim or victims. Homicide is thereby viewed as a final means through which they exert control over them. On the other hand, when women kill their male intimate partners, homicide tends to be seen as an extreme response to their abuser. A response that aims at women regaining some control for themselves. Theoretical explanations of domestic homicide are discussed in more depth in other chapters though and we should therefore move now on to the second form of homicide identified here. Essentially, homicide in *public spaces* takes place in streets, licensed premises, such as nursing homes, hotels, and lodging houses, open outdoor areas, such as the areas around pubs and restaurants, and other public spaces, such as car parks. This form of homicide is usually confrontational and thereby predominately involves male offenders and victims. Looking at recent statistical data confirms this assumption, as we notice that 52 per cent of all male victims died in public spaces for the year ending March 2019, as opposed to only 21 per cent of female victims who died in a public area.

Further considering the circumstances under which homicide takes place, scholars have drawn our attention to homicide committed in the course of some other crime (Polk, 1994). The Home Office does acknowledge these circumstances by making specific reference to homicide committed in furtherance of theft or gain, thereby including such criminal behaviours as burglary, robbery and armed robbery. In these instances, homicide plays a secondary role in the sense that offenders aim at committing one of the aforementioned crimes and only resort to killing their victim under specific circumstances, such as when their threats of violence are not taken seriously or when their victims attempt to defend themselves or their property. It should be noted that the offenders involved in the initial crime might also end up being killed if the victim resorts to physical violence. Polk (1994) draws particular attention to both scenarios, explaining that this form of homicide usually involves offenders and victims that are unknown to each other. Of course, this is down to the fact that crimes such as armed robbery usually take place amongst strangers. We can therefore see how in these events the nature of homicide tends to be consistent with the nature of the crime in the course of which it was committed. We can further understand this connection by exploring homicide in relation to other criminal offences, such as stalking which, as we have already noted, appears to be on the rise. The focus here is specifically placed on femicide that is preceded by stalking, an interrelation that has been barely explored by academics. Having touched upon femicide earlier in this chapter, we should now explain what stalking means. Despite an existing absence of a universally accepted definition, stalking can be defined as a series of unwanted and persistent actions directed at an individual by another which result in personal harassment (Sheridan, 2001). Heavy press coverage of stalking cases back in the mid-1990s in the UK resulted in the Protection from Harassment Act 1997, which constitutes the first legal framework aimed at regulating stalking behaviours (Ellison and Akdeniz, 1998). However, public concern and doubt about the extent to which this Act dealt with the issue adequately led to the Protection of Freedoms Act 2012, which now regulates a wider range of stalking offences (Reilly, 2017). Interestingly, irrespective of its classification as a criminal offence, a legal definition of stalking (i.e. as opposed to harassment which is defined by the 1997 Act) is yet to be reached. Despite the absence of a unified definition, stalking has been the subject of academic theorising. For instance, Mullen et al (1999) have described five different types of stalkers based on their psychological motivations. These are the rejected stalker, the intimacy seeker, the incompetent, the resentful, and the predatory. Much like homicide, stalking is by and large a male phenomenon, considerably more prevalent though, which explains why only a small portion of stalking cases end up with the killing of the victim.

Research conducted by Smith, Szymanska and Haile (2017) has explored femicide cases, highlighting that stalking behaviours were identified in an alarming 94 per cent of these. The focus here is primarily placed upon male homicide offenders who killed an ex-partner, after showcasing behaviours such jealousy, obsession, fixation and control. In these cases homicide is viewed as an escalation of the emotional journey stalkers embarked upon. Killing their victim is the ultimate means through which the offenders exerted control over them.

The case of the murder of Shana Grice effectively helps us to understand the dynamics between stalking and femicide. Shana was murdered by her ex-boyfriend, Michael Lane, in August 2016 after he had stalked her following their break-up. He could not accept the end of their relationship, much less the fact that Shana had moved on to a new one. Michael would thereby fall under the rejected stalker category. He indeed engaged in various stalking behaviours, such as putting a tracker device on her car so that he would know of her whereabouts, sending her unwanted flowers, snatching her phone, grabbing her hair, entering her home, calling her from a blocked number, wandering outside her home. His controlling behaviour escalated on August 25 when he once again let himself into Shana's house, this time in order to slit her throat before setting fire to her bedroom.

We can see here that the lines between stalking and femicide are considerably blurred, as the two criminal behaviours co-exist, driven by the same pervasive emotions of rejection, fixation and control. Lane lost control of his actions and did not know what he was doing. Rather, the killing was planned and premeditated, as he waited for her to be alone in the house. Murdering Shana was simply the ultimate means through which he would control her, an escalation of his stalking journey. What is also noteworthy is that Shana had raised most of these incidents with the police, who did not it seems take her complaints seriously and even dismissed her by giving her a fixed penalty notice.

Generally, stalking incidents tend to be under-reported and, when they do get reported, they might be dismissed, as certain behaviours that constitute stalking, such as receiving flowers or phone calls, may appear to be innocent. The main point that should be noted here is that stalking can be a key indicator for homicide, thereby necessitating more academic attention to be placed upon its inter-relation with homicide.

Conclusion

This chapter has focused on single homicide with specific references to its trends and types. The main purpose has been to provide an outline of the scale and nature of the phenomenon. Single homicide remains a relatively rare type of crime despite its more recent statistical growth. It is for the most part a male phenomenon both in terms of offending and victimisation.

From a theoretical perspective, homicide has been explored from a variety of different angles. Each angle is essentially providing us with specific forms of homicide. This is why it was deemed necessary to touch upon the various typologies such as murder, manslaughter, infanticide, juvenile homicide, male-perpetrated, female-perpetrated, confrontational, revenge, sexual homicide, and mercy killings, as well as domestic homicide and homicide in the streets. What should be noted is that these typologies are not exhaustive, meaning that homicide can be divided in more ways than the ones discussed here. For example, based on the form of violence involved in the homicide event, we could further distinguish homicide into expressive and instrumental, concepts outlined in the introduction to this textbook. Similarly, based on the stage of police investigation, we could consider homicides that are solved or unsolved. The latter are usually committed under unspecified circumstances and result in the omission of relevant data, such as key socio-demographic characteristics of the offender. There are indeed plenty of typologies we could be referring to. They are all useful as each one sheds light on a different corner of homicide, enabling an in-depth analysis of the phenomenon once information is collated.

Questions to consider
- Why do media reports on homicide tend to perpetuate its apparent statistical rise?
- What are the key benefits and limitations of being preoccupied with typologies?
- Should the age of criminal responsibility be raised in England and Wales?
- Should mercy killing and euthanasia be legalised in the UK?
- What other crimes constitute key indicators for homicide?

References

Brookman, F. (2005), *Understanding Homicide*, London: Sage.

Brookman, F., Maguire, E. R., Maguire, M. (2017), *The Handbook of Homicide*, New Jersey: Wiley & Sons.

Bonn, S. (2014), *Why We Love Serial Killers: The Curious Appeal of the World's Most Savage Murderers,* New York: Skyhorse Publishing.

Daly, M. and Wilson M. (1988), *Homicide*, New York: Aldine de Gruyter.

Dobash, R. E. and Dobash, P. D. (2015), *When Men Murder Women*, New York: Oxford University Press.

Eisner, M. (2017), 'Interpersonal Violence on the British Isles, 1200–2016,' in Liebling, A., Maruna, S., McARA, L. (eds.), *The Oxford Handbook of Criminology*, pp. 565–586, Oxford: Oxford University Press.

Ellison, L. and Akdeniz, Y. (1998), 'Cyberstalking: The Regulation of Harassment on the Internet,' *Criminal Law Review* (December Special Edition, 'Crime, Criminal Justice and the Internet'), pp. 29–48.

Government UK (2019), Funding for Violence Reduction Units announced: https://www.gov.uk/government/news/funding-for-violence-reduction-units-announced (Accessed 20 December 2019).

Hammond, L., and Ioannou, M. (2015), Age Effects on Juvenile Homicide Perpetration, *Journal of Criminal Psychology*, 5(3), pp. 163–176.

Jackson, E. and Keown, J. (2012), *Debating Euthanasia*, Oxford and Portland Oregon: Hart Publishing.

Kerr, K. J., Beech, A. R. and Murphy, D. (2013), 'Sexual Homicide: Definition, Motivation and Comparison with other Forms of Sexual Offending,' *Aggression and Violent Behavior*, 18(1), pp. 1–10.

Monckton-Smith, J. (2012), *Murder, Gender and the Media. Narratives of Dangerous Love*, New York: Palgrave Macmillan.

Monckton-Smith, J. Szymanska, K., Haile, S. (2017), *Exploring the Relationship Between Stalking and Homicide*, Suzy Lamplugh Trust.

Mullen, P. E, Pathe, M. Purcell, R. and Stuart, G. W. (1999), 'Study of Stalkers,' *American Journal of Psychiatry*, 156(8), pp. 1244–9.

Office for National Statistics (2020), *Homicide in England and Wales: Year Ending March 2019*, London: Office for National Statistics.

Office for National Statistics (2020), *Appendix Tables: Homicide in England and Wales*, London: Office for National Statistics.

Polk, K. (1994), *When Men Kill: Scenarios of Masculine Violence*, Cambridge: Cambridge University Press.

Reilly, A. (2017), *Legislative Position on Stalking and Relevant Statistics in the UK and the Republic of Ireland*, Northern Ireland Assembly, pp. 1–40.

Rodway, C., Norrington-Moore, V., While, D., Hunt, I. M., Flynn, S. and Swinson, N. (2011), 'A Population-based Study of Juvenile Perpetrators of Homicide in England and Wales', *Journal of Adolescence*, Vol. 35, pp. 19–28.

Sheridan, L., Davies, G., Boon, J. (2001), 'Stalking Perceptions and Prevalence,' *Journal of Interpersonal Violence,* 16(2), pp. 151–167.

CHAPTER 3

Explanations of Homicide

'Evil begins when you begin to treat people as things'

Terry Pratchett, author

Introduction

Our culture is saturated with representations of homicide. It is the staple topic of crime drama and documentaries, crime novels and internet streaming series, it grabs news headlines. There is an intrinsic, irrevocable and irreversible sense of harm involved in the act of one person killing another. Stories of the causes and consequences of homicide provide the basic ingredients for the kind of morality tales that inform our sense of collective identity as members of society. Homicide is a subject we all converge around in what Seltzer (2008) calls a 'wound culture.' We all have an opinion on it, we all believe that it is, to varying degrees, wrong and should be avoided.

Homicide is an important barometer for good and evil. Pure and dangerous. Explanations of this harm are stories of our social reality, they help us make sense of the world and other people's behaviour, they point us towards who is 'like us' and away from who is not, who is an 'outsider.' We use them to set and maintain standards of what a good citizen looks like, of what socially acceptable behaviour is. Homicide is not the 'cold-blooded' act that fiction writers and television script writers often portray it as. It is not about strangers randomly attacking. It is rather a 'hot-blooded' conflict that most often involves a victim and a perpetrator who are known to each other. This is the very essence of what the sociologist C Wright Mills described when he talked about private troubles that become public issues. The aim of this chapter is to explore how theory can help us explain homicide and to consider potential answers to the question, 'Why do people kill?' In so doing, it draws upon three theoretical frameworks: micro; macro; and integrated.

Micro, Macro and Integrated

The distinction between micro and macro, agency and structure, the personal and the collective — is well-established in the social sciences. The 'micro' focuses upon the individual. In criminology, we often talk of 'psychopathology': the things we perceive to be *wrong* with a person that impacts upon their behaviour. Some micro approaches emphasise the ability of individuals to exercise free will and self-determination. Others are more *deterministic* — looking at forces internal or external to the individual which *compel* them to behave in certain ways. Micro approaches can be seen in biological perspectives on crime and within some branches of psychology. The 'macro' on the other hand explores how wider forces like the economy, political system and culture shape and influence human behaviour. This approach can often be seen in fields such as social and evolutionary psychology, as well as sociology. Integrated approaches attempt to bring micro and macro together, bridging the vast chasm between these two schools of thought.

A range of theoretical standpoints have been used to make sense of homicide. They are based on a plethora of factors, including different assumptions about human nature: are people fundamentally good, fundamentally bad, or neither? Are they completely free and active agents, constructing their own social realities in their interactions with others around them? Are they puppets on strings, their behaviour determined by forces outside of their control? Is it a combination of both? These are intrinsic dilemmas for social sciences and criminology. When we examine the most extreme end of human behaviour — homicide — we have an opportunity to consider these questions in a more meaningful and revealing way than is possible when looking at other types of human action. It's important to remember when examining explanations of homicide that particular approaches are favoured at specific points in history. There are periods in which one type of approach emerges as dominant. These trends and fashions are not coincidental. How society explains homicide can be revealing about the very nature of society itself — for example in terms of the relationship between the citizen and the State, and how that society is organized and governed. Throughout this chapter, as we look at different explanations for homicide, we consider the broader context in which these explanations have become popular. We begin with micro explanations.

Micro Explanations for Homicide

Micro explanations focus on individual attitudes, beliefs and behaviours. Such approaches emphasise factors that are internal to an individual and include things like their psychology and biology. They tend to position offenders as pathological, as fundamentally different from the rest of us. Those who take the lives of others are considered aberrant and abnormal. There is a clear dichotomy between 'us and them.' This is a popular way to theorise about homicide in a society which places an emphasis on individualism and personal responsibility and believes that the role of the State in the lives of private citizens should be a minimal—or *laissez-faire*—one. These approaches were prominent at the dawn of criminology in the 1800s—for example in the work of Cesare Lombroso, who examined the physiological characteristics of criminals. Micro explanations reappeared again from the 1970s, a period in which neoliberal governments rose to power across the Western world and placed the onus on individual citizens to look after themselves and their families, minimising their reliance on the State. During this period, micro approaches gained traction not just in terms of criminal justice but also in relation to mainstream media—very rarely did news stories or reports look beyond the individual psychology in trying to explain why people kill. Within this section, we explore two varieties of micro explanation—biological and psychological.

Biological Explanations

Biological explanations of homicide fall within the paradigm of individual positivism. This approach assumes that criminality is generated largely by forces within the individual and that a homicide offender is a distinct category of person with a predisposition to violence and aggression. The work of Cesare Lombroso, mentioned above, is a key example of individual positivism. At the time Lombroso was developing his studies, phrenology had gained significant traction as a way of explaining people's behaviour. It is based on the premise that the contours of the human skull reflect individual character and, as such, criminals would be physically different from non-criminals because their character was influential in their offending behaviour. Criminal behaviour was built on a physiological foundation.

Lombroso studied the facial features of over 4,000 criminals and concluded that the appearance of someone's head was a powerful predictor of what crimes they would commit. He stated that criminals in general had features such as large ears, sloping foreheads and protruding jaws and that murderers would have bloodshot eyes and curly hair. Lombroso argued that these people were 'born criminals'—their fate was sealed by their physiology—an approach also known as *biological determinism*. They were othered and considered 'less than,' atavistic throwbacks who had not evolved to the same extent as other human beings. Later studies, which drew attention to the importance of situation, culture and environment in offending led to Lombroso's work falling out of favour and it is now considered to be the crudest form of biological explanations of homicide. However, remnants of his approach can be found in some contemporary biological theories. Indeed, theories which examine the biology of homicide offenders and consider the ways in which they are physiologically different from those who have not committed this crime have seen something of a resurgence in recent years due to advances in genetics and the neurological sciences. These contributions will now be considered.

Neurology is a branch of medicine which explores the central nervous system. Neurological explanations of homicide examine the brain and consider the extent to which brain dysfunction is associated with behaviours that result in harm to other people—for example, aggression, violence and homicide. One part of the brain explored in such studies is the frontal lobe. The frontal lobe includes different components, for instance the amygdala, considered to be the emotional processing centre of the brain. The frontal lobe is important in decision-making, choosing a course of action and making judgements. This part of the brain is like a set of brakes on a car. In people whose brakes are not in good order, the likelihood of impulsive behaviour—which includes violence and aggression—is greater.

One field of study which emerged in the 1980s explored the impact of head injuries on homicidal behaviour. Based on the premise that frontal lobe injuries can cause difficulties in behavioural control, multiple studies began to explore such trauma in convicted killers. Freedman and Hemenway (2000) found that 75 per cent (12 out of 16) of death row homicide offenders in their study had experienced a traumatic brain injury in their early lives. In seven of these cases, the offenders had received multiple head injuries or head injuries that caused a loss of consciousness, severe headaches, blackouts, mood changes and heightened impulsivity which dated from the time of the injury. Studies of prison inmates serving sentences for murder found prevalence rates of brain injury of between ten per cent and 75 per cent of the samples (see Fabian, 2010). This compares to a rate of brain injury in the general population of one-to-two per cent (Jennett and MacMillan, 1981) suggesting that there may be a link between this type of injury and homicidal behaviour.

In his 2013 book, *Anatomy of Violence,* Adrian Raine reported upon the findings of various studies which involved scanning the brains of participants. Raine argued that when examining the brain scans of murderers, he consistently noted reduced activity in the frontal lobes of their brains. According to Raine, homicide *does* have a biological element. However, he does not believe that aggression, violence or indeed homicide are inevitable outcomes of people with reduced functioning in their frontal lobe and argues that brain functioning can change with improvements in the environment of the individual. For example, he describes a longitudinal study in which three-year-old children took more exercise and were given better nutrition and enhanced cognitive stimulation (opportunities to improve their perception, memory, judgement and reasoning). At age eleven, these children had better brain functioning and, at age 23, they had a 35 per cent reduction in criminal offending when compared with groups without these improvements to their environment. Raine's work does not feature the same degree of biological determinism as the work of earlier scholars like Lombroso. He argues that the making of a killer is not simply about *either* biology *or* environment alone — it is a combination of *both*.

Raine's work is important in ensuring that micro explanations do not stand in isolation or revert to crude determinism. Indeed, it may be true that amongst those who have committed serious harms there is a disproportionate prevalence of neurological dysfunction. However, Raine's contribution invites further questions and challenges the *causation* thesis, i.e. that the neurological dysfunction led to the homicidal behaviour and this behaviour was *determined* and *proscribed* by physiological factors. After all, if brain injuries or dysfunctions really cause someone to kill, all people with such conditions would be homicidal—which is clearly not the case.

Looking beyond the individual to their environment, as Raine suggests, leads us to further avenues to explore the roots of their behaviour. For example, how might a brain injury or a brain dysfunction come about in the first place? Physical abuse at the hands of parents? Neglect? Were killers born with abnormal brain functioning or did their brains develop in this way because of a range of factors within their environment? Brain development occurs not just in a biological context but also within a social one. In sum, whilst the early biological theories were *determinist* in nature—that one's biology led to violent behaviour—more recent theories are better at acknowledging biology as one part of the violence jigsaw puzzle. Within the next section, we explore another variety of micro explanations, those emerging from the discipline of psychology.

Key Term: Determinism
- The idea that people's behaviour is driven by factors beyond their control, which may be internal or external to them.

Psychological Explanations

Psychological theories are largely located within the positivist tradition, assuming that the violent offender is somehow distinct from other individuals, and trying to identify what factors make them different. There are many varieties of psychological explanation but within this section we focus upon two which appear to have become increasingly popular in recent years—psychopathy and psychodynamic theory.

The notion of the psychopath emanates from a school of thought examining the role of personality in the development of violent offenders. Personality can be understood as the collection of attributes, qualities and traits which combine to form our distinct character as an individual. Personality theories explore clusters of particular features which result in different types of character and shape the conduct and behaviour of the individual. The notion of the *personality disorder* describes someone with a cluster of features which combine to result in them feeling, acting and behaving in a way that is considerably different from the 'average' person. Psychopathic personality disorder or psychopathy are terms often evoked in the attempt to explain homicidal behaviour.

Psychopathy is assessed using Hare's Psychopathy Checklist Revised — or PCL-R — which lists 20 interpersonal, emotional and behavioural deficits. Psychologists apply a score of 'o' if the item does not apply at all, 'I' if it applies sometimes and '2' if it applies all of the time. These traits and behaviours include: glibness/superficial charm, grandiose sense of self-worth, proneness to boredom/need for stimulation, pathological lying, conning/being manipulative, lack of remorse or guilt, shallow affect, callousness/lack of empathy, poor behavioural control, lack of realistic long-term goals, impulsivity, irresponsibility, failure to accept responsibility for one's own actions. Psychopaths, it is sometimes argued, commit homicide because the presence of some of these characteristics combines with the absence of others to create an individual with a unique type of subjectivity who acts as if the rules of society — both formal and informal — do not apply to them. For example, the presence of a grandiose sense of self and the absence of feelings of remorse.

At the heart of psychopathy is a disregard for the rights and feelings of others. Psychopaths do not possess the same range of complex emotions as non-psychopaths but become proficient in reading other people's emotions and delivering socially appropriate responses in given situations to get what they want. Psychopaths do not have the distorted perceptions of reality that are often associated with *psychosis* — commonly confused with psychopathy in popular culture through the slang term 'psycho.' Psychopaths are lucid, aware of what they are doing and capable of distinguishing between right and wrong. People experiencing psychotic episodes are not, they suffer delusions — over which they have no control — which compel them to behave in particular ways. The prevalence rate of psychopathy in the general population is around one per cent (Hare, Hart and Harpur, 1991). However, some studies have shown that among homicide offenders, rates are significantly higher (Firestone, Bradford, Greenberg, Larose and Curry, 1998). Hodgins et al (1996) claimed that just over one-third of homicide offenders had high psychopathy scores and Gray et al (2003) noted that psychopathic murderers did not react as negatively to depictions of violence as non-psychopathic murderers, suggesting that their personalities and belief systems were distinctly different from 'the rest of us.' However, not all homicide offenders are psychopaths. Furthermore, not all psychopaths kill, and many such individuals do not engage in psychical violence at all—let alone the most extreme form of it. Furthermore, personality theories can be helpful in describing the character of some killers, but this focuses very much on the personality *in the present* and does not examine how such a personality comes to develop in the first place. However, psychodynamic approaches begin to ask these questions.

Also known as psychoanalytical theories, psychodynamic approaches grew from the work of the psychologist Sigmund Freud. Within this school of thought, homicide is seen as the result of internal mental activity—conscious or subconscious—which results from disruption within a child's psychosexual development. This approach places a strong emphasis on early childhood experiences and tends to implicate the acts and omissions of parents and caregivers in the making of a killer. These approaches draw attention to the fact that childhood trauma in the form of consistent abuse and maltreatment is common amongst offenders convicted of violent offences like homicide. To this end, psychodynamic theories have some overlap with attachment theory (Bowlby, 1969), which claims that the nature of the relationship between a child and their caregiver is influential in the development of perceptions and expectations of themself and others and that this provides the basis for the relationships they go on to have with other people. Gilligan's (2000) research drew on life history interviews with men convicted of violent offences. He argued that his participants' internal conflicts were rooted in feelings of shame. As a result of the violence they experienced as children, they were embarrassed, humiliated and came to see themselves as weak. However, they did not express these feelings to the outside world, instead putting on a veneer of toughness and aggression to conceal them. Gilligan argues that those who go on to be violent towards others do so because they see it as the only way of tackling their feelings of shame. In addition, they lack the depth of attachment to other human beings which in other individuals acts as a barrier to violence.

Similarly, the work of Stein (2007) emphasises the importance of serious physical, violent and sexual trauma within the childhoods of people later convicted of serious violent crimes including homicide. Stein's work offers an explanation of *how* people with such biographies come to harm others. She places particular significance on the concept of *dissociation*—when someone feels a sense of disconnection from the self and the world around them, they experience a detachment of sorts. Whilst physically present, they are psychologically absent from events in the here and now. Stein argues that dissociation is a natural reaction to coping with stress and trauma and that we *all* engage in dissociation to one degree or another. However, those who have experienced the most extreme maltreatment in childhood draw heavily on dissociation as a survival mechanism throughout their abuse which comes to impact upon future behaviour. Abused children cannot make sense of the violence inflicted upon them, so they escape it at the time through dissociation. Their future violent behaviours are essentially attempts to create meaning. Stein explains:

> '...it is the pathological disengagement precipitated by early, intense and repetitive trauma that most strongly facilitates the streaming of an unprocessed violent past into the present...dissociative processes circumvent symbolization, attacks cannot be reflected on or learned from...Consequently, urges toward aggressing are difficult to mediate and are frequently impossible to diffuse. Dissociated violence seems destined to be replayed in an endless loop, like the very cheapest pornography...' (Ibid, p. 4)

The work of Gilligan and Stein are important because they do not suggest that this one factor — childhood trauma — writes a fixed script for future violence. Gilligan argues that some individuals with such experiences do *not* see violence as the only route to restoring their sense of self-esteem and worth — they pursue non-violent ways of securing a sense of pride in themselves. Furthermore, some *do* feel a sense of attachment to other people which serves to prevent violent conduct. Stein argues that violence is not the only way in which individuals might seek to give meaning to their own trauma. Whilst early experiences of abuse at the hands of caregivers is a factor in explaining homicide, not all — indeed relatively few — children who are abused go on to fatally harm other people

Micro Explanations — An Assessment

Despite their usefulness in identifying some common individual features of homicide offenders — frontal lobe dysfunction, early childhood trauma and psychopathic personalities — the micro approaches considered here do not help us make direct causal links between these factors and homicidal behaviour.

Whilst they help us to understand why *some* individuals kill, the absence of these characteristics from *all* killers suggests that other factors are at play. Micro approaches have not yet identified any single physiological or psychological driver of homicidal behaviour. These approaches help us to add to a list of common features in the backgrounds of killers rather than build explanations. In addition, micro studies do not only fail to ascertain *if* particular factors cause homicidal behaviour but also *how* they do so. In emphasising the abnormal and the deviant, micro studies position killers as fundamentally different from *non-killers* or *everyone else*—however, what do we mean by *non-killers* and *everyone else*? This taken for granted notion of the 'normal' perhaps requires further attention. Whilst several micro studies emphasise that we should not neglect factors beyond the individual—for instance Raine's valuing of the environmental context of violence—they have not engaged in a critical analysis of the bigger picture and the roots of our comparisons between those who kill and those who do not. The macro approaches described in the next section begin to tackle some of these issues.

Case Study: The murder of James Bulger

In February 1993, two-year-old James Bulger was abducted, tortured and murdered by two ten-year-old boys. His killing evoked disgust and outrage among the British public, who desperately sought out explanations as to how two individuals—who were children themselves—could do such a terrible thing to an innocent, vulnerable toddler.

Sense-making in mainstream media drew heavily upon the micro approach. The *Today* newspaper ran the headline 'Born to Kill', implying that James' killers were aberrant and inherently evil. They were presented as different from the rest of us, defective freaks of nature. Commentators were also quick to locate the blame for the boys' behaviour at the hands of their parents, presenting them as feckless, deficient and unfit. Very rarely did analysis go beyond the individual and the familial. The book *As If* by Blake Morrison, published in 1997, *did* begin to engage with broader structural themes of poverty, inequality and contemporary masculinity—and was widely criticised for 'excusing' the boys' behaviour.

The Bulger case led to the revision of a long-established legal principle relating to children's culpability. In England and Wales, no child under the age of ten can be found guilty of an offence on the presumption of *doli incapax* (meaning 'incapable of evil'). Children under this age cannot be held legally responsible for acts that would constitute criminal behaviour in older children or adults. Prior to this case, it was incumbent upon the prosecution to demonstrate that children between the ages of ten and 14 who found themselves charged with a criminal offence understood that their actions were wrong. In the Bulger case, the prosecution were able to establish this and James' killers were tried as if they were adults. However, this rule was abolished in 1998 under section 34 Crime and Disorder Act, so now any child aged ten or above is deemed to be criminally responsible.

The micro explanations of the Bulger case were based on well-established tropes of the rational actor. The argument that we are all equally rational and in control of our decisions and choices. The assumption that we all begin from the same starting line. The view that life in society is a level playing field and a meritocracy in which we all have the same opportunities to thrive. Those who do not thrive, and indeed those who engage in fatal harm towards others, have only themselves to blame.

Why were micro explanations so appealing in this case? Could it be that they are easy to grasp and reproduce? Notions of mad/bad and good/evil enable a compact and efficient news product with a clear message (Jewkes, 2015). Is it because they are effective in separating the law-abiding 'us' from the criminal 'them'? In believing that James' killers were born bad and inherently evil, does this reinforce the view that their homicidal behaviour was inevitable and that nothing could have been done to prevent it?

Macro Explanations for Homicide

Whilst micro explanations are focused upon individual factors, macro explanations 'zoom out' to identify wider, social and cultural factors which create the conditions in which violent crimes like homicide occur. Taking such a broad focus inevitably involves the introduction of new themes and ideas—for instance statistical data about homicide rates, the nature of the relationship between the individual and the State and social divisions like social class, ethnicity, age and gender.

The structural approach draws upon the work of sociologist Emile Durkheim (1888–1951), who identified a relationship between the economy and the suicide rate. At times when the economy was booming, the suicide rate was lower than at times when it was in recession. Durkheim suggested that acts which were seemingly private and personal were influenced by broader social forces. Macro explanations made a resurgence in the 1960s—a time when many social movements were challenging systemic inequalities like poverty, sexism and racism through the labour movement, second wave feminism and the civil rights movement. The structural school of thought has since drawn upon international comparative studies to identify homicide peaks and troughs at specific places during particular time periods, highlighting associations between homicide rates and political, economic, social and cultural change (LaFree et al, 2015; Mares, 2009; Nivette and Eisner, 2013; Pridemore, 2007; Stamatel, 2014; Roth, 2009). In turn, this has led to the identification of social groups at heightened risk of victimisation, particularly in relation to serial homicide

(Leyton, 1986; Grover and Soothill, 1999; Wilson, 2007). Within this section, we will explore two approaches which identify the importance of structural factors in explaining particular types of homicide. Firstly, we will consider feminist perspectives in terms of explaining femicide before moving on to look at the structural approach to explaining serial homicide. Finally, we will critically consider the thesis of the 'crime decline' in making sense of contemporary trends in national homicide rates.

Feminist Perspectives on Femicide

One persistent homicide trend is that when women are killed; the suspect is most likely to be a partner or an ex-partner. Drawing on official homicide statistics in England and Wales from the 18-year period 2001–2019, Yardley (2020a) noted that the total number of female homicide victims who knew their killer was 2,682. Of these female victims, 60.1 per cent (N = 1,611) had been killed by a partner or ex-partner. Male victims of homicide on the other hand, were highly *unlikely* to have been killed by their female intimate partners. During the same time period, of the 3,948 male victims who knew their killer, only 9.1 per cent (N = 358) were killed by a partner or ex-partner (Ibid, 2020a). When examining cases of victims killed by partners or ex-partners over nearly two decades, the proportion of women killed by this suspect group was over six times that for men.

Key Term: Femicide
- The killing of women by men.

Feminist researchers point to social structural factors in explaining these key differences and begin with a criticism of the term *homicide* itself. Instead, they use the term *femicide,* which describes the killing of women by men, arguing that this specific terminology is needed because terms like homicide, murder and manslaughter deny the gendered nature of these women's deaths. Femicide is distinct in drawing attention to female victimisation and encouraging a focus on the broader social, cultural, political and economic forces in which violence against women is denied and minimised (Ingala-Smith, 2018). Feminist researchers argue that the reason for the disparity in the proportion of men and women killed by intimate partners or ex-partners is a structural one. They claim that society is built upon inherently *patriarchal* power structures, in which men dominate women and masculinity is more valued and valuable than femininity (Renzetti, 2018). Gender, feminists argue, is the most important and influential social division shaping people's lives and experiences. Within patriarchal societies, women are viewed as subordinate and 'less than' men, they are seen as the property of men, giving men a sense of entitlement to abuse and violate them. Traditional models of patriarchal control include the male breadwinner and female caregiver, where men go out to work whilst women take care of the domestic environment, raising children and keeping the home in order. Patriarchy creates the conditions in which men can kill women.

It is clearly not the case that all men are potential abusers at risk of killing their female partners, but it is argued that all men benefit from the *patriarchal dividend* (Connell, 2005): in a society run by men, in the interests of men, all men will have a privileged position. Feminist researchers not only identified patriarchal power structures as a key part of understanding femicide victimisation patterns, they also highlighted that most cases of femicide follow on from clear patterns of abusive, controlling and coercive behaviour towards the victim and other women before her. For example, Monckton-Smith (2020) identified eight sequential stages discovered in all cases of femicide within a model termed 'The Homicide Timeline.' This directly challenged mainstream modes of sense-making around the killing of women by men, notably the considerable force of the 'crime of passion' discourse, which emphasises traditional gender roles, norms of heterosexual romantic love and differences in expectations, responsibilities and behaviours of men and women. In this frame of reference, femicide perpetrators 'snap' and the violence comes 'out of the blue' in a moment of madness, evoking terms like 'red mist,' which serve to deny their responsibility (Adams, 2007; Dobash and Dobash, 2009). This approach interprets femicides as spontaneous incidents, in which an otherwise 'normal' man has been compelled to kill by forces beyond his control.

Perpetrator past histories of abuse of women, common in femicide, are absent from the crime of passion discourse (Stark, 2007; Dobash and Dobash, 2015). There is a focus upon the victim's behaviour—their alleged nagging, infidelity and/or failure to live up to expectations of who women are and how they should behave (Lees, 1997; Monckton-Smith, 2012). The focus on victim behaviour means that those killed by their current or former partners are accorded the lowest status in a victim hierarchy where levels of sympathy are contingent upon the nature of the woman's relationship with the perpetrator (Greer, 2007; Monckton-Smith, Williams and Mullane, 2014). The 'popular imagery' (Dobash and Dobash, 2015, 123) of sexual murder, where a woman is attacked by a stranger — often late at night in a dark area — causes outrage. The tendency of mainstream media to sympathetically cover 'ideal victims' (Christie, 1986; Van Wijk, 2013) means that women killed by men with some degree of legitimate access to them — through a marriage or intimate partnership — are seen in a less sympathetic light, evoking questions like 'Why didn't she just leave?' and victims are held accountable for their own deaths. Feminists argue that the question should be, 'Why did he decide to kill her?'

Feminist perspectives are an important example of the value of a structural approach, emphasising the importance of value systems and ideologies — notably patriarchal ones — in explaining femicide. They have drawn attention to the heavily gendered nature of women's victimisation and challenged mainstream sense-making around men who kill female partners or ex-partners. However, feminist approaches have come under criticism for the heavy emphasis they place on gender at the expense of other social characteristics like ethnicity and social class. Whilst some strands of feminism explore these additional factors, considering how they overlap or *intersect* (Crenshaw, 1990) to shape women's experiences, it is argued that there is still a lack of a comprehensive framework that fully appreciates how the range of differences between women may impact upon their homicide victimisation. Furthermore, the extent to which patriarchy persists unaltered in the twenty-first century is debatable. Is it as influential as it was in previous historical periods or has it been displaced by other power structures in late-capitalist society? Yardley (2020b) argues that patriarchy does indeed continue but it does so with a new lease of life in neoliberal society. Identifying an ideological hybrid termed *neoliberal patriarchy*, she argues that neoliberal notions of individual responsibility, hostile competition, self-reliance and meritocracy serve to reinforce misogyny through holding women responsible for their own victimisation.

Case Study: Guidelines for reporting domestic homicide

We Level-Up, a feminist organization challenging sexism in the UK, has introduced a set of guidelines for journalists covering cases of homicide in which women have been killed by men (We Level Up, 2018). The guidelines aim to encourage accurate and sensitive reporting which challenges the 'crime of passion' discourse and honours the victims of fatal domestic abuse. The five key messages from the guidelines are summarised below.

  I.   Accountability: Place the responsibility solely on the killer.
 II.   Accuracy: Name the crime as domestic violence.
III.   Dignity: Avoid sensationalising language, invasive or graphic details that compromise the dignity of the deceased woman or her surviving children and family members.
 IV.   Equality: Avoid insensitive or trivialising language or images.
  V.   Images: If you are reporting on domestic violence more generally, avoid using stock images that reinforce the myth that it's only a physical crime.

Will the guidelines work? If yes, why? If not, why not? What else needs to change? Why do journalists draw upon the existing 'crime of passion' discourse in reporting cases of domestic homicide?

Structural Perspectives on Serial Homicide

Theorising around serial killers has tended to fall into the 'micro' category of theory. Within the serial homicide literature this is known as the 'medical-psychological' (sometimes called medico-psychological) approach. Focused on locating the reasons for serial homicide within the individual offender, it has gained much traction both in academia, criminal justice and mainstream media (Yardley, 2020c). Techniques to emerge from the medical-psychological tradition include *offender profiling*, a staple element in crime drama and film, in which the expert tries to 'get inside the mind of the serial killer.' However, such approaches are not the only school of thought in the study of serial homicide. Another perspective — the *structural approach* — goes beyond the individual to identify broader social and cultural factors that facilitate this extreme form of killing.

In the mid-1980s, Leyton (1986) suggested that serial homicide was a form of homicidal protest influenced by the way society was organized at particular points in history. He identified the *modern epoch* as the historical period after World War II and a distinct time when serial killers targeted victims in higher social class groups than themselves. Working-class perpetrators would target middle-class victims, middle-class perpetrators would target upper-class victims. Leyton argued that these homicides were borne out of frustration and resentment among these social groups — working and lower-middle-class men felt that they could not progress up the social class ladder, they were stuck and sought vengeance upon those occupying positions they felt entitled to access. Leyton claimed that the normalisation and acceptance of men's violence — which might also be linked to the feminist perspective above — made physical harm a legitimate response to such feelings. Leyton's work was important in broadening the scope of the study of serial homicide, encompassing the broader factors that the micro medical-psychological approach neglected.

In testing Leyton's thesis, Grover and Soothill (1999) agreed that structural factors were important but disagreed with his stance that the less privileged targeted the more privileged. To the contrary, they discovered that victims of serial homicide tended to come from society's most marginalised and vulnerable groups. Indeed, middle-class victims were the minority. Wilson (2007) developed these ideas in exploring the social context within which society's least privileged were becoming the target of serial killers. He drew attention to factors that had driven marginality and polarisation since the 1970s. At the core was the rise of neoliberal philosophy in government, which led to a more distant relationship between the individual and the State, fewer protections for the vulnerable through the welfare system and a focus on the maximisation of wealth and individual 'freedoms.' This eroded the social-democratic consensus of the post-war years, which had provided support through State services like social security. In an increasingly individualistic society, where a sense of collective responsibility for the well-being of others had faded, those unable to achieve conventional success in a hostile and competitive political economy became isolated and vulnerable, blamed for their own demise and devalued by society. As societies become less equal, hostility within them increases. Inequality has a negative impact upon social relationships of trust, respect and reciprocity. It is no coincidence, argued Wilson, that the elderly, sex workers, gay men, 'runaways and throwaways' and babies and infants are the groups most targeted by serial killers in contemporary society.

This focus upon victimology brought the voices of feminist scholars into the structural debate around serial homicide. Feminists argued that patriarchy was particularly relevant when examining the victimisation of sex workers. Bland (1992) argued that Peter Sutcliffe, the so-called 'Yorkshire Ripper' who killed in excess of a dozen women between 1975 and 1980, was able to get away with killing for so long because he was the embodiment of stereotypical, hegemonic masculinity. There was a tendency to victim-blame through focusing on the fact that these women were out in public places alone, late at night — and as such were not conforming to idealised traditional femininity — rather than upon the decisions and actions of the perpetrator in killing them (Wattis, 2017; Bland, 1992; Smith, 2013). Feminist perspectives argue that both femicide and serial homicide are outcomes of patriarchal social structures. Women who fail to conform to idealised notions of femininity are problematised, stigmatised and blamed for their own victimisation.

Fewer Homicides — The 'Crime Decline'?

There is a further important area of debate around homicide that must be considered when examining explanations for this most serious of violent acts. This proceeds from an acceptance of the idea that homicide rates have *declined* as societies have developed and evolved. Throughout modern history, there has been a general reduction in the number of homicides — and thankfully for most of us our lives and the lives of our loved ones will never be touched by this devastating crime. From the 1300s, beginning in England and appearing later in Europe, interpersonal violence in public places consistently declined up until the mid-1950s — and a similar thing happened in other capitalist nations. Some argue that this was an indicator of society becoming more civilised. No longer were we in a situation akin to philosopher Thomas Hobbes' theoretical *state of nature* in which it was every person for themselves, living in constant threat of violence from others in their attempts to secure the resources they needed to live. As nations began to organize themselves around the principles of centralised government, clearer rules and codes around behaviour began to take root and were formalised through criminal law (Pinker, 2012). The State emerged as a protector of the people and citizens agreed to give up some of their freedoms through deferring to the authority of the State. The State would protect people through mechanisms such as the Criminal Justice System and, in return, they would behave in a civilised manner. Indeed, Elias (1987) described the *civilising process*—where the State became the only social actor who could legitimately use violence through punishment and war—in the interests of keeping all citizens safe. The State therefore had a *monopoly* on the use of violence which, Elias argued, led to greater self-control and fewer violent altercations. When people know what the rules are, know what is expected of them and know what will happen if they disobey them, they will be considerably less likely to engage in acts like homicide.

However, crime decline has been questioned by many. Some scholars argued that whilst there may have been an overall decline in violence and homicide, this was not evenly distributed across the social class spectrum or throughout all localities within nations. Indeed, there were significant spikes in homicide rates in particular spaces and places, which went against the overall trend of decline (Leyton, 1986; Mares, 2009; LaFree et al, 2015). Offering an explanation, Leyton (1986) argued that the vast majority of people who kill are from the lowest social spectrum or the 'underclass' as he called them. He claimed that they had not been successfully socialised and formed part of a lower working-class who continued to value violence long after others had developed alternative ways of dealing with conflict. To use Elias' terminology, the *civilising* process had not filtered down to all and there remained an uncivilised element. The lowest social strata, Leyton (1986) claimed, still featured remnants of 'manly vengeance,' a hangover of sorts from the feudal era—and these groups continued to have the least to lose and most to gain from such behaviour.

Perhaps the most interesting observations about the 'crime decline' in modern times are offered by Hall (2012), who argues that existing sense-making around this is missing the point. Hall proposes an alternative interpretation, which he terms *pseudo-pacification*, which centres on the idea that harm in the form of fatal violence may have declined but in other forms it continues to exist. The values and beliefs that underpinned people's decisions to kill have not gone away—they have simply been repositioned and repurposed. Hall claimed that the decline in fatal violence was not due to the factors Pinker and Elias suggest. This was not attributable to civility or progress but out of necessity to create favourable conditions for a market economy. Trade could not prosper if people felt the constant threat of physical violence from others. In order to do business, a non-violent environment was required. Legal frameworks which outlawed physical violence emerged, paving the way for trade and exchange in the early days of capitalist, market economies. However, the individualistic pursuit of profit also meant that people could not simply act in kind, altruistic ways in their dealings — if so, their businesses would not survive. Therefore, people retained elements of aggression, but this did not manifest as physical violence. It emerged as competition cloaked in performances of politeness, 'good manners' and etiquette — a much more *civilised* form of conflict. Violence is akin to a form of energy, which cannot be destroyed: it simply changes in shape and form. Whilst we retain our harmful libidinal drives, its enactment shifts. Indeed, whilst homicide rates steadily declined throughout modernity, property crimes and unethical behaviour *increased* (Ellis, 2019). In Hall's terms, we have not been *civilised* or *pacified*, we have been *pseudo-pacified*. Hall's thesis draws attention to the nature of political economy in understanding individual subjectivity — something altogether neglected by Elias and Pinker. Neoliberal capitalism, Hall and Wilson (2014) argue, contains inherently harmful elements and as such, those who harm and kill cannot be understood as aberrant deviations from 'the rest of us' but the extreme embodiment of and conformity to the ideologies and values which guide contemporary life. More recently, Ellis (2019) has applied the pseudo-pacification thesis to an understanding of the increase in homicide rates in England and Wales 2014–2018. Ellis argues that government austerity policies in the aftermath of the 2008 financial crash have fundamentally changed the nature of the relationship between the individual and the State, whereby older universalistic and collectivist approaches to governance have been replaced with a much more individualistic and atomised perspective. The already marginalised and disconnected became increasingly likely to act on violent impulses:

> 'The latest increases in lethal and serious violence do not represent subcultural deviations amongst "outsiders" from a "civilizing" value system that restrains primal violent urges and maintains civilizing sensibilities. Rather, they appear as unrestrained and often quite extreme manifestations of liberal capitalisms' disavowed dark heart.' (Ellis, 2019, p. 874)

Key Term: Pseudo-Pacification
- The idea that people have not simply become less violent as society has developed and evolved but that their violence has changed in shape and form.
- Non-physical forms of aggression have replaced embodied violence to facilitate and maintain the market economy.

Macro Explanations — An Assessment

The macro approaches enable us to apply a different lens, emphasising the broader social forces which create the conditions in which homicide takes place. Rather than looking *down*, which characterises the micro school of thought, macro interpretations force us to look *up*. The areas of study and themes explored within this section reveal how the ways in which we make sense of homicide can be based on stereotypical myths of individual behaviour formed on assumptions around social class, gender and ethnicity.

Many have challenged the extent to which these truisms are true at all, arguing that they simply serve to distract us from the structural forces behind harmful and homicidal behaviour. The structural approaches force us to look at the landscape in which homicide takes place and identify particular features of that terrain — inequality, patriarchy, political economy — that make some more vulnerable to both homicide perpetration and victimisation. In this sense, they fill in many of the gaps around micro approaches. However, questions still remain. Whilst structural factors are helpful in developing our understanding of homicide beyond individual pathology in identifying the cultural backdrop to this harm, simply saying that such factors *explain* homicide would be inaccurate. Whilst the ideologies and values within contemporary society might facilitate, enable and minimise homicide, they do not *cause* it. The structural approach does not provide answers to the question, 'Why do people kill?' Many people find themselves in marginalised social locations yet do not go on to harm, let alone kill others. A minority of men abuse their female partners and an even smaller minority of this population go on to kill them. Whilst macro approaches offer significant potential to examine factors that micro approaches omit, we still do not have a comprehensive explanation of why people kill. However, new developments in criminological theory offer a way forward through integrating insights from micro and macro approaches. One example of this, integrated theory is considered in the following section.

Integrated Theory — A Multi-level Framework

Throughout this chapter thus far we have explored a range of micro and macro explanations of homicide, all of which come with their advantages and disadvantages. Might it be possible to take the best parts of each approach and combine them to create new insights into homicide that may finally begin to provide us with answers to the questions, 'Why do people kill?', and more specifically — 'Why do only *some* people kill?' A new perspective — ultra-realism, offers potential to shed new light on homicide and begin to connect the micro and the macro. Ultra-realism aims to locate harmful subjectivities within the political-economic context of neoliberal consumer capitalism and explain why it is that *some* people harm others in pursuit of their own interests rather than seeking solidarity with them.

Ultra-realism proceeds from the observation that in the last 50 years, societies across the globe have experienced change at an unprecedented pace and scale. In Western economies, the industrial capitalism of the nineteenth and much of the twentieth century has made way for consumer capitalism. Some argue that, in so doing, it has fundamentally changed human subjectivity and as such carries considerable implications for violence and homicide (Winlow and Hall, 2017). Neoliberal consumer capitalism values competitive individualism, which may be beneficial for the economy, but has had a damaging impact upon how individuals see themselves and each other. Competitive individualism fuels hostility, envy, narcissism, cynicism and *amour propre* — success premised on the failure of others, which in turn creates an undercurrent of anxiety and insecurity (Winlow and Hall, 2017). The stable and secure work of the industrial economy has made way for precarious employment and zero hours contracts. Whilst the inhabitants of the former industrial heartlands no longer form a significant part of the economy's *supply* side, their stake in society is located in the *demand* side of contemporary consumer capitalism — often financed through debt (Ellis, 2019; Winlow and Hall, 2017). It is in this context that homicide has become theoretically barren, a preoccupation with micro theories—premised on the assumption that killers are aberrations in an otherwise pro-social order—continue to dominate. Such theories are well-suited to the simplification demanded by mainstream media and offer individualistic—inherently neoliberal answers—to the question, 'Why do people kill?' Ultra-realists argue that we can no longer apply the theoretical frameworks of the twentieth century to an understanding of harms in the twenty-first century and in relation to homicide—they propose a new integrated approach of macro, meso and micro (Hall and Wilson, 2014).

At the macro-level, Hall and Wilson (2014) consider the *pseudo-pacification process*—discussed earlier—as fundamental to making sense of homicide. The 'pacified form of social competition that fuelled consumer culture and increased demand in burgeoning markets' (Ibid, p. 644) was the incubator for *special liberty*. Under special liberty, some citizens internalise the individualistic ethos of neoliberal consumer capitalism, developing an inherent narcissism which justifies their transgression of law and ethics and enables them to risk harm to others in pursuing their interests (Hall, 2012). The neoliberal State advocates personal responsibility and individual freedom, creating opportunities for the exercise of special liberty—which in turn creates the conditions for increased rates of homicide and multiple homicide.

Hall and Wilson (2014) also identify the importance of the meso-level—a 'middle ground' of exchange between macro level structures and micro level norms, attitudes, beliefs and behaviours. These locales and situations feature the organizational manifestations of social institutions—for instance the home, school, workplace and church as embodiments of family, education, economy and religion respectively. An emphasis on the nature of relationships with and expectations of others in these spaces could help shed light on why some choose to engage in harmful behaviours like homicide whilst others do not. Better ascertaining how these social environments reinforce, challenge and/or subvert neoliberal truisms is an important part of the theoretical landscape in explaining homicide.

Furthermore, digital online spaces represent an important layer at the meso-level and as such, are deserving of scholarly attention. For example, literature exploring the technology of gender-based violence has identified virtual locations where abuse of women and girls is validated and encouraged, embodied most clearly within the contemporary 'incel' movement (Scaptura and Boyle,

2019; Van Valkenburgh, 2018). This is of particular importance given that online spaces are subject to minimal — if any — regulation by neoliberal States and may be important locales of the facilitation and legitimisation of the crime of passion discourse. These environments also tend to be the sites where neoliberal freedoms — like freedom of speech — are evoked, whereby the freedom of some to do harm exceeds other's right to be protected from harm (Yardley, 2020b).

Mindful of the macro and micro contexts, ultra-realists have cast new light on the micro-level of analysis in explaining homicide. They argue that the forces driving harmful subjectivity at the individual level are the same as those driving other types of harm (Hall and Wilson, 2014). The roots of the urge to kill are far from abnormal. Those who kill are the embodiment rather than the antithesis of mainstream values. Applying this to serial homicide, Hall and Wilson argue:

> '…the serial killer cuts through everyday hypocrisy to act out a pure mani-
> festation of the pre-symbolic human drives — envy, fear, prejudice, hatred,
> sadism, hedonistic pleasure — that fuel the systemic violence of the socio-
> economic system and its attendant culture of special liberty.' (Ibid, p. 650)

In explaining why only a minority of individuals within neoliberal society choose to kill, ultra-realists cite research noting the importance of individual trauma (see, for example, Winlow, 2009). Of particular importance is the way in which trauma is understood and perpetuated *within* macro and meso contexts. Ultra-realists begin to help make sense of the fact that whilst many people experience abuse, neglect and violence at the hands of caregivers during their childhoods, only a proportion of such individuals will go on to harm others.

The empirical studies conducted by ultra-realist researchers with persistently violent men in the deindustrialised regions of the north of England are particularly valuable in this regard (see, for example, Ellis, Winlow and Hall, 2017; Winlow, 2012, 2014; Winlow and Hall, 2009). When trauma occurs in a context where violence is valued, expected and a way of 'getting things done,' a readiness to physically harm others is always present. Feelings of guilt, shame and failure at *not* evoking the violent cultural scripts in response to abuse lead to a lifelong project to take back control and protect themselves from further victimisation, not able to trust or rely on anyone but themselves (Ellis, Winlow and Hall, 2017; Winlow, 2014; Winlow and Hall, 2009). This isolation and atomisation clearly resonates with the 'macro' neoliberal tropes of self-reliance and individualism. Not all individuals with biographies of such trauma will go on to harm and kill. Some engage in acts of violence towards the self—for example substance misuse, self-harm and destructive social or intimate relationships, *internalising* their trauma (Winlow, 2014). Others may respond by relocating to areas where a violence-affirming local culture is absent—or at least *less* prevalent (Ellis, Winlow and Hall, 2017). Others may engage in supportive and secure intimate relationships and friendships where one's value is not premised on their capacity for violence. Therefore victimisation does not *cause* people to commit homicide but given the presence of childhood trauma in the lives of violent offenders, 'it is inescapable that these men are both harmful and harmed' (Ellis, 2016, p. 127). In bringing together the structural, local and individual, the integrated analysis proposed by Hall and Wilson (2014) questions the conceptualisation of killers as inherently abnormal and antithetical to mainstream values. In so doing, it offers more sophisticated understandings of the values and world views of those who kill, exploring how neoliberal ideologies are locally manifested in violence-affirming cultures—and offering ways forward in identifying how the extreme enactment of such ideologies can be challenged and resisted by the individual.

Conclusion

This chapter has considered micro, macro and integrated approaches to theorising around homicide, trying to develop a satisfactory answer to the question, 'Why do people kill?' The advantages and disadvantages of these approaches have been considered and the chapter has revealed that the way in which we make sense of homicide at any given point in history is indicative of 'mainstream' social values around subjectivity. If we are to push theorising further forwards, we must move beyond dichotomies. Rather than adopting an *either/ or* positioning on micro and macro, we need to consider the value of a *both/and* framework which considers the importance of structure, agency and the meso spaces in which these are reconciled in real-world situations. Ultra-realism is still in its infancy and whilst it has explored what might be termed male-on-male 'honour contest violence' (Polk, 1994), there are multiple types of homicide that it has not directly considered—for example femicide. However, the integrated approach of ultra-realist scholars could be the foundation upon which we build more convincing and comprehensive understandings of homicide in the twenty-first century.

Questions to consider:
- Are all individuals convicted of homicide offences equally 'rational'?
- Are macro explanations for homicide simply 'excuses' which justify and minimise fatal violence?
- Women are most likely to be killed by their male intimate partners or ex-partners—why?
- Is anyone 'born to kill'?

References

Adams, D. (2007), *Why Do They kill? Men Who Murder their Intimate Partners,* Nashville, TN: Vanderbilt University Press.

Bland, L. (1992), 'The Case of the Yorkshire Ripper: Mad, Bad, Beast or Male?,' in J. Radford and D. E. H. Russell (eds.), *Femicide: The Politics of Women Killing,* Buckingham: Open University Press, pp. 233–252.

Bowlby, J. (1969), *Attachment and Loss: Attachment,* Basic Books.

Christie, N. (1986), 'The Ideal Victim,' in E. A. Fattah (ed.), *From Crime Policy to Victim Policy: Reorienting the Justice System* (17–30), Basingstoke: Macmillan.

Connell, R. W. (2005), *Masculinities,* Cambridge: Polity.

Crenshaw, K. (1990), 'Mapping the Margins: Intersectionality, Identity Politics, and Violence Against Women of Color,' *Stanford Law Review,* 43, p. 1241.

Dobash, R. E. and Dobash, R. P. (2009), 'Out of the Blue: Men Who Murder an Intimate Partner,' *Feminist Criminology,* 4(3), pp. 194–225.

Dobash, R. E. and Dobash, R. P. (2015), *When Men Murder Women,* Oxford: Oxford University Press.

Durkheim, E. (1951), *Suicide: A Study in Sociology* (J. A. Spaulding, Trans.), New York: Free Press.

Elias, N. (1987), *The History of Manners: The Civilizing Process,* Pantheon Books.

Ellis, A. (2016), *Men, Masculinities and Violence,* Routledge.

Ellis, A. (2019), 'A De-civilizing Reversal or System Normal? Rising Lethal Violence in Post-recession Austerity United Kingdom,' *British Journal of Criminology*, 59(4), pp. 862–878.

Ellis, A., Winlow, S., and Hall, S. (2017) '"Throughout my life I've had people walk all over me": Trauma in the Lives of Violent Men,' *Sociological Review,* 65(4), pp. 699–713.

Fabian, J. M. (2010). 'Neuropsychological and Neurological Correlates in Violent and Homicidal Offenders: A Legal and Neuroscience Perspective,' *Aggression and Violent Behavior*, 15(3), pp. 209–223.

Firestone, P., Bradford, J. M., Greenberg, D. M., Larose, M. R., and Curry, S. (1998), 'Homicidal and Nonhomicidal Child Molesters: Psychological, Phallometric, and Criminal Features, *Sexual Abuse: A Journal of Research and Treatment*, 10(4), pp. 305–323.

Freedman, D., and Hemenway, D. (2000), 'Precursors of Lethal Violence: A Death Row Sample,' *Social Science and Medicine*, 50(12), pp. 1757–1770.

Gilligan, J. (2000), *Violence: Reflections on Our Deadliest Epidemic*, Jessica Kingsley Publishers.

Gray, N. S., MacCulloch, M. J., Smith, J., Morris, M., and Snowden, R. J. (2003), 'Forensic Psychology: Violence Viewed by Psychopathic Murderers,' *Nature*, 423(6939), pp. 497–498.

Greer, C. (2007), 'News Media, Victims and Crime,' in Davies P, Francis P and Greer C (eds.), *Victims, Crime and Society,* pp. 20–49, London: Sage

Grover, C. and Soothill, K. (1999), 'British Serial Killing: Towards a Structural Explanation,' *British Criminology Conferences: Selected Proceedings (Vol. 2)*.

Hall, S. (2012), *Theorizing Crime and Deviance,* Sage.

Hall, S., and Wilson, D. (2014), 'New Foundations: Pseudo-pacification and Special liberty as Potential Cornerstones for a Multi-level Theory of Homicide and Serial Murder,' *European Journal of Criminology*, 11(5), pp. 635–655.

Hare, R. D., Hart, S. D. and Harpur, T. J. (1991), 'Psychopathy and the DSM-IV Criteria for Antisocial Personality Disorder,' *Journal of Abnormal Psychology*,100(3), pp. 391–398.

Hodgins, S., Mednick, S. A., Brennan, P. A., Schulsinger, F., and Engberg, M. (1996), 'Mental Disorder and Crime: Evidence from a Danish Birth Cohort, *Archives of General Psychiatry,* 53(6), pp. 489–496.

Ingala-Smith, K. (2018), 'Femicide,' in Lombard N (ed.), *The Routledge Handbook of Gender Based Violence*, pp. 158–170, London: Routledge.

Jennett, B., and MacMillan, R. (1981), Epidemiology of Head Injury, *British Medical Journal* (Clinical Research Edition), 282(6258), pp. 101–104.

Jewkes, Y. (2015), *Media and Crime* (3rd edn.), Sage.

LaFree, G., Curtis, K., and McDowall, D. (2015), 'How Effective are Our "Better Angels"? Assessing Country-level Declines in Homicide Since 1950,' *European Journal of Criminology*, 12(4), pp. 482–504.

Lees, S. (1997), *Ruling Passions: Sexual Violence, Reputation and the Law,* Buckingham: Open University Press.

Leyton, E. (1986), *Hunting Humans. The Rise of the Modern Multiple Murderer,* Toronto: McClelland & Stewart.

Mares, D. M. (2009), 'Civilization, Economic Change, and Trends in Interpersonal Violence in Western Societies,' *Theoretical Criminology*, 13(4), pp. 419–449.

Mills, C.W. (1959), *The Sociological Imagination*, Oxford: Oxford University Press.

Monckton-Smith, J. (2012), *Murder, Gender and the Media: Narratives of Dangerous Love,* Basingstoke: Palgrave Macmillan.

Monckton Smith, J. (2020), 'Intimate Partner Femicide: Using Foucauldian Analysis to Track an Eight Stage Progression to Homicide', *Violence Against Women*, 26(11), pp. 1267–1285.

Monckton-Smith, J., Williams, A. and Mullane, F. (2014), *Domestic Abuse, Homicide and Gender: Strategies for Policy and Practice,* Basingstoke: Palgrave Macmillan.

Nivette, A. E. and Eisner, M. (2013), 'Do Legitimate Polities have Fewer Homicides? A Cross-national Analysis,' *Homicide Studies*, 17(1), pp. 3–26.

Pinker, S. (2012), *The Better Angels of Our Nature: Why Violence Has Declined*, Penguin.

Polk, K. (1994), *When Men Kill: Scenarios of Masculine Violence*, Cambridge: Cambridge University Press.

Pridemore, W. A. (2007), 'Change and Stability in the Characteristics of Homicide Victims, Offenders and Incidents During Rapid Social Change,' *British Journal of Criminology*, 47(2), pp. 331–345.

Raine, A. (2013), *The Anatomy of Violence: The Biological Roots of Crime*, Penguin.

Renzetti, C. (2018), 'Feminist Perspectives,' in Lombard N (ed.), *The Routledge Handbook of Gender Based Violence*, pp. 74–82, London: Routledge.

Roth, R. (2009), *American Homicide*, Cambridge, MA: Harvard University Press.

Scaptura, M. N., and Boyle, K. M. (2020), 'Masculinity Threat, "Incel" Traits, and Violent Fantasies Among Heterosexual Men in the United States,' *Feminist Criminology*, 15(3), pp. 278–298.

Seltzer, M. (2007), *True Crime: Observations on Violence and Modernity*, Taylor & Francis.

Smith, J. (2013), *Misogynies: Reflections on Myth and Malice*, New York: Fawcett Columbine.

Stamatel, J. P. (2014), 'Explaining Variations in Female Homicide Victimization Rates Across Europe,' *European Journal of Criminology*, 11(5), pp. 578–600.

Stark, E. (2007), *Coercive Control: How Men Entrap Women in Personal Life*, Oxford: Oxford University Press.

Stein, A. (2007), *Prologue to Violence: Child Abuse, Dissociation and Crime*, Routledge.

Van Valkenburgh, S. P. (2018), 'Digesting the Red Pill: Masculinity and Neoliberalism in the Manosphere,' *Men and Masculinities* (ePub ahead of print).

Van Wijk, J. (2013), 'Who is the "Little Old Lady" of International Crimes? Nils Christie's Concept of the Ideal Victim Reinterpreted,' *International Review of Victimology*, 19(2), pp. 159–179.

Wattis, L. (2017), 'The Social Nature of Serial Murder: The Intersection of Gender and Modernity,' *European Journal of Women's Studies*, 24(4), pp. 381–393.

We Level Up (2018), 'Media Guidelines': https://www.welevelup.org/media-guidelines (Accessed 2 October 2020).

Wilson, D. (2007), *Serial Killers: Hunting Britons and Their Victims, 1960 to 2006*, Winchester: Waterside Press.

Winlow, S. (2012), '"All that is Sacred is Profaned": Towards a Theory of Subjective Violence,' in: S. Hall and S. Winlow (eds.), pp. 199–215.

Winlow, S. (2014), 'Trauma, Guilt and the Unconscious: Some Theoretical Notes on Violent Subjectivity,' *Sociological Review*, 62(S2), pp. 32–49.

Winlow, S. and Hall, S. (2009), 'Retaliate First: Memory, Humiliation and Male Violence,' *Crime Media Culture*, 5(3), pp. 285–304.

Winlow S and Hall S (2017), 'Criminology and Consumerism,' in P. Carlen and L. A. Franca (eds.), *Alternative Criminologies*, Abingdon: Routledge, pp. 116–133.

Yardley, E. (2020a), 'The Killing of Women in "Sex Games Gone Wrong": An Analysis of Femicides in Great Britain 2000–2018,' *Violence Against Women* (publication pending).

Yardley, E. (2020b), Technology-facilitated Domestic Abuse in Political Economy: A New Theoretical Framework,' *Violence Against Women* (ePub ahead of print).

Yardley. E. (2020c), 'Serial Killing,' in Loucks, N., Smith-Holt, S. and Adler, J. R., *Why We Kill: Understanding Violence Across Culture and Disciplines* (2nd edn.), Abingdon: Routledge, pp. 57–75.

CHAPTER 4

Serial Homicide

'I am simply not interested in any particular serial killer—his background, his relationships with family members and friends, what his schooldays might have been like, whether he prefers jam to marmalade. Rather, I want to understand whom he (it is almost always a "he") was able to kill.'

David Wilson, *A History of British Serial Killing*

Introduction

Arguably, one of the most exciting subjects for those with an interest in criminology is serial homicide. We seem to be fascinated by the stories of these individuals who have killed repeatedly, we hold a genuine interest in understanding their motives and entering their minds so as to see what is so different about them. Stories featuring serial killers have been the subject of news media reports, films and TV shows, with audiences always eager to consume true crime and fictional narratives. At the same time, however, we view serial homicide as the most heinous of crimes, we tend to feel empathy for the victims and we demonise the perpetrators, essentially perceiving them as entities who exist and function outside our moral spheres. The label *serial killer* alone is enough to provoke these diametrically opposed feelings of fascination and repulsion, usually in a simultaneous manner. From a scholarly perspective, this label has been the cause of considerable, longstanding controversy among academics, researchers and law enforcement professionals, who do not seem to agree on a unified definition. There are indeed historical and contemporary debates surrounding the term and questions which still seek conclusive answers. For example, how many victims should someone leave in order to be labelled 'serial killer'? Is it important that there is a cooling-off period between each killing? Should the killing acts be premeditated to constitute serial homicide? What other elements should we be taking into account? And why are these important?

This chapter places particular attention on these debates, and the context in which they emerged, in an attempt to explain how our understanding on serial homicide is informed. Further to this, this it explores the two dominant theoretical traditions criminologists have employed, in order to make sense of this enigmatic criminal behaviour. The first one is known as the *medical-psychological* tradition that takes as its focus the psyche of serial homicide offenders. In that regard, attention is placed upon early life experiences, motivations, *modus operandi* (that is the specific method used to commit the crime), evidence from the crime scene, potential mental health problems and personality disorders. The second one, known as the *structural tradition,* examines serial homicide through a sociological lens. Its focus is thereby placed upon the socio-economic context in which serial killers operate, the power relations in society that make certain groups more vulnerable than others, contributing to their victimisation. This perspective essentially examines the extent to which there is a link between structural issues and serial homicide. Preceding this discussion however, we need to provide a thorough definition of serial homicide that should act as a point of reference for our discussion.

Key Term: Cooling-Off Period
- This refers to the timeframe in which serial killers abstain from the behaviours which led them to commit murder. Instead, they re-integrate into their lives, engaging in non-offending activities. There is no consensus in academic literature as to whether this time element should be taken into account when defining serial homicide. In our opinion, however, it is of crucial importance, as it helps differentiate serial homicide from other types of multicide, such as spree and mass homicide that are characterised by continuity, as the perpetrators do not disconnect from killing (Wilson, Yardley and Lynes, 2015).

Defining Serial Homicide — Historical and Contemporary Debates

Serial homicide is an intriguing criminal behaviour that has been the subject of extensive theorising and analysis. During the past 40 years, scholars, researchers and law enforcement professionals have attempted to define the phenomenon, resulting in a plethora of contested definitions (Ferguson et al, 2013). Robert Kenneth Ressler, a Federal Bureau of Investigation (FBI) agent specialising in offender profiling, is credited with coining the term *serial killer* back in the 1970s to refer to offenders such as John Wane Gacy, David Berkowitz and Ted Bundy who were active at that time. It was during the 1980s however that the label was embedded in public consciousness. In 1984, specifically, the FBI aimed at developing a programme that would deal with violent offenders, such as serial killers. In order to get funding for their endeavour, it was claimed that approximately 5,000 people per year were thought to be killed by serial killers (Hickey, 2006). This figure was of course inflated and not factual, as we now know that serial homicide accounts for approximately one per cent of all homicide victims. Back then however, the publicised figure shocked the public, who were led to believe that serial homicide had reached epidemic proportions (Jenkins, 1994). The primary reason for the exaggerated reaction was that academic theorising on serial killers was at a primitive stage at the time, as serial homicide was a relatively new phenomenon.

The use of contested labels such as *repeated killer* or *stranger killer* to describe the individual, who committed murders repeatedly, highlights the initial theoretical struggle to conceptualise this particular type of crime (McDonald et al, 2013). It also indicates how the terms *serial homicide* and *serial killer* are socially constructed. They are decided by social groups, they are subjective, fluid, and prone to change and interpretation. The socially-constructed nature of these terms becomes further evident when one considers the various ways in which they have been defined. Serial homicide has indeed been examined from completely different and unrelated perspectives, with scholars usually defining the term so that it fits the aims of their studies. One of the first definitions that the FBI proposed considered serial homicide to be committed by an offender in ten or more separate and distinguishable incidents. The FBI (2008) have revisited the definition of the term however, arguing that serial homicide is the unlawful killing of two or more victims by the same offender in separate events. This definition does provide a numeric threshold, which constitutes a step forward from previous definitions. Its application however on an international but also national level is hindered by the use of the word *unlawful,* as there is no consistency among countries and States in relation to what constitutes unlawful killing (Adjorlolo and Chan, 2014). Other scholars who have made considerable contributions to our understanding of serial homicide and have produced their own definitions are Eric Hickey, Kevin Haggerty, Ronald Holmes and Stephen Holmes.

Hickey (2006) claimed that a serial murderer is any offender, irrespective of gender or motive, who kills three or more people over time. This definition notably accounts for the sex of the perpetrator, who can indeed be male or female, thus addressing perpetuated stereotypes that serial killers are all male. A more minimalistic definition comes from Holmes and Holmes (2010), according to whom a serial killer is an individual who has killed three or more people. Here, much like in the definition of Hickey, we see a numeric threshold that is different to what the FBI had proposed, an indication of the longstanding debate in relation to the minimum number of victims that are required to constitute serial homicide. Most definitions require either a minimum of two or three victims, but as of today there is no actual agreement on the matter. The difference appears to be an insignificant one, but, in fact, it considerably impacts the way in which serial homicide cases are understood and reported. For instance, offenders such Ed Gein and Scott William Cox should not be considered serial killers if we follow definitions that require a minimum of three victims, as they were both convicted of killing two victims each. At the same time, however, the threshold of two victims makes serial homicide appear more prevalent than it actually is and, as history has shown, this can result in disproportionate reactions. Therefore, considering that the role of the social scientist is to obtain a balanced understanding of the nature, scale, and impact of phenomena, we find the minimum requirement of three victims to be the most appropriate one.

Examining serial homicide from a different perspective, Haggerty (2009) defined serial killers as individuals who have killed three or more people, previously unknown to them. The assumption put forward here that serial killers only target strangers does not quite help us make sense of serial homicide, as it poses the risk of under-including cases. If we were to follow this assumption, then offenders such as Frederick and Rosemary West, Beverley Allitt, and even Harold Shipman would not be considered serial killers, as they all knew their victims. As a matter of fact, this previously established relationship was proven to be an integral aspect of their *modus operandi*. Harold Shipman, for instance, one of the most prolific serial killers on a global scale, who was found responsible for the deaths of as many as 215 people, was a trusted GP, who would normally visit his patients at their homes before injecting them with lethal doses of diamorphine. So not only had Shipman established a more personal relationship with his patients, but this relationship was instrumental in terms of his criminal behaviour, as it gave him access to his victims, the opportunity to kill them, falsify their medical records, and get away with his crimes for approximately 23 years, from 1975 to 1998. It is due to cases like this one that we argue that serial killers might actually target people they previously knew. They are perfectly capable of taking advantage of well-established relationships, be these of a personal or professional nature.

Considering the key strengths and weaknesses of existing definitions of serial homicide, Adjorlolo and Chan (2014) argued that serial homicide incidents should be linked from a forensic standpoint and be committed in separate events over a period of time by the same offender, whose predominant motive is personal gratification. This definition unifies scientific and legal approaches, essentially aiming to eliminate the current absence of a widely accepted definition. Particular consideration is placed upon the notion of intentionality, an element that is consistent within academic discourse, as serial homicide is generally viewed as a crime that requires premeditation and planning (Egger, 1998). Expecting individual incidents to be linked from a forensic standpoint, in order to talk about serial homicide can be deemed problematic though and lead to under-inclusion of cases. The reason is that we have witnessed serial homicide cases unfold whose separate events were not linked forensically. Trevor Joseph Hardy, for instance, was found responsible for the deaths of three women between 1974 and 1976. Thereby, he has been rightfully perceived to be a serial killer. His crimes were not linked from a forensic standpoint though, as his *modus operandi* varied. Specifically, his first victim, Janet Lesley Stewart was stabbed to death, his second Wanda Skala was hit over the head with a brick, whereas his third victim Sharon Moshoph was strangled (Wilson, 2011).

We therefore suggest that serial homicide events do not necessarily have to be forensically linked.

Along similar lines in terms of considering commonly applied criteria on serial homicide definitions, Wilson, Yardley and Lynes (2015) concluded that a serial killer is an individual who has killed three or more people in a time period greater than 30 days, thereby highlighting the cooling-off period as an integral element of serial homicide. Whilst there is no consensus in academic discourse in relation to this time element, it should be noted that it is very important when defining but also understanding serial homicide, as it separates it from mass and spree homicide. Mass homicide is characterised by spatial and temporal proximity in killings (Dietz, 1986), whereas spree homicide involves a spatial and temporal separation between killings (Holmes and Holmes, 2001). Neither of these include a cooling-off period however, as they are continuous and contained in nature (Yardley and Wilson, 2015). Drawing upon existing definitions and for the purposes of this textbook, we propose that *a serial killer is an individual who has killed at least three people, in a period greater than 30 days, and whose motive is personal gratification.*

The importance of the numeric threshold and of the time element has been outlined above. With regard to the proposed motive however, we need to explain that we chose the word *personal,* because it implies a motivation that is intrinsic, thereby coming from within the individual to express an interest in the act of killing. This helps separate serial killers from hitmen, who also kill repeatedly, but whose motives are extrinsic, as they kill for profit, under a 'contractual' obligation when an external source asks them to complete their task (Wilson, Yardley and Lynes, Ibid, 2015). Similarly, the word *gratification* was chosen as it is broad enough to encompass the array of motives, which lead serial killers to commit their crimes and this will be discussed later in this chapter.

The Importance of a Unified Definition

Criminologists tend to be preoccupied with constructing and de-constructing definitions, creating typologies, putting information into neat categories, as ways of making sense of criminal behaviour. While there remain debates in relation to what we mean when we label someone a *serial killer*, criminologists have put forward the idea that academic discourse on serial homicide would benefit from a unified definition of the term, one that could potentially be applied to the whole world (Lynes, 2017). From a theoretical standpoint, an agreed upon definition would enable more productive communication amongst academics, researchers, and law enforcement officials, as all sides would have the same thing in mind when referring to serial killers. This could subsequently enable, on a more practical level, empirical research on the subject to be conducted in a more consistent manner. Specifically, identifying, comparing and contrasting trends would be considerably easier on both a national and international level. Social scientists would also be able to make better sense of statistics, as these now seem to vary based on how serial homicide is defined in each jurisdiction. A single, agreed upon definition of serial homicide would thereby contribute to a more comprehensive understanding of the phenomenon, helping us see it in its actual proportions. Towards that particular end, criminologists have employed two different theoretical perspectives to examine serial homicide, the medical-psychological and the structural tradition that this chapter should now take as its focus.

The Medical-Psychological Tradition

The first perspective that we are going to explore is the medical-psychological tradition that examines serial homicide in relation to the genetics, background, personality, mental health and *modus operandi* of the perpetrator. It draws upon positivistic approaches to explaining crime, essentially viewing serial homicide as individual pathology. It therefore places the perpetrators at the heart of its focus, seeking to address the question of *what is wrong with them*. In that sense, it is very much consistent with the stereotypical notion that to understand serial homicide one needs to *enter the mind of the serial killer* and examine what makes them so different to the rest of us.

Serial Homicide and Biological Determinism

These ideas can be traced back to the nineteenth century when the father of criminology, Cesare Lombroso, who we alluded to in *Chapter 3*, first put forward the assumption that criminals were physiologically different to non-criminals.

Criminal behaviour was thought to have physiological roots, meaning that individuals who carried certain characteristics were predetermined to commit crime. Drawing upon these assumptions, examining head injuries of serial homicide offenders has been a common approach (Norris, 1988). This is based on the assumption that brain damage can result in cognitive and personality issues, and specifically impact self-regulation in terms of increasing impulsivity and aggression, both of which are viewed as risk factors. There have been indeed certain serial homicide offenders, such as Frederick West and Henry Lee Lucas who suffered head injuries.

These case studies alone do not allow us to draw firm conclusions with regards to the link between physiological issues and serial homicide though. This is predominately down to the fact that other offenders did not sustain such injuries. The neurological examination of Ted Bundy, for instance, produced no evidence of abnormality (Reid, 2007). This rationale explains why contemporary criminologists are sceptical when it comes to biological explanations of serial homicide. A similar positivist approach that should be noted, however, relates to the genetics of offenders. Men normally have one X and one Y chromosome. Researchers have identified, however, a rare genetic condition in small proportions of the male population, in which men are born with an extra Y chromosome (therefore XYY). The assumption that was put forward here is that these men, who have a super-male or hyper-male condition, known as Jacob's Syndrome, are more likely to be violent and subsequently commit crime. This does not quite help us make sense of serial homicide though, as most serial killers do not have the Jacob's Syndrome (Reid, 2007). The inability of biological determinism to produce conclusive answers in relation to the causes of serial homicide explains why scholars of the medical-psychological tradition examined the phenomenon from various different perspectives.

The MacDonald Triad

A particular approach to that end requires the consideration of early life experiences of serial killers, as these are thought to have shaped their offending behaviour. A framework that aimed at predicting violent and predatory behaviour based on a combination of childhood behaviours is known as the MacDonald Triad or the Homicidal Triad. Forensic psychiatrist John Marshall MacDonald (1963) examined 100 patients from the Colorado Psychopathic

Hospital in the US, who claimed that they had threatened to kill someone. He suggested that animal cruelty, bed-wetting past the age of five (enuresis), and fire-setting in childhood are indicators of later aggressive and violent behaviour, such as serial homicide. The MacDonald Triad can be seen as a starting point but also a milestone for the medical-psychological tradition. As such, it is commonly taught in criminology and psychology courses, whereas forensic practitioners take it into account in assessing risk, thereby validating it as a time-enduring framework. Despite its positive aspects, however, this piece of research does come with certain limitations that we need to consider when evaluating its usefulness. First, the sample used was considerably small and unrepresentative, a fact which set limits to its predictive power. Second, the patients who were tested had only threatened to kill and there is no evidence to suggest that they had actually acted upon these threats. This simply means that the research findings cannot be applied to homicide offenders (Wilson, Yardley and Lynes, 2015). In this context, the proposed triad of behaviours does little in terms of predicting serial homicide that is the topic at hand. Given these limitations, future studies are needed aimed at empirically validating the MacDonald triad by examining its individual characteristics.

In 1987, animal cruelty was included in the *Diagnostic and Statistical Manual of Mental Disorders*. It has been commonly viewed by criminal investigators to be a predictor for future serial killers. This is based on the assumption that killing animals is a means to end, thereby a way for serial killers to prepare for their subsequent crimes, essentially a rehearsal for killing humans (Wright and Hensley, 2003). Studies, however, challenge this assumption and suggest that explanations for animal cruelty are far more complex and diverse. These can include controlling the animal, expressing aggression, thrill-seeking, amusing others, retaliation, sadism, and prejudice against specific species (Kellert and Felthous, 1985). It should also be noted that research has only managed to link animal cruelty to antisocial behaviour, which of course does not necessarily mean violent behaviour.

Similarly, enuresis is primarily linked to psychological functioning and is viewed as a consequence of stress, anxiety and pressure, usually located within dysfunctional home environments (Parfitt and Alleyne, 2018). Along the same lines, fire-setting co-exists with aggressive behaviour, scholastic difficulties, conduct disorders and is primarily linked to abusive family environments, traumatic childhood experiences and interpersonal difficulties. In terms of linking fire-setting to future criminal behaviour, literature vaguely suggests that childhood fire-setters might engage in aggressive or non-aggressive crimes (Mehregany, 1993). Therefore there is no direct link between these individual behaviours and serial homicide. It should also be noted that no empirical research, as of today, has produced conclusive answers in relation to the three behaviours occurring together, meaning that fire-setting, enuresis and animal cruelty are not linked to each other.

Typologies of Serial Homicide

Much like single homicide, serial homicide can be divided in all sorts of ways. Taking as our focus the sex of the offenders for instance, we can discuss male-perpetrated and female-perpetrated serial homicide. The first thing that needs to be outlined is that serial homicide is by and large a male phenomenon with approximately 85 per cent of all offenders being male, opposed to only 15 per cent female (Hickey, 2006). Miller (2004) describes the typical male serial killer as white, 20-to-40-years-old, predominately targeting individuals from the same ethnic group as himself or herself, meaning that his or her crimes are usually intra-racial in nature. Male serial killers tend to collect trophies from the crime scene that they keep as mementos, they leave their characteristic signature on the body of their victims, and they sometimes engage in *post-mortem* mutilation or cannibalism. On the contrary, female serial killers are usually in their early thirties, white, and in many instances with no prior criminal record (Hickey, 2006). They can be described as educated, middle-class, predominately target-ing individuals who are socially, emotionally, or professionally close to them (Gurian, 2011). Their primary method of killing their victims is through poison-ing. There are exceptions to these rules, however, that we need to be mindful of. Aileen Wuornos, for example, unlike the typical female serial killer, had below average education, came from a disadvantaged background, and chose to shoot all her six victims that she had no prior relationship with. This indicates that serial homicide is a type of crime better examined on a case-by-case basis.

Focusing on the personalities of the offenders it should be noted that person-ality disorders have chronically been identified amongst both male and female serial killers (Egger, 1998; Harrison, Murphy, Bowers and Flaherty, 2015). Psychopathy, specifically, is a personality disorder that is characterised by antisocial behaviour and is commonly associated with serial killers. Superficial charm, manipulation, irresponsibility, impulsivity, lack of empathy, lack of remorse, insincere speech, overconfidence, selfishness and violence are some key characteristics. Psychopaths are perfectly aware of their actions, they understand the difference between right and wrong, and they know how to perform in a socially acceptable manner in any given situation. We can identify these traits in such serial homicide cases as those of Ted Bundy, Dennis Rader, Aileen Wuornos, Harold Shipman, Paul Bernardo, and Ian Brady to name a few. Ted Bundy specifically would put on display his identity as law school student, he knew how to be charming, and he would politely offer his victims a drive with his car, before raping and killing them.

The Hare Psychopathy checklist, currently known as the PCL-R (R = revised) was developed by Robert Hare and accounts for the interpersonal, emotional and behavioural deficits of psychopaths. It is a standardised method which yields a quantitative score with regards to the degree of psychopathy of the individual under examination (Wilson, Yardley and Lynes, 2015). The evaluation is based upon clinical interviews and an extensive review of records. It should be noted though that not every serial killer is a psychopath. For example, there is no conclusive evidence to suggest that Beverley Allitt, who was found responsible for killing four children in 1991, is a psychopath. Her crimes are rather attributed to her suffering Munchausen Syndrome by Proxy that led her to falsify illness in the children under her care so that she would attract attention for herself. Along the same lines, it should be noted that not all psychopaths are potential serial killers. An individual might be diagnosed with psychopathy and still be able to function without ever engaging in criminal activity.

Considering serial homicide in terms of the *modus operandi* we can distinguish serial homicide offenders as organized and disorganized, geographically stable and transient, those who act alone and team killers. Focusing on the first category that emerges here, organized serial killers are usually characterised by above average intelligence and a self-perceived sense of superiority. They tend to be meticulous in most aspects of their lives and the way they choose to commit their crimes reflects that (Miller, 2014). Their killings are carefully planned and executed with precision, paying particular attention to the concealment of evidence. This explains why they tend to evade police investigations for considerably more time than disorganized offenders. Harold Shipman, for example, would rely on his status as a trustworthy GP not only to approach and kill his victims, but also to falsify their medical records as a means of escaping detection, which explains how he managed to leave victims in the span of three decades. Disorganized serial killers, on the other hand, are usually below average in intelligence and lacking in social skills. They tend to feel inadequate, have low self-esteem and they are quite messy when it comes to planning and committing their crimes (Miller, 2004). Their attacks are impulsive and hectic and they are rarely concerned about concealing evidence.

An example of a disorganized serial killer would be none other than Jack the Ripper who was responsible for killing at least five sex workers back in the late-nineteenth century. His crimes are characterised by overkill, as he would quickly kill his victims and later stab their bodies multiple times. He would engage in *post-mortem* mutilation, never caring about concealing evidence, or simply hide the dead bodies. All of his victims were found within hours after their deaths. Jack the Ripper was also geographically stable in the sense that he only left victims in the area of Whitechapel in London's East End that he was very familiar with. By contrast, geographically transient serial killers travel to different areas to commit their crimes. Peter Sutcliffe, who worked as a lorry driver is a perfect example. His *modus operandi* had an impact on the investigation of the police, who struggled to link what appeared to be distant and separate incidents.

Finally, considering the third forensic distinction, it should be noted that team killers or couple killers or partner killers tend to commit their murders as a duo (Miller, 2014). The planning and execution of the attack usually draws upon the relationship of the offenders and overarching themes of dominance and submission. The dominant partner, that is usually the male, is perceived as the mastermind behind the attack. The primary motivation in these cases is sexual gratification. Women, viewed as being more submissive, take part in the killings to please their partners, frequently having a secondary role in the killing, in the sense that they are predominately concerned with baiting or seducing the victim. A typical example falling under this category would be Ian Brady and Myra Hindley who were found responsible for killing five children and sexually assaulting four between 1963 and 1965. Hindley has specifically stated that her role in the killings was to lure and abduct the children, following the wish Ian Brady had expressed in 1963 to commit the perfect murder (Downing, 2013). The couple are known to have suffered from the mental disorder *folie à deux*, meaning madness generated and exacerbated within a relationship between two people, indicating how the madness of Brady was transmitted to Hindley.

In terms of what drives serial killers to commit their crimes the most frequently cited typology in academic discourse belongs to Holmes and DeBurger (1988) who identified four different types, the visionary, the missionary, the hedonistic and the control-oriented type. Visionary serial killers commit their crimes in response to the command of imagined voices which they think to be real. They usually kill within the context of a psychotic break from reality. A typical example would be David Berkowitz, who was found responsible of killing 13 people in New York in 1976 and 1977 and who claimed to have committed his crimes in response to Satan ordering him to kill. Missionary serial killers believe their crimes serve a higher purpose of eliminating certain groups within society. They tend to target those such as the elderly, sex workers and gay men. An example would be Colin Ireland, known as the Gay Slayer, who targeted and killed five gay men back in 1993.

The hedonistic type refers to serial killers who usually derive sexual satisfaction from the murders. This would include individuals such as Ted Bundy who was convicted of raping and killing at least 30 women between 1974 and 1978. Finally, control-oriented serial killers derive pleasure from being able to exert control over their vulnerable victims. Despite controversy as to why he killed as many as 215 of his patients, the most frequently attributed motivation of Harold Shipman is that he committed his crimes as a means of controlling his helpless victims, who relied upon his scientific knowledge and treatment. Shipman would therefore fall under the control-oriented type.

As Hickey (2006) suggests the typology produced by Holmes and DeBurger is quite helpful in terms of classifying data and understanding what led certain offenders to commit their crimes. We need to be mindful though that these types might overlap one another. There are indeed serial killers who fall into more than one of the outlined categories. Peter Sutcliffe, for example, would be classified as visionary killer as he was diagnosed with paranoid schizophrenia, following his claims that it was the voice of God that pushed him commit his crimes. He would also fit the missionary type however, as he predominately targeted sex workers, even stating that he was on a mission to kill them. We should be therefore applying existing typologies to serial homicide cases with caution as these are not mutually exclusive.

The Structural Tradition

The structural tradition shifts the focus of our attention from the offenders and places it upon the social forces that contribute to the victimisation of certain social groups. It thereby widens the scope in which serial homicide is discussed and understood. This approach seeks to explore how social changes are responsible for producing serial killers during specific time periods. Leyton (1986), for example, was one of the first scholars to examine serial homicide through a sociological lens, viewing the phenomenon as a form of 'homicidal protest.' He specifically argued that multiple homicide offenders of the modern era, therefore those who operated post-World War II, predominately came from working-class or lower middle-class backgrounds and they targeted those belonging in the privileged middle-class. Their killings were viewed as a conduit through which they expressed their internalised frustration over the restrictions and pressures social arrangements had placed upon them. A critique of this thesis came from Grover and Soothill (1999) who noticed that British serial killers did not target individuals of higher social classes. They preyed upon the vulnerable ones instead.

Focusing upon the victims of serial homicide, we can indeed discover that marginalised social groups such as the elderly, sex workers, gay men, and children who run away from home have consistently and persistently been targeted by serial killers (Wilson, 2007). Such serial killers as Peter Sutcliffe, Steve Wright and Stephen Griffiths have predominately targeted sex workers. Michael Copeland, Dennis Nielsen, Colin Ireland, Peter Moore and Stephen Port have all preyed upon gay men. Ian Brady, Myra Hindley, Frederick West, Rose West, Robert Black and Beverley Allitt have all been responsible for killing children or young people, and finally such serial killers as Patrick Mackay, Kenneth Erskine, Colin Norris and of course Harold Shipman have targeted the elderly (Wilson, 2011).

What structural scholars take as a given is that there will always be individuals who will want to kill repeatedly. The key question to address is why society allows them to do so. In this context, negative societal values and attitudes towards sex workers, gay men, the elderly, and runaways are viewed as permissive. Serial killers target these socially marginalised groups, knowing society does not adequately value their lives. They are perfectly aware that this element of social exclusion can potentially allow them to get away with their crimes for a considerable amount of time, as has been the case in many instances.

Structural scholars have additionally utilised comparative studies that draw comparisons between serial homicide rates and changes in the political, economic and social landscape. The year 1986 constitutes the peak for serial homicide in Britain in terms of numbers of offenders and victims. During that year four serial killers were active at the same time, these being John Duffy, Kenneth Erskine, Robert Black and Harold Shipman, who collectively killed a total of 29 victims (more if you count suspected victims) (Wilson, 2011).

We could be focusing on the offenders in an attempt to find out what is wrong with them, but as mentioned above the structural approach would ask us to zoom our lenses out and focus on the broader politico-economic context instead. Throughout the 1980s, Margaret Thatcher served as Prime Minister of the United Kingdom, implementing *laissez-faire* economic policies known as Thatcherism. These would include low inflation, privatisation, free markets and government deregulation, solidifying consumer capitalism as the overarching economic philosophy. There was indeed promotion of the private sector, less government intervention, and less provision for those who were poor and unemployed (Wilson, 2011). Individualism, competition, success based on the failure of others remain key components of consumer capitalism as of today. In that context, humans tend to depend for their personal well-being and contentment on the level of personal consumption that typically involves the purchase and acquisition of material goods (Wright and Rogers, 2015). Humans are essentially converted into consumers, feeling entitled, pursuing their own interests even at the expense of others.

According to Jarvis (2007), serial killers, much like contemporary consumers, are defined by a sense of incompletion, a rigid sense of lacking they need to respond to. The argument here is that our consumerist culture with the insatiability and individualism it encompasses enables violence and—when taken to extremes—serial homicide. Wilson (2007) has further noted how consumer capitalism has resulted in widening social inequalities and a decline in collective social life. Drawing upon this, Lynes, Kelly and Uppal (2019) have highlighted how British serial killers have predominately been situated in the lower levels of the socioeconomic sphere. They resort to crime as a means of standing out, displaying autonomy from society, gaining some form of recognition for themselves, eventually shaping their self-identity; aims that they would not be able to achieve through monetary means given their disadvantaged position in society. These arguments are not to say that consumer capitalism is to blame for serial homicide. They are rather indicative of how this seemingly private and aberrant criminal behaviour alarmingly embodies norms and values that are very much mainstream.

It is finally worth-noting that the structural approach to the study of serial homicide relates to the occupational choice of offenders. Lynes (2017) has highlighted how British serial killers fall under five categories in terms of employment. There are those who were unemployed at the time of their killings and those who held legitimate employment in one of the following sectors: business, healthcare, driving, and public and personal service. In many instances, the occupational choice of serial killers facilitated their crimes. For example, healthcare serial killers, such as Beverley Allitt, Harold Shipman and Colin Norris, had access to both harmful substances and vulnerable patients who relied upon their medical assistance (Wilson, Yardley and Lynes, 2015). This gave the offenders the opportunity to commit their crimes and avoid suspicion for a considerable length of time given their professional status. Along similar lines, driving and transitory dependent work proved to be instrumental in the crimes of such serial killers as Peter Sutcliffe, Robert Black and Steve Wright, to name a few. Peter Sutcliffe, for example, would use his lorry to approach his victims, kill them in a safe space, move their bodies to a different location, and subsequently flee the crime scene (Ibid). His occupation notably equipped him with knowledge of road networks which resulted in him leaving victims in separate and distant locations, thereby hindering police investigation and avoiding detection. The work of Lynes (2017) specifically focuses on driving and transitory depended work in relation to serial homicide, a subject that had not been explored by contemporary criminologists to any considerable extent by that point.

Conclusion

This chapter has provided a concise outline of the academic discourse in relation to serial homicide. Longstanding debates with regards to the definition of the term were considered, before concluding that serial homicide occurs when an individual kills at least three people in a time-period greater than 30 days as a means of achieving personal gratification. Explanations of serial homicide draw upon two contested theoretical traditions—the medical-psychological and the structural. The former places at the heart of its focus the offenders and psychological factors which impact their crimes. The latter focuses on the victims and social forces which are thought to enable serial killers. It is suggested that a synthesis of both approaches can help us understand what drives serial killers to commit their crimes and why the rest of us, who view ourselves as different to them, sustain attitudes that are very much permissive.

Questions to consider
- How would you define serial homicide?
- Should we continue striving for a unified definition of the term?
- What are the key strengths and limitations of the medical-psychological tradition?
- What are the limitations of using typologies when attempting to categorise serial homicide?
- Which of the outlined traditions do you find the most useful in explaining serial homicide?

References

Adjorlolo, S., Chan, H. C. O. (2014), 'The Controversy of Defining Serial Murder: Revisited,' *Aggression and Violent Behavior*, 19(5), pp. 486–491.

Dietz, P. E. (1986), 'Mass, Serial and Sensational Homicides,' *Bulletin of the New York Academy of Medicine*, 62(5), pp. 477–491.

Downing, L. (2013), *The Subject of Murder*, London: University of Chicago Press.

Egger, S. A. (1998), *The Killers Among Us*, New Jersey: Simon & Schuster.

Federal Bureau of Investigation (2008), *Serial Murder: Multi-disciplinary Perspectives for Investigators*, Washington DC: Behavioral Analysis Unit, National Center for the Analysis of Violent Crime, US Department of Justice.

Ferguson, C. J., White, D. E., Cherry, S., Lorenz, M., Bhimani, Z. (2003), 'Defining and Classifying Serial Murder in the Context of Perpetrator Motivation,' *Journal of Criminal Justice*, 31, pp. 287–29.

Gurian, E. A. (2011), 'Female Serial Murderers: Directions for Future Research on a Hidden Population,' *International Journal of Offender Therapy and Comparative Criminology*, 55(1), pp. 27–42.

Haggerty, K. D. (2009), 'Modern Serial Killers,' *Crime, Media, Culture*, 5(2), pp. 168–187.

Harrison, M. A., Murphy, E. A., Bowers, T. G., and Flaherty, C. V. (2015), 'Female Serial killers in the United States: Means, Motives, and Makings, *The Journal of Forensic Psychiatry and Psychology*, pp. 1–24.

Hickey, E.W. (2006), *Serial Murderers and their Victims,* Belmont, CA: Thompson Wadsworth.

Holmes, R., M. and DeBurger, J. (1998), *Serial Murder,* Newbury Park, CA: Sage.

Holmes, R., M. and Holmes, S. T. (2001), *Murder in America* (2nd edn.), Thousand Oaks, CA: Sage.

Holmes, R., M., and Holmes, S.T. (2010), *Serial Murder*, Los Angeles, CA: Sage.

Jarvis, B. (2007), 'Monsters Inc: Serial Killers and Consumer Culture,' *Crime, Media, Culture*, 3(3), pp. 326–344.

Jenkins, P. (1994), *Using Murder: The Social Construction of Serial Homicide*, New York: Aldine de Gruyter.

Kellert, S. and Felthous, A. (1985), 'Childhood Cruelty Towards Animals Among Criminals and Noncriminals,' *Human Relations*, 38, pp. 113–129.

Lynes, A. (2017), *The Road to Murder*, Hook, Hampshire: Waterside Press.

Lynes, A., Kelly, C., Uppal, P. (2018), 'Benjamin's "Flâneur" and Serial Murder: An Ultra-Realist Literary Case Study of Levi Bellfield,' *Crime, Media, Culture*, 15(3), pp. 1–21.

MacDonald, J. (1963), 'The Threat to Kill,' *American Journal of Psychiatry*, 120, pp. 125–130.

MacDonald, A. (2013), *Murders and Acquisitions: Representations of the Serial Killer in Popular Culture,* London: Bloomsbury Academic.

Mehregany, Donna V. (1993), 'Firesetting in Children,' *Jefferson Journal of Psychiatry*, pp. 18–28.

Miller, L. (2014), 'Serial Killers: I. Subtypes, Patterns, and Motives,' *Aggression and Violent Behavior*, 19(1), pp. 1–11.

Norris, J. (1988), *Serial Killers,* Garden City, NY: Doubleday.

Parfitt, C. H. and Alleyne, E. (2018), 'Not the Sum of its Parts: A Critical Review of the MacDonald Triad,' *Trauma, Violence and Abuse*, pp. 1–11.

Reid, S. (2017), 'Development Pathways to Serial Homicide: A Critical Review of Biological Literature,' *Aggression and Violent Behavior*, 35, pp. 52–61.

Wilson, D. (2007), *Serial Killers: Hunting Britons and their Victims 1960–2006,* Winchester: Waterside Press.

Wilson, D. (2011), *A History of British Serial Killing,* London: Sphere.

Wilson, D., Yardley, E., Lynes, A. (2015), *Serial Killers and the Phenomenon of Serial Murder*, Hook, Hampshire: Waterside Press.

Wright, J. and Hensley, C. (2003), 'From Animal Cruelty to Serial Murder: Applying the Graduation Hypothesis,' *International Journal of Offender Therapy and Comparative Criminology*, 47(1), pp. 71–88.

Wright, E. O., Rogers J. (2015), *American Society*, New York, NY: Norton.

Yardley, E. and Wilson, D. (2016), *Female Serial Killers in Social Context,* Bristol: Policy Press.

CHAPTER 5

Mass and Spree Homicide

'Multiple homicide offenders (MHOs), defined as criminal defendants who murder more than one person during a criminal episode, occupy a peculiar place in criminology. Because of their lethality, MHOs are presumably deserving of study, but scholarly investigations of them are far exceeded by journalistic, popular, or true-crime treatises'

Delisi and Scherer, 2016, p. 367

Introduction

Complementing our discussion on serial killers, this chapter takes as its main focus mass and spree killers in order to provide students with a thorough overview of multiple homicide. These forms of offending constitute social issues and they are important to explore for various reasons. Multiple homicide cases generate unthinkable horror due to the unpredictable and seemingly random nature of the violence they involve. Their impact on primary and secondary victims is profound. The psychological consequences of experiencing an incident of mass killing, for instance, have been well-documented, involving post-traumatic stress disorder, anxiety, nervousness, irritability, feelings of helplessness and major depression (Norris, 2007). Mass homicide also impacts the community in which it occurs, chronically resulting in debates on gun control, offender accountability, especially in terms of mental health issues and dangerousness, as well as those regarding the inadequate responses of the Criminal Justice System.

With regard to spree homicide incidents, the action of an apparently demented individual who decides to engage in a killing spree results in the public feeling vulnerable, considering that they might well have been victims of this seemingly random attack. Media representations further fuel these public concerns and fears, essentially perpetuating stereotypical notions that MHOs are different to 'ordinary' humans (Wright et al, 2008). This results in the offenders being viewed as monsters, devils, larger-than-life entities that we should be afraid of. What is more, media tend to use the terms serial, mass and spree interchangeably, as they are rarely, if ever, concerned with what type of multicide has been committed (Holmes and Holmes, 2009). This invites us to identify and outline key similarities and differences between these forms of offending, in order to address any confusion surrounding these classifications and thereby develop a comprehensive understanding. Serial, mass and spree are indeed three distinct categories by chronology, location and motivation (Enzo, 2019). This chapter therefore includes definitions of mass and spree homicide, and outlines key characteristics of the perpetrators, in an attempt to shed light on the specifics of these criminal behaviours. Following the approach of previous chapters, case studies are utilised, in order to reinforce the conceptual frameworks that our discussion builds upon.

Defining Mass Homicide

For reasons outlined in *Chapter 4*, there is no single and agreed upon definition of the term 'mass homicide.' Chronically a wide range of criteria have been applied such as victim count, location and time period. The Federal Bureau of Investigation (FBI) defines mass homicide as the killing of four or more people at one time, a definition that is widely accepted in academia (Fox and Levin, 2003; Morton, 2008; Rush, 2003). *At one time* indicates that the killings take place in the same incident without a cooling-off period between them. This time element helps us differentiate mass homicide from serial homicide. Along similar lines, Dietz (1986) offers a somewhat minimalistic definition arguing that mass homicide is the premeditated killing of multiple victims in a single incident. Importantly, this definition highlights the premeditated nature of this form of offending, as mass killers usually plan out their attacks and only in rare instances do they act in spontaneous rage. Indeed, mass homicide is viewed as an individually motivated criminal behaviour as the killings are usually driven by intrinsic and expressive motivations (Hickey, 2006). Further to this, Holmes and Holmes (2009) have defined mass homicide as the killing of three or more people in one time and one place, a definition that, as we see, deviates from the proposed numeric requirement of the FBI. Much like we discussed in our previous chapter, numeric thresholds are important in terms of determining the increase or decrease of the frequency of multicide events. This explains why this numeric element has been the subject of considerable debate and constant re-evaluation amongst academics and law enforcement officials.

At this point, we should outline in clear terms that discussion in this chapter draws upon the comprehensive definition proposed by Holmes and Holmes (2009). The main issue that we identify in the definition proposed by the FBI is how the threshold of four victims to constitute mass homicide would simply leave the killings of three people in one time and one location unclassified. All things considered, mass homicide is a relatively rare form of crime, albeit more common than serial homicide (Hickey, 2006). It can take place in various locations such as domestic settings, workplaces, schools, campuses, movie theatres, shopping malls and churches. There have also been incidents of suicide-mass killings in airplanes whereby pilots or co-pilots caused deliberately the plane crash, as was the case with Germanwings Flight 9525 in March 2015 that resulted in 150 fatalities.

Key Characteristics of Mass Murderers

Despite their lethality, MHOs have received more attention from news media than by criminologists (Fox and Levin, 1998). This is predominately due to mass homicide being a relatively rare form of offending (Hickey, 2006) which potentially indicates that it is less deserving of scholarly investigation than instances of single homicide. Further to this, additional empirical issues involve limited access to data as criminal justice agencies might not share information with researchers. According to Delisi and Scherer (2006), this results in criminologists relying upon media reports to collect and analyse data. Alternatively, they work on specific case studies, concerned with providing criminal profiles of offenders which are indeed very informative but rather difficult to generalise and apply to other cases of mass homicide. With that being said, studies that have been conducted so far enable us to obtain an initial understanding in terms of key characteristics, motivations and *modus operandi*.

In terms of key characteristics, MHOs are primarily male, white, they usually plan out their attacks and they use firearms to kill victims in an abrupt and swift manner (Delisi and Scherer, 2006; Hickey, 2006; Messing and Heeren, 2004). In terms of victim selection, they usually target specific victims, for instance in cases of family annihilation. In public shootings, however, more people who happen to be in the location might be killed alongside the intended targets. Unlike serial killers who manage to get away with their crimes for a considerable amount of time, mass killers are usually quickly apprehended or killed by the police. In some cases they are only concerned with carrying out the attack, so they subsequently either turn themselves in to the authorities or they commit suicide (Hickey, 2006). In other cases, they put themselves in a vulnerable position so as to be killed by the police, a behaviour known as suicide by proxy (Holmes and Holmes, 2009).

Considering killers' motivations and inner drives, these are varied and diverse including rejection, failure, revenge, need to control and, in rarer instances, profit and sexual gratification (Hickey, 2006). Key risk factors include mental health issues such as depression, psychosis, paranoia (Delisi and Scherer, 2006), or personality disorders such as psychopathy and narcissism (Dutton, 2013; Mullen, 2004). Inconsistent parenting, dysfunctional family structures, social isolation, marginalisation, inability to cope with stress, preoccupation with weaponry, impulsivity and obsessive beliefs have also been documented (Bondu and Scheithauer, 2014; Delisi and Scherer, 2006). Research also suggests aggression, misogyny and prior abusive behaviour, especially against women, as risk factors (Marganski, 2019). The range of potential explanations for mass homicide unfortunately hinders conclusive answers as to what drove these individuals to this severe form of targeted violence, which results in a lack of consistent offender profiling. Verlinden, Hersen and Thomas (2000) have attempted to categorise these factors at four different levels, these being the individual, family, peers and environmental.

Importantly, when focusing upon individual factors, in other words on the psyche of mass homicide offenders, particular attention should be placed upon their narcissism. Key characteristics of narcissistic personality disorder involve a constant need for attention and validation, a sense of grandiosity, superiority, entitlement, sensitivity to criticism and rejection, inability to accept fault, tendency to claim victim status, manipulative, controlling behaviour, and lack of empathy (Bondu and Scheithauer, 2014). This analysis, of course, contradicts common perceptions that narcissists are confident, self-absorbed individuals who love themselves. It is quite the opposite, actually. They are insecure, over-sensitive to critique, they care to be seen as something important, they care to impress. When this sense of superiority is not acknowledged nor validated, narcissists resort to abusive behaviour as a means of responding to the rejection they feel they experience. This partially explains why narcissism is frequently identified amongst MHOs. They are individuals who remain obsessed with rejection and subsequently exaggerate their responses to it (Dutton, White and Fogarty, 2013). Their narcissistic traits can also be identified in their *modus operandi*, as they decide to inflict harm on others and then, to put it simply, go down on their own terms. As mentioned above, they either kill themselves, or turn themselves in to the authorities or place themselves at risk so that they are killed, which proves their tendency to remain in control of their behaviour and its consequences. Considering this analysis, it should additionally be noted that mass media have been argued to be contributing to mass homicide (Hickey, 2006) in the sense that they provide narcissistic supply to mass murderers given the attention that their crimes receive, a fact that these individuals are very much aware of. Therefore, media attention and subsequent public recognition provide an incentive for mass killers to commit their crimes, so that they are eventually placed in the pantheon of the MHOs that society has such a fascination with.

Further considering individual characteristics, scholars have produced classifications with regard to MHOs applying a wide range of criteria. Holmes and Holmes (2009) have introduced a typology that is useful in terms of providing an initial understanding as to why or in which context MHOs commit their crimes. They specifically list:

- The Disciple Killer that is an individual who commits crime following instructions of a leader that is viewed as charismatic. An example would be the Manson Family who thought Charles Manson to be the manifestation of Jesus Christ and killed at his behest.
- The Family Annihilator, that is a person who kills family members and usually commits suicide afterwards. An example would be Christopher Foster who in August 2008 shot his wife and daughter

in the family home in Maesbrook before setting the property on fire and killing himself.

- The Disgruntled Employee that is used to describe an angry employee who seeks revenge from employers or co-workers due to actual or perceived mistreatment. In the US workplace mass shootings occur twice every year with approximately 12 people being killed every year (Lee and McCrie, 2012).

- The Ideological Killer who persuades others to commit crime, much like cult leader Charles Manson did back in the summer of 1969 when he orchestrated the Tate-LaBianca murders.

- The Set and Run Killer that is an individual whose deviates from our analysis above, as they intend to evade police detection before or after their attacks. Their method of killing usually involves setting timers on bombs, food poisoning and setting fires (arson).

- The Disgruntled Citizen who much like the disgruntled employee category seeks revenge for imagined or actual wrongs that they have experienced. Their victim selection tends to be random as they are solely preoccupied with letting their anger out.

- The Psychotic Killer who is suffering psychosis and is considered legally insane.

- The School Shooter that is a person who targets students and members of staff in schools and colleges. An example would be Thomas Watt Hamilton whose case we discuss in detail later in this chapter.

Dietz (1986) has also referred to 'pseudo-commando' shooters, individuals who commit murder due to their fascination with guns. Existing typologies help us classify data into neat categories and quickly make sense of specific cases studies that share key characteristics. However, we do need to be mindful of certain limitations. The basis upon which these classifications are built is considerably varied. Some refer to the motivations of the offender (Disgruntled Employee, Disgruntled Citizen), and others to their intention to escape (Set and Run Killer). Some refer to the location of the killings (School Shooters), and others to their context (Family Annihilator, Disciple Killer). Lack of coherence in terms of the elements upon which existing classifications are constructed results in them overlapping one another. For instance, a School

Shooter could as well fit the Disgruntled Employee category. Similarly, a Disciple Killer might as well fall under the Set and Run killer typology, as long as there is a plan to get away with the attack. We therefore need to be mindful when we apply these typologies to mass homicide incidents, as they are not mutually exclusive.

Finally, in terms of exploring how we shape our understanding of mass homicide, attention should be placed upon the role of the media. This is deemed necessary as the public is informed of such incidents through mass media platforms, but also because much criminological inquiry on mass homicide has relied upon news media reports as a means of collecting relevant data. As discussed in *Chapter 3*, mass media tend to focus on micro explanations in their representation of homicide. It comes as no surprise that when reporting mass killings considerable focus is placed upon the mental health issues of the offender. This unavoidably creates a dichotomy in public perception—we view these individuals as different to us because of their mental health issues. However, it needs to be stressed that MHOs are not an alien other, they are individuals who are very much embedded in the community. Besides, mental health issues alone do not adequately explain mass homicide, or any other form of crime for that matter. There are people who are suffering mental health issues and they never engage in criminal activity. We should therefore shift our focus of attention from *why* mass homicide offenders kill to *how* they kill. According to Hickey (2006, p. 17) 'invariably, handguns, semiautomatic guns, and rifles are the weapons used to kill suddenly and swiftly.' This indicates that access to firearms is key to making sense of mass homicide (Dutton, White and Fogarty, 2013). The following case study helps us reinforce this point.

Case Study: The Dunblane Massacre

Location: Dunblane Primary School near Stirling, Scotland.

Time: 13 March 1996.

The Victims: Sixteen children aged five and six, and their teacher, were gunned down by a local man in what is often described as an unexplained and unprecedented attack.

The Suspect: The perpetrator was Thomas Watt Hamilton, who was 43-years-old at the time he committed this mass murder. Leading up to the event there had been several complaints to police regarding Hamilton's behaviour towards the young boys who attended the youth clubs he directed. Claims had been made of him having taken photographs of semi-naked boys without parental consent. In the 1970s, there were also several complaints made about his leadership in the scouts, including two occasions when scouts were forced to sleep with Hamilton in his van during hill-walking expeditions. In 1974, Hamilton's scout warrant was withdrawn, with the county commissioner stating that he was suspicious of his moral intentions towards boys (Cusick, 1996). In later years, Hamilton claimed in letters that rumours and stories about him and his reported behaviour resulted in his shop closing for business in 1993. Specifically, he claimed that his kitchen-fitting business, which relied on orders from the Dunblane area, had been destroyed by the hint of scandal (Cohen, 1996). Only a few months prior to the tragic event, Hamilton complained that he was being targeted by local police and the scout movement in an attempt to stop him from organizing a boys' club (Ibid). In the months before the murders, a gun club refused to let Hamilton join. Two members knew him and said the club should have nothing to do with him (Seely, 1996). Whilst there has been much speculation within both mainstream media and academic circles, to this day we are no closer to determining the reason why Hamilton decided to target and kill such young children and their teacher.

The Event: On the morning of Wednesday, 13 March 1996, Hamilton drove approximately five miles to Dunblane. He arrived at the grounds of Dunblane Primary School at around 9.30 am and parked his van near a telegraph pole in the car park of the school. Hamilton cut the cables at the bottom of the pole, which served nearby houses, with a set of pliers before making his way across the car park towards the school buildings. After entering the school, he made his way to the gymnasium armed with four legally-held handguns. He was also carrying 743 cartridges of ammunition. In the gym was a class of 28 Primary 1 pupils preparing for a PE lesson in the presence of three adult members of staff. Gwen Mayor, the teacher of the Primary 1 class, was shot and killed instantly. From entering the gymnasium and walking a few steps, Hamilton had fired 29 shots with one of the pistols, killed one child, and injured several others. He then went towards the centre of the gym, firing 16 shots at point-blank range at a group of children who had been incapacitated by his earlier shots. Hamilton then left the gym briefly through the fire exit, firing another four shots towards the cloakroom of the library, striking and injuring Grace Tweddle, another member of staff at the school. In the mobile classroom closest to the fire exit where Hamilton was standing, Catherine Gordon saw him firing shots and instructed her Primary 7 class to get down onto the floor before Hamilton fired nine bullets into the classroom, striking books and equipment. One bullet passed through a chair where a child had been sitting seconds before. Hamilton then re-entered the gym. He put the barrel of the gun in his mouth, pointed it upwards, and pulled the trigger, killing himself. A total of 32 people sustained gunshot wounds inflicted by Hamilton over a three-to-four minute period, 16 of whom were fatally wounded in the gymnasium, which included Gwen Mayor and 15 of her pupils. One other child died later while being transported to hospital.

The aftermath of the Dunblane massacre sparked intense debates concerning the sale and availability of firearms. The Cullen Reports, the result of the inquiry into the massacre, recommended that the government introduce tighter controls on handgun ownership and consider whether an outright ban on private ownership would be in the public interest (Barnett, 2017). The Gun Control Network was founded in the aftermath of the shootings and was supported by some parents of the victims of the Dunblane shooting (Squires, 2016). In response to this public debate, the Conservative Government of John Major introduced the Firearms (Amendment) Act 1997, which banned all cartridge ammunition handguns with the exception of .22 calibre single-shot weapons in England, Scotland and Wales, and following the 1997 General Election, the Labour government of Tony Blair introduced the Firearms (Amendment) (No. 2) Act 1997, banning the remaining .22 cartridge handguns as well. A similar ban was introduced in Australia, where in 1996 (the same year as the Dunblane massacre) the Port Arthur massacre took place, in which 35 people were killed (Wahlquist, 2016). After the Port Arthur massacre, the National Firearms Agreement was made, which included a ban on all semi-automatic rifles and all semi-automatic and pump-action shotguns, and a system of licensing and ownership controls. The 'gun buy-back scheme' started on 1 October 1996 and concluded on 30 September 1997 (Wallace, 2019). Whilst North America is continually debating tighter regulation of guns, with a primary focus on assault rifles, both the UK and Australia have witnessed considerably fewer cases of mass murder (with the use of a firearm), which provides a compelling reason as to why gun control is an effective and practical step in preventing such tragedies from occurring.

Within the context of the US, it is important to note that it has the largest civilian-owned stock of guns in the world. At the end of 2017, the Small Arms Survey reported there were an estimated 393 million firearms in the US (excluding arms used by the military and police) — This 'represents 45.8 per cent of the world's civilian-owned guns' (Ibid). This is only further compounded when we consider that, in 2019 alone, there were more mass shootings than days in North America (Silverstein, 2020). Specifically, by the end of 2019, there were 417 mass shootings in the US, according to data from the non-profit Gun Violence Archive (GVA), which tracks every mass shooting in the country (Ibid). So many cases of mass murder has resulted in many being neglected or ignored by the media, but such incidents in 2019 included a shooting at Walmart in El Paso, Texas with 22 people killed with another 24 wounded, a shooting in a municipal building in Virginia Beach where a former city employee killed 12 people and wounded four, and a drive-by shooting spree in Odessa and Midland, Texas that left seven people dead and 24 wounded. While it is important to acknowledge that there has been increasing support for the regulation and banning of certain firearms, it is essential to stress that the US Constitution (in the form of the Second Amendment) protects the right to bear arms. So too, the National Rifle Association (NRA) have become an increasingly powerful lobbying arm that has significant political influence. The NRA has a membership of five million Americans and significant economic resources—funding politicians and lobbying for and against legislation.

While many Americans may have a nuanced approach to gun laws, the NRA just says 'no' to proposed controls (BBC News, 2020). For instance, during the 2016 general election, the NRA spent a record $54 million on 86 Republican candidates. In doing so they often produced advertisements in support of the Republican candidate and criticising their Democratic opponent (Reinhard and Ballhaus, 2016). Among the 535 current members of Congress, 307 have received either direct campaign contributions from the NRA and its affiliates or benefited from independent NRA spending on advertising supporting their campaigns (Ibid). A huge symbiotic relationship between politicians and the NRA has developed, effectively putting a barrier in front of gun control efforts in the face of the growing death toll.

Defining Spree Homicide

The term spree homicide is yet another social construction as various labels and definitions have chronically been developed to describe this form of offending. An initial label 'disorganised asocial lust murderer' was proposed by Hazelwood and Douglas (1980) in order to describe offenders who killed randomly without a set plan of action. This label places particular attention on the impulsivity that characterises spree killers, as they tend to commit their crimes in an unplanned, non-methodological and spontaneous manner (Delisi et al, 2008). Additional labels such as 'rampage killers' and 'killing machines' (Hickey, 2006) have also been applied in order to highlight the unpredictable and frantic manner in which these individuals engage in their killing sprees. Specifically, viewing spree killers as killing machines helps us understand how they are very much preoccupied with carrying out the attacks, paying little to no attention to the implications of their actions. This explains why their crimes do not last for a prolonged period of time—caring only to attack but not to conceal their crimes, they tend to be arrested or killed by the police very quickly. Considering that spree killers carry out their killings in a relatively short period of time, Delisi et al (2008) also referred to them as 'hybrid cases,' in order to highlight how criminological inquiry situates these offenders somewhere between mass murderers, who kill in one specific location, at one specific time, and serial killers whose crimes span over months, years and, in some instances, decades. Yaksic (2019) describes spree killers as 'rapid sequence homicide offenders' as a means of highlighting the swift and bombastic nature of their killings. This time element between the attacks has been an integral part of spree homicide definitions. Delisi et al (Ibid, p. 40) define spree killers as 'homicide offenders who committed their crimes in a time span that was greater than one day and less than 14 days inclusive,' thereby placing particular attention on the lack of an emotional cooling-off period between the crimes. This essentially means that the killings of spree killers are viewed as one incident only, in the sense that these offenders do not abstain from their criminal behaviours. This constitutes a key difference between spree and serial homicide. According to Holmes and Holmes (2009), a spree killer is a person who has killed three or more people within a 30-day period. This chapter draws upon this definition due to its consistency with our proposed definition of the term *serial killer* that is an individual whose crimes last for a time period greater than 30 days.

Key Characteristics of Spree Killers

In terms of their key characteristics, spree killers can be considerably instrumental, as they tend to target individuals who meet their personal needs at the time (Hickey, 2006). They usually kill for necessities such as money or drugs and they tend to select victims randomly, ranging from acquaintances to random bystanders. This partially explains why spree homicide is frequently committed in conjunction with other crimes such as robbery, burglary, abduction and sexual assault (Jenkins, 1992). Empirical research conducted by Delisi et al (2006) confirms that spree killers tend to commit more robberies, burglaries, abductions, assaults and weapon offences than any other multiple homicide offender. This helps us differentiate spree from serial and mass homicide and thereby understand why this unique form of offending needs to be examined separately.

Along similar lines, whilst serial killers predominately seek sexual gratification, spree killers are usually motivated by feelings of resentment, rejection, and disappointment which results in an emotional state of anger. Their crime sprees are therefore viewed as conduits through which they respond to life stressors (Howard, 2017). This is a process through which spree homicide offenders perceive to be regaining control over their lives, re-evaluating their self-concept.

They are no longer frustrated individuals, immobilised by the pressures social institutions have placed upon them. They are forces to be reckoned with, they react, choosing to harm others, to dominate instead of being dominated. As Yaksic (2019, p. 140) puts it 'maladaptive patterns of cognition, emotion and behaviour result in interpersonal problems and eventually transform into an outward expression of social dominance.'

In terms of their *modus operandi*, spree killers tend to be spontaneous, impulsive, having little to no concern over the consequences of their actions, facts that further differentiate them from serial killers that tend to be calculating, stoic and very much concerned with avoiding suspicion and detection (Yaksic, 2015). However, there should be an acknowledgement that there might be some shared features and characteristics amongst MHOs, especially when considering spree homicide on a case-by-case basis. This predominately relates to risk factors that underpin spree homicide. Much like other forms of multicide, mental health issues and antisocial behaviour are prevalent amongst spree killers (Holmes and Holmes, 2009). Further to this, much like serial and mass homicide, there is no consensus as to whether a prior criminal record should be viewed as predictive of spree homicide. Another similarity that should be noted is that spree homicide is by and large a male phenomenon. This partially explains why the rare instances of female perpetrators generate much media attention and evoke emotional public reactions. The case of Joanna Dennehy helps support this assumption.

Case Study: The Peterborough ditch murders
Location: Cambridgeshire, England
Timeframe: 19-to-29 March 2013
The Victims: The first victim was Lukasz Slaboszewski, a Polish national, who was killed on 19 March. John Chapman, a housemate of the perpetrator, was killed on the 29 March along with Kevin Lee, a property developer. Lee's body was found dressed in a black sequined dress, which the perpetrator placed on Lee before disposing of his corpse. All victims were found with multiple stab wounds. After the killings, the perpetrator was driven by an accomplice, Gary Stretch, to Hereford where she stabbed two men, chosen separately and at random, both of whom survived.
The Perpetrator: Joanna Dennehy was born in 1982 in St Albans, Hertfordshire. She was raised in a four-bedroom house in the wealthy commuter town of Harpenden in that county. Growing-up she regularly played school hockey and netball. Joanna had two children and, it has been reported, there were few warning signs of the behaviour she would later exhibit in March 2013. However, she has been diagnosed with several psychopathic and antisocial disorders, including borderline personality disorder. After her arrest she was also diagnosed with paraphilia sadomasochism, where sexual excitement is derived from pain and humiliation. Leading-up to the murders, Kevin Lee had been trying to evict Slaboszewski, Chapman and Dennehy in the weeks before the killings. Toni Roberts, who used to live in the house, told the court that the tenants had been served an eviction notice by him ordering them out by the 25 April so the house could be renovated. The court was told that she then had a 'thirst for blood' and while on the journey to Hereford the court heard that Dennehy said that 'I want to have my fun' and that she 'wanted nine victims' (*The Telegraph*, 2017).
The Trial: In November 2013, Dennehy pleaded guilty to all three murders and two further attempted murders (BBC News, 2013). Two men, Gary Stretch (formerly known as Gary Richards), 47, and Leslie Layton, 36, stood trial charged with a range of crimes for assisting Dennehy. On 10 February, Richards was found guilty of attempted murder and Layton was found guilty of perverting the course of justice. On 28 February

2014, at the Old Bailey, Dennehy was sentenced to life imprisonment (Dodd, 2014). The trial judge, Mr Justice Spencer, recommended that she should never be released due to the premeditation of each murder. The judge said further that Dennehy was sadomasochistic, and lacked the normal range of human emotions (McKinney, 2015). Due to the perceived severity and brutality of the crimes committed, she joins serial murderers Myra Hindley and Rosemary West as the only women to receive such a punishment.

It is important that we consider the media representation of Joanna Dennehy. Not only do many media accounts of this case incorrectly define her as a serial murderer due to the perceived newsworthiness of such a label, but there is significant attention towards her gender. Female offenders are often considered as being 'doubly deviant, doubly damned' as they are not only judged for transgressing the criminal law, but more importantly, the 'laws' governing acceptable forms of femininity (Lloyd, 1995).

Representations of female offenders often become entrenched with over-simplistic categories such as 'mythical monster,' 'bad mother' and/or 'mad' or 'bad' (Ballinger, 2000; Jewkes, 2015; Jones and Wardle, 2008). Those female offenders who are constructed as bad, as in the case of Dennehy, are viewed to be inherently evil and wilfully defiant of their gender role expectations (Berrington and Honkatukia, 2002). Dyer (1993, p. 14) argues that these representations encourage us to create overly simple 'short-cuts' regarding explanations for female offending. Due to the perceived abnormality of female offending (Naylor, 2001; Young, 1999), journalists often use overly simplistic and gendered discourses and language to 'explain' female criminality (Jewkes, 2015). Othering emphasises polarisations, such as 'insiders' and 'outsiders,' 'normal,' and 'deviant' and thus serves to create distinct boundaries between 'us and them,' who are in this case female offenders. Young (1999, p. 104) argues essentialism is vitally important when creating 'others', as 'it separates out human groups on the basis of their culture or nature.' This notion is particularly important for this current case study, as images and depictions of female offenders, such as Dennehy, encourage the categorisation of 'other' on the basis of physical appearance, thus again highlighting the continued influence and impact of Lombroso's (1893) work. Whilst all offenders are to some extent viewed to be 'others,' female criminals are more readily ascribed this label, due to the perceived abnormality of the female offender and the additional layer of gendered deviancy, in comparison to male counterparts (Heidensohn, 1996; Lloyd, 1995).

Conclusion

This chapter has provided an overview of academic discourse and research findings on mass and spree homicide. Discussion has specifically focused upon definitional issues and key characteristics attributed to the perpetrators. Despite their lethality and devastating consequences, these criminal behaviours have been somewhat overlooked by criminological inquiry. Criminologists have been preoccupied with constructing definitions and classifications, which hinders a more critical understanding of these forms of offending. Stereotypical media representations contribute to uncritical thinking as they focus on simplistic micro-explanations, persistently describing the offenders as demented monsters who kill at random. This creates a sense of othering — it is them against us. It is important to understand though that multiple homicide offenders, as scary and uncomfortable as that feels, are individuals who are very much embedded in the community. Further to this, scholars have outlined an array of motivations and risk factors which makes it difficult, if not impossible, to draw firm conclusions as to why these offenders decide to attack multiple individuals. Subsequently predicting and preventing mass and spree homicide are deemed considerably challenging.

There is a solid basis upon which to build, however, as we are now able to highlight key differences and similarities between serial, spree and mass homicides. We can therefore differentiate these distinct forms of multicide and examine each one of them in their own right. For reasons outlined in *Chapter 3*, future research should essentially aim at an integrated approach to explaining mass and spree homicide, combining micro, meso and macro explanations. We are in need of a multi-level research framework which will help us address questions that scholarship has so far left unanswered.

Questions to consider:
- Should we strive for unified definitions of mass and spree homicide?
- How is narcissism different to psychopathy?
- What are the key differences between mass and spree killers in terms of their *modus operandi*?
- Why is serial homicide more newsworthy than spree homicide?

References

Ballinger, A. (2000), *Dead Woman Walking*, Aldershot: Ashgate.

Barnett, D. (2017), 'Firearms Act: Twenty Years On, Has It Made a Difference?,' *Independent*, 16 December: https://www.independent.co.uk/news/long_reads/firearms-act-twenty-years-has-it-made-difference-dunblane-port-arthur-a8110911.html

BBC News (2013), 'Peterborough ditch deaths: Joanna Dennehy pleads guilty,' 18 November: https://www.bbc.co.uk/news/uk-england-24987953

BBC News (2020), 'US gun control: What is the NRA and why is it so powerful?', 6 August: https://www.bbc.co.uk/news/world-us-canada-35261394

Berrington, E., and Honkatukia, P. (2002), 'An Evil Monster and a Poor Thing: Female Violence in the Media,' *Journal of Scandinavian Studies in Criminology and Crime Prevention*, 3, pp. 50–72.

Bondu, R. and Scheithauer, H. (2014), 'Kill One Or Kill Them All? Differences Between Single and Multiple Victim School Shootings,' *European Journal of Criminology*, 12(3), pp. 277–299.

Cohen, N. (1996), 'The Life and Death of Thomas Watt Hamilton,' *Independent*, 17 March: https://www.independent.co.uk/news/uk/home-news/the-life-and-death-of-thomas-watt-hamilton-1672323.html

Cusick, J. (1996), 'Dunblane Killer was "Blacklisted" after Chaotic Trip,' *Independent*, 5 June: https://www.independent.co.uk/news/dunblane-killer-was-blacklisted-after-chaotic-trip-1335501.html

Delisi, M. and Hochstetler, A., Scherer, A. M., Purhmann, A., Berg, M. T. (2008), 'The Starkweather Syndrome: Exploring Criminal History Antecedents of Homicide Crime Sprees,' *Criminal Justice Studies*, 21(1), pp. 37–47.

Delisi, M. and Scherer, A. M. (2006), 'Multiple Homicide Offenders: Offense Characteristics, Social Correlates and Criminal Careers,' *Criminal Justice and Behaviour*, 33, pp. 367–391.

Dietz, P. E. (1986), 'Mass, Serial and Sensational Homicides,' *Bulletin of the New York Academy of Medicine*, 62(5), pp. 477–491.

Dodd, V. (2014), 'Joanne Dennehy given whole-life jail sentence for triple murder,' *Guardian*, 28 February: https://www.theguardian.com/uk-news/2014/feb/28/joanna-dennehy-whole-life-jail-sentence

Dutton, D. G., White, K. R., Fogarty, D. (2013), 'Paranoid Thinking in Mass Shooters,' *Aggression and Violent Behaviour*, 18, pp. 548–553.

Dyer, R. (1993), *The Matter of Images: Essays on Representation*, London: Routledge.

Fox, J. A. and Levin, J. (2003), 'Mass Murder: An Analysis of Extreme Violence,' *Journal of Applied Psychoanalytic Studies*, 5, pp. 47–64.

Hazelwood, R. R. and Douglas, J. E. (1980), 'The Last Murderer,' *FBI Law Enforcement Bulletin*, 49, pp. 18–22.

Heidensohn, F. (1996), *Women and Crime* (2nd edn.), Basingstoke: Macmillan.

Holmes, R. M. and Holmes, S. T. (2009), *Serial Murder*, London: Sage

Howard, R. C. (2017), 'Refining the Construct of Anger in Relation to Personality Disorders,' *Journal of Behaviour*, 2(3), pp. 1013–1019.

Jenkins, P. (1992), 'A Murder Wave? Trends in American Serial Homicide, 1940–1990,' *Criminal Justice Review*, 17, pp. 1–19.

Jewkes, Y. (2015), *Media and Crime* (3rd edn.), London: Sage.

Jones, P., and Wardle, C. (2008), '"No Emotion, No sympathy": The Visual Construction of Maxine Carr,' *Crime, Media and Culture*, 4, pp. 53–71.

Lee, S. and McCrie, R. (2012), *Mass Homicides by Employees in the American Workplace*, Alexandria, VA: ASIS Foundation Inc.

Lloyd, A. (1995), *Doubly Deviant, Doubly Damned: Society's Treatment of Violent Women*, London: Penguin.

Lombroso, C., and Ferrero, G. (2004/1893), *Criminal Woman, The Prostitute, and the Normal Woman*, Durham, NC: Duke University Press.

Marganski, A. J. (2019), 'Making a Murderer: The Importance of Gender and Violence Against Women in Mass Murder Events,' *Sociology Compass*, 13(9), e12730.

McKinney, E. (2015). 'Birmingham criminologist to probe mind of UK's first female serial killer Joanne Dennehy', *Birmingham Live*, 31

January: https://www.birminghammail.co.uk/news/midlands-news/birmingham-criminologist-probe-mind-uks-8553466

Messing, J. T. and Heeren, J. W. (2004), 'Another Side of Multiple Murder: Women Killers in the Domestic Context,' *Homicide Studies*, 8, pp. 123–158.

Morton, R. J. (2005), 'Serial Murder: Multi-disciplinary Perspectives for Investigators,' National Center for the Analysis of Violent Crime, Critical Incident Response Group, Federal Bureau of Investigation: https://www.fbi.gov/stats-services/publications/serial-murder

Mullen, P. E. (2004). 'The Autogenic (Self-generated) Massacre,' *Behavioural Sciences and the Law*, 22, pp. 357–374.

Norris, F. (2007), 'Impact of Mass Shootings on Survivors, Families and Communities,' *National Center for Post-traumatic Stress Disorder*, 18(3).

Reinhard, B. and Ballhaus, R. (2016), 'NRA Shows Its Support for Donald Trump With Big Ad Spending,' *Wall Street Journal*, 25 October: https://www.wsj.com/articles/nra-shows-its-support-for-donald-trump-with-big-ad-spending-1477431363

Rush, G. E. (2003), *The Dictionary of Criminal Justice*, New York: Dushkin/McGraw-Hill.

Seely, R. (1996), 'Dunblane Kids' Killer Had Been Denied Gun Club Membership,' *AP News*, 14 March: https://apnews.com/article/55806fde638951f5c1dde991c852ac54

Silverstein, J. (2020). 'There were more mass shootings than days in 2019,' CBS News, 2 January: https://www.cbsnews.com/news/mass-shootings-2019-more-than-days-365/

Squires, P. (2016). 'Dunblane massacre 20 years on: how Britain rewrote its gun laws — and the challenge it faces now,' *The Conversation*, 11 March: https://theconversation.com/dunblane-massacre-20-years-on-how-britain-rewrote-its-gun-laws-and-the-challenge-it-faces-now-55896

Verlinden, S., Hersen, M., Thomas, J. (2000), 'Risk Factors in School Shootings,' *Clinical Psychology Review*, 20(1), pp. 3–56.

Wahlquist, C. (2016), 'It took one massacre: how Australia embraced gun control after Port Arthur,' *Guardian*, 14 March: https://www.theguardian.com/world/2016/mar/15/it-took-one-massacre-how-australia-made-gun-control-happen-after-port-arthur

Wallace, L. (2019). 'Could a national gun-buyback program reduce the 393 million firearms on America's streets?,' ABC News, 5 August: https://www.abc.net.au/news/2019-08-05/us-shootings-gun-buy-back/11383084

'Who is serial killer Joanna Dennehy?' (2017), *Telegraph*, 28 July: https://www.telegraph.co.uk/news/0/serial-killer-joanna-dennehy/

Wright, K. A., Pratt, T. C., Delisi, M. (2008), 'Examining Offending Specialisation in a Sample of Male Multiple Homicide Offenders,' *Homicide Studies*, 12(4), 381-398.

Yaksic, E. (2015), 'Addressing the Challenges and Limitations of Utilizing Data to Study Serial Homicide,' *Crime Psychology Review*, 1(1), pp. 108–134.

Yaksic, E. (2019), 'Moving Past Sporadic Eruptions, Discursive Killing, and Running Amok: Recognizing the Convergence of the Serial and Spree Killer,' *Journal of Criminal Psychology*, 9(3), pp. 138–146.

Young, J. (1999), *The Exclusive Society*, London: Sage.

CHAPTER 6

Genocide

'Why is the killing of a million a lesser crime than the killing of an individual?'

Raphael Lemkin, Polish lawyer

Introduction

The above quote from Raphael Lemkin who coined the term 'genocide' upon losing 49 relatives during the course of the Holocaust has never been more poignant than in today's celebrity obsessed mediascape. For instance, the media ignites into a frenzy whenever there is a serial murderer on the loose, or when a famous celebrity commits homicide (such as in the case of American record producer, musician, songwriter, and convicted murderer Phil Spector) or is the victim of such a crime (for example, the murder of former Beatles member John Lennon). While the media is preoccupied in the reporting on famous celebrities who commit acts of murder or, in the case of serial murderers, providing celebrity status to such individuals (Wilson et al, 2010), violent and brutal acts carried out by the hands of various States are either briefly touched upon or omitted entirely. As Communist and Soviet Leader Joseph Stalin stated, 'a single death is a tragedy; a million deaths is a statistic.' While such a quote for many may be distasteful and merely an attempt to provide a justification, for the deaths of millions of people sanctioned by Stalin it would unfortunately appear that such sentiments towards mass murder are shared by the mainstream media.

Key Term: Holocaust
- The World War II genocide of the European Jews.
- Between 1941 and 1945 across German-occupied Europe, Nazi Germany, aided by local collaborators, systematically murdered some six million Jews, around two-thirds of Europe's Jewish population.
- The government of Nazi Germany also targeted other groups for various discriminatory reasons due to their ethnicity, religion, political beliefs, or sexual orientation.
- In total, including the six million Jewish deaths, the total number murdered during the Holocaust is estimated at 17 million.

The above is only further compounded when we consider that there are currently, according to Genocide Watch — the coordinator of the Alliance Against Genocide — eight countries listed under 'genocide emergency', including Yemen, Myanmar, Iraq, Nigeria and Sudan (Genocide Watch, 2019). A 'genocide emergency' is declared when the genocidal process has reached the stage of genocidal massacres and other acts of genocide. These listed countries are, at the time of writing, currently engaged in the extermination of certain groups that exist and live within them, yet are routinely ignored in the face of more 'newsworthy' stories and headlines designed to maximise sales and profit (Jewkes, 2004).

It would appear that, despite the world uniting in the form of the Declaration of Human Rights (1948) to ensure that something as horrific as the Holocaust would never scourge the Earth again, the Political Instability Task Force estimated that, between 1956 and 2016, a total of 43 genocides took place, causing the deaths of about 50 million people (Anderton and Brauer, 2016). The United Nations High Commissioner for Refugees also estimated that a further 50 million had been displaced by such episodes of violence up to 2008 (Ibid). Taking these points into consideration, this chapter aims to shed light onto this repeatedly neglected form of murder. In doing so it will explore the various definitional debates surrounding genocide, the numerous theoretical frameworks that attempt to makes sense of such heinous crimes, and synthesise these key points in the form of a case study of reserve police Battalion 101 and their involvement in the 'Final Solution' in Poland.

Defining Genocide: A Hotly Debated and Contested Issue

Few major human rights concepts have as clear a point of origin as the concept of genocide does (Courthoys and Docker, 2008). While the Holocaust during World War II prodded the international community to recognise and pledge to prevent genocide, the term itself was coined by Raphael Lemkin. He defined genocide as 'the destruction of a nation or an ethnic group.' He built the word 'from the ancient Greek word *genos* (race, tribe) and the Latin *cide* (killing), thus corresponding in its formation to such words as tyrannicide, homicide, infanticide, etc. He wrote,

> 'Genocide is directed against the national group as an entity, and the actions involved are directed against individuals, not in their individual capacity, but as members of the national group.' (Lemkin, 2008)

A key dimension of genocide is that the intent of violence is to destroy groups. So too, Lemkin argued that genocide is not just murder, but also acts that destroy the social, economic, cultural, religious, and moral foundations of a group.

Lemkin worked tirelessly to promote his term genocide at an international level, and the first official use of the term was during the Nuremberg trials. These consisted of the indictments of 24 leading Nazi officials who were charged with a series of crimes against humanity, including 'deliberate and systematic genocide.' The next development came in the form of a resolution in the 1946 United Nations General Assembly. The resolution formally recognised genocide as a crime under international law and called for the Convention on the Prevention and Punishment of the Crime of Genocide. Article 2 of the convention outlines the following acts that constitute genocide:

(a) Killing members of the group;

(b) Causing serious bodily or mental harm to members of the group;

(c) Deliberately inflicting on the group conditions of life calculated to bring about its physical destruction in whole or in part;

(d) Imposing measures intended to prevent births within the group; or

(e)   Forcibly transferring children of the group to another group.

Despite this recognition and awareness of the various means in which a group could become victim to genocide, there was a debate as to what exactly genocide entails and how it should be defined. For instance, the first draft of the convention included political killings, but the Soviet Union along with some other nations would not accept that actions against groups identified as holding similar political opinions or social status would constitute genocide, so these stipulations were subsequently removed in a political and diplomatic compromise. One of the central rationales for why the USSR was so adamant at the removal of political groups was due to the recent catastrophic death toll caused by Joseph Stalin. Stalin, as leader of the Soviet Union, set in motion events designed to cause a famine in the Ukraine to destroy the people there seeking independence from his rule. As a result, an estimated seven million persons perished in this farming area, known as the breadbasket of Europe, with the people deprived of the food they had grown with their own hands.

With the all-too-recent devastation caused by World War II, world leaders — tired and weary — succumbed to the Soviet Union's demands. Before continuing, it is worth framing this discussion with the acknowledgement that *Time* magazine put Stalin on its cover eleven times, and that Russian public opinion polls rank him near the top of the greatest leaders of Russian history. While we may never know the exact number of individuals killed by Stalin's orders (numbers range between six-to-20 million), Historian Norman Naimark provides some possible answers as to why Stalin does not appear to be met with the same level of revilement as other leaders responsible for genocidal acts. Specifically, Naimark alludes to the possibility that almost every family had not only victims but perpetrators. 'A vast network of state organizations had to be mobilised to seize and kill that many people.' Naimark wrote, approximating that tens of thousands were accomplices (Haven, 2010).

Despite these contentions and political debates, the genocide convention was the first binding international human rights treaty to emerge from the post-war United Nations. Nonetheless, embedded in the concept of genocide and the convention are issues that limit the power of innovation and thus progress in the quest to prevent such atrocities from occurring in the future. In particular, genocide, as previously discussed, is a contested concept with important ambiguities around the types of groups this treaty is supposed to protect. To account for these ambiguities and attempt to move beyond the tired debates, scholars have proposed other terms. For instance, terms such as 'politicide' were generated in order to 'capture' the systematic targeting of those individuals tied to a particular political movement or ideology. In particular, politicide is the deliberate physical destruction or elimination of a group whose members share the main characteristic of belonging to a political movement. It is a type of political repression, and one means of the political cleansing of a population, with another being forced migration (Sharpe, 2011).

Another key concept to emerge was 'democide,' which constitutes 'the intentional killing of an unarmed or disarmed person by government agents acting in their authoritative capacity and pursuant to government policy or high command' (Rummel, 1994, p. 42; see also Harff, 1996). Another important term generated was that of mass killings, which is defined as 'the killings of substantial numbers of human beings, when not in the course of military action against the military forces of an avowed enemy, under the conditions of the essential defencelessness and helplessness of the victims' (Esteban et al, 2010, p. 6). Lastly, another key concept to emerge amongst scholars is that of 'classicide.' This is the deliberate and systematic destruction, in whole or in part, of a social class through persecution and violence (Mann, 2002). Examples includes Joseph Stalin's mass killing of the affluent middle-class peasant Kulaks who were identified as 'class enemies' by the Soviet Union. As stated by Weiss-Wendt (2008), any attempts to develop a universally accepted terminology describing mass killings of non-combatants has continually been met with 'complete failure.'

Due to this lack of consensus as to what constitutes genocide and other forms of mass killings at the hands of the State, there is no set, or universally agreed, definition of genocide. With this ambiguity comes a general lack of clear or specific enforcement mechanisms that could trigger action to stop such atrocities from occurring. The conceptual ambiguities and weak enforcement provisions make debates about whether acts constitute genocide frequently irresolvable and often without dramatic practical consequences. For instance, the 1994 mass murders in Rwanda sparked debate among rich nations and appeared to turn more on the semantic question of whether events technically qualified as 'genocide,' rather than on formulating any practical response. This is primarily due to the fact that calling such killings genocide would force action. Member States can call on the United Nations to try to prevent genocide and are bound by treaty to stop genocide from taking place within their own borders. Due to intense political issues, generally interwoven with economic interests, countries tend to fall back on the ambiguity of genocide, riled by recurrent debates, in order to not take action. This 'crime against humanity', which was promised never to occur again after the horrors of World War II, continues to occur to this day.

Stages of Genocide

Whilst there is intense political debate regarding contemporary cases of mass murder at the hands of the State, and whether or not they constitute genocide, it is universally accepted that the mass extermination of Jews and other so-called 'undesirables' at the hands of Nazi Germany was an act of genocide. This section explores the various stages that resulted in the most industrialised form of mass murder that was ever committed, and examines — through a case study of the reserve police Battalion 101 — how seemingly 'ordinary men' participated in such atrocities.

Before continuing it is important to provide historic context behind the rise of the Nazi party in Germany, and identify the structural factors that increased far-right sentiments and which were monopolised and weaponised by the Nazis — ultimately leading them to power and total control of the country.

World War I took place from the 28 July 1914 to the 11 November 1918. An estimated 20 million people died. It was a global war fought between the Allies (the French Empire, the British Empire, the Russian Empire, the USA and others) and the Central Powers (the German Empire, Austro-Hungarian Empire and the Ottoman Empire). As the war drew to a close in 1918, German supplies and troops were exhausted from four years of warfare. In contrast, by 1918, the British had improved their tactics and equipment and the US had arrived to support the Allied Powers on the battlefields. It was a combination of these factors that led to the Allied Powers achieving victory (Wawro, 2018). Losing the war caused far reaching upheaval in Germany. Home to a number of extreme political parties born out of the public's resentment towards its leaders, Germany entered a peace treaty (Neiberg, 2019). This became known as The Treaty of Versailles. It was signed on the 28 June 1919. It is important to note here that Germany was not permitted to contribute to this treaty. Under clause 231, the 'War Guilt Clause,' Germany had to accept complete responsibility for the war. It lost 13 per cent of its land and 12 per cent of its population to the Allies (Prichard, 1958). This land made up 48 per cent of Germany's iron production and a large proportion of its coal production, limiting its economic power. The German army was also limited to 100,000 soldiers. As financial compensation for the war, the Allies also demanded large amounts of money known as 'reparations.' This treaty was very unpopular in Germany and viewed as extremely harsh. Faced with the revolutionary atmosphere at home, and shortages from the conditions of war, the German government reluctantly agreed to accept the terms. Many Germans were outraged by the Treaty of Versailles. They regarded it as a 'diktat' — dictated peace (Sharp, 2008).

Despite the war drawing to an end and with the treaty having been signed, conditions in Germany did not dramatically improve. Initially, Allied forces still blocked shipments of food and supplies from entering Germany (Bessel, 1995). What food did get through was sparse and therefore expensive. While there were significant changes made to political structures, the new proportional representation system of voting in the Weimar Republic caused political instability (Henig, 2002). Whilst the new system was intended to reduce political conflicts, it in fact resulted in many different parties gaining a small number of seats in the *Reichstag* (the German Parliament). This meant that no one party had an overall majority, and parties joined together to rule in coalitions. In these coalitions, each party had different aims which often led to disagreements on policy. These disagreements made it difficult for the *Reichstag* to govern. In the early-1920s there were many changes of government, which made managing Germany's growing political and economic problems very difficult (Ibid). So too, the detested restitutions costs, which Germany was obligated to pay via the Treaty of Versailles, put an enormous economic burden on the government (Keynes, 2007).

These issues were only further compounded when we consider that, throughout the war, the German currency — the *Reichsmark* — fell considerably in value. In 1914, one British pound was equivalent to 20 German marks and by 1919 one British pound was equivalent to 250 marks (Ibid). In order to mitigate the post-war condition, the government made the decision to print more currency (Guttmann and Meehan, 1976). This subsequently had an adverse consequence and further reduced the value of the *Reichsmark*. Germany continued to endeavour to pay the restitutions as outlined by the treaty. The restitutions had to be paid in gold marks, as gold maintains value, whilst the German currency further deteriorated. This made it more and more expensive to pay (Ibid). Due to Germany's inability to pay restitutions, in 1923 France and Belgium invaded the Ruhr, an important province of Germany containing numerous factories (Gomes, 2010). This only compounded worsening sentiments and living situations. By the autumn of 1923 a loaf of bread cost two hundred thousand million marks ('Hyperinflation', John D Clare, n.d.).

Gustav Stresemann, in this dire moment, was elected Chancellor in September 1923. Stresemann worked to develop Germany's international associations. In the Locarno Pact of 1925, France, Belgium and Germany agreed to respect each other's borders (Zabecki, 2015). The Dawes Plan, alongside a rapid influx of foreign loans, aided the German economy to stabilise and flourish. Those in work saw real developments as salaries increased and working hours were reduced. However, unemployment was still worryingly high with two million people unemployed in 1926 (Fergusson, 1975). Furthermore, the abrupt introduction of foreign loans had left Germany reliant on revenue that it could not regulate nor control. Despite these various issues, Germany had made momentous strides towards recovery between 1924 and 1929. Regrettably, this came to an unforeseen end with the Wall Street Crash of 1929 in the US (Klein, 2003). As the world economies were linked through international business, the crash resulted in an international depression. As a consequence, the US requested return on their international loans. Germany had relied on these loans to rebuild its economy after the war and deal with its hyperinflation crisis, and as the USA removed this investment Germany slipped into another economic emergency.

Before the inception of the Great Depression, in Germany the National Socialist German Workers' Party (Nazi Party) was a minor party on the radical right of the political spectrum. In the *Reichstag* election of May 2, 1928, the Nazis received only 2.6 per cent of the national vote, a proportionate decline from 1924, when the Nazis received three per cent of the vote. As a result of the election, a 'Grand Coalition' of Germany's Social Democratic, Catholic Centre, German Democratic, and German People's parties governed Weimar Germany into the first six months of the economic downturn. The international economic downturn had devastating ramifications, and millions of people were out of work. The unemployed were joined by millions of others who linked this grim economic situation to the perceived humiliation felt after defeat in World War I. For many, the blame for this situation was to be placed on the current coalition government, who failed to come to the aid of its people. Widespread economic depression, dread, anxiety, and perception of worse times to come offered fertile ground for the rise of Adolf Hitler and his Nazi Party. Hitler, aware of this anger and powerlessness experienced by a large number of Germans, attracted a wide following who were desperate for change. The Nazi party vowed to re-establish German national values, reverse the necessities dictated by the Treaty of Versailles, provide more employment opportunities, and return Germany to its 'rightful position' as a world power (Waite, 1993). Hitler and other Nazi propagandists were highly successful in directing the population's anger and fear against the Jews; against the Marxists; and against those the Nazis held responsible for signing the Versailles treaty. As a result of the Nazis' mass support, the then German president Paul von Hindenburg appointed Hitler as Chancellor on January 30, 1933. His appointment paved the way to the Nazi dictatorship after Hindenburg's death in August 1934.

Hitler and the Nazi party, fully aware of the structural obstacles faced by the German people, targeted the perceived threat and limitation to individual agency felt by almost all in the nation. Unfortunately, the Jewish people, amongst other groups Hitler considered to be 'undesirable', were the target towards which he channelled this resentment and anger. While the entirety of events during the course of the World War II are far beyond the remit of this book, we will instead examine how the aforementioned series of events created the conditions in which the first stage of genocide could commence, i.e. *classification*.

Classification consists of the differences between people not being respected. There is also a division of 'us and them', which can be carried out using stereotypes, or excluding people who are perceived to be different (Burnet, 2012). Whether about ethnicity, race, religion or nationality, genocides always start with the idea of 'us and them' — it is what sets the rest in motion. Societies which are the most split and fragmented are seen as the most vulnerable, in this case Hitler targeted predominantly the Jewish population as the source of anxiety, insecurity and frustrations felt by many Germans within a post-World War I context. What generally follows this first step is what is considered as *symbolisation*. Names, caricatures, and colours are just some of the ways this classification is symbolised and further engrained. The symbols slowly become less about identification, and more about identifying 'outcasts' (Stanton, 1998). The yellow star for Jews under Nazi rule is a prime example of how they are applied in order to dehumanise real people. Likewise, the clothing or symbols of a community can be outlawed, thereby denying people the right to identify. Inversely, the use and promotion of symbols such as Nazi *Swastikas* can make the wearers feel superior and justified. Here we can perhaps see the importance and role of cultural violence. As stated by Galtung (1990), these representations of symbolic violence serve to legitimise direct and structural violence and to inhibit or suppress the response of its victims. Cultural violence also serves to provide justifications for individuals to destroy each other and to be rewarded for doing so. In the case of Nazi Germany, the structural violence that spawned from World War I was distorted and weaponised against large swathes of the population via the means of cultural violence. So too, as the Nazi war machine developed and tightened its grip on power, these previously discussed forms of structural violence were reshaped to accommodate the will of the Nazi agenda. For instance, the Nazis created a society whose structure oppressed others via government, culture, labour, terror, and propaganda. Most reminiscent of this violence were the Nazi concentration camps. These camps imprisoned 'enemies' of the Nazi party, people whose very existence was threatened by Nazi ideology. Those imprisoned in such camps suffered harsh living conditions and were subjected to forced labour amongst other hardships and atrocities. Thus, Nazi Germany committed structural violence through its imposition of the system of concentration camps upon wrongfully accused people.

The very same embodiment of cultural violence that resulted in the engrained mentality of 'us and them' also provided the means necessary to justify prevailing attitudes and beliefs that legitimised both this new form of structural violence and various forms of direct violence that resulted from it, making it seem as though it was natural or unavoidable. This, as a result, made the possibility of 'pushing' against this agenda incredibly difficult, and little to no sympathy or support from those in society, including those within the upper echelons of power, was present or capable of preventing such multi-faceted forms of violence.

The third stage in genocide is *discrimination* (Stanton, 1998). The structural violence alluded to in the previous stage did not begin in the concentration camps. Once classification and negative symbols are in place, discrimination becomes all-too-possible. The targeted group becomes powerless, loses civil rights, and is often deprived of basic citizenship. For example, the Nuremberg Laws of 1935 stripped the Jewish population of the right to employment at any government institution or university (Majer, 2003). By targeting a group in such a way, an individual's ability to achieve and realise individual agency begins to erode, becoming powerless in the process. This sense of individual agency is further threatened by the fourth stage: *dehumanisation.* Through such a process, those who exist outside of the targeted population, are unable, or choose not to, recognise the individual agency of members of the targeted group. For instance, the Nazis described Jews as *Untermenschen,* or sub-humans. In doing so, the Nazi-generated propaganda often referred to the Jewish people as rats and other forms of rodents (Smith, 2012). While one may interpret this representation as a metaphor, David Smith, author of *Less than Human* (2012), argues that the Nazis did not mean it metaphorically; '[T]hey didn't mean they were *like* sub-humans. They meant they were *literally* subhuman' (Smith cited in NPR News, 2011). With the language of eugenics often being applied, the perpetrators defined the victim group as being outside the universe of moral obligation (Fein, 1979). Smith extrapolates further, stating that:

'The Nazis were explicit about the status of their victims. They were Untermenschen—sub humans—and as such were excluded from the system of moral rights and obligations that bind humankind together. It's wrong to kill a person, but permissible to exterminate a rat. To the Nazis, all the Jews, Gypsies and others were rats: dangerous, disease-carrying rats.' (Ibid, p. 15)

With a target group now firmly established, the fifth stage, *organization,* is implemented. In the case of the Holocaust, the Nazis trained special army units and militias in order to suppress the Jews and follow through with their preparations. Constructed upon Nazi ideology, the *Schutzstaffel* (often just 'SS') was a criminal organization that assisted the Nazis in providing security for all Nazi party members, mainly Adolf Hitler. After gaining control of Germany's police forces, the SS expanded their responsibilities. Heinrich Himmler commanded the SS and divided it into three sections: The Security Section, the Military Section, and the Concentration Camp Section (Worth, 2005). This was in order to ensure utmost structural efficiency and operational effectiveness at each stage.

> **Key Term: Eugenics**
> * Eugenics is a set of beliefs and practices that aim to improve the genetic quality of a human population by excluding certain genetic groups judged to be inferior, and promoting other genetic groups judged to be superior.

The sixth stage of genocide indicates extreme forms of *polarisation*. An endless stream of dividing propaganda was presented to the German public in forms of open speeches, posters, and newspaper advertisements (Kallis, 2005). These various iterations of propaganda were under Nazi control and the powerful effects of the media were used to its maximum potential. The Nuremberg Laws prohibited Jews from marrying or having a sexual relation with persons of German or German-related blood to prevent their 'disease' from spreading (Rees, 2012). Again, we can witness the powerful and often under-acknowledged ramifications of cultural violence, in which repressed individuals are seemingly powerless to address matters and resist.

Stages seven and eight are *preparation* and *persecution*. Preparation consists of ensuring that at an operational level, soldiers and other necessary personal are instrumentally equipped for the actions that are ahead, along with details of victims, often in the form of lists which are published (Stanton, 1998). Another key element of preparation is that, due to the results of the previous stages, such personnel are psychologically and motivationally equipped and primed. Stage eight, *persecution*, involves the removal of the victim group from the rest of the population. After the Nazis occupied Poland in 1939, they began segregating Jews in ghettos, usually in the most run-down area of a city (Trunk, 1996). By mid-1941, nearly all Jews in occupied Poland had been forced into these overcrowded districts. In the Warsaw ghetto, 490,000 Jews and a few hundred Roma and Sinti struggled to survive despite extreme hardship (Hayes, 2015). In larger centres, ghettos were shut in by walls, fences or barbed wire. Each community was ordered to set up a *Judenrat* (Jewish Council), which would be responsible for enforcing German orders (Trunk, 1996). With these previous eight stages now complete, stage nine, *extermination*, commences.

Stage nine, *extermination*, consists of a deliberate campaign of direct violence, precipitated and enabled through the various forms of structural and cultural violence present in the aforementioned stages. While we may know a lot about how the Germans carried out the extermination component of the Holocaust, we know remarkably little about the ordinary Germans who made the Holocaust happen. While we may also be aware of those in the higher echelons of power that gave the orders, we often neglect to consider the tens of thousands of conscripted soldiers and policemen from all walks of life, many of them middle-aged, who rounded up millions of Jews and methodically shot them, one-by-one, in forests, ravines and ditches. With this in mind, the following case study of reserve police Battalion 101 explores some of the reasons why these 'ordinary men' (Browning, 1992) committed the acts that they did, and this supposed 'banality of evil' (Arendt, 1963).

Case Study: Reserve police Battalion 101 — the 'ordinary men'
Background: In the 1960s Battalion 101 was investigated for its activities by West German prosecutors. In the process, 210 former members were interrogated, and 125 of the testimonies were detailed enough to enable Christopher Browning, examining the records, to piece together not only how the unit operated but also how its members felt about their participation in its work. These testimonies formed the basis for Browning's seminal work, *Ordinary Men* (1992).
Role of the Battalion: The battalion consisted of 500 policemen. Most were in their 30s and 40s and of middle or lower-class backgrounds. They included men who, before the war, had been professional policemen as well as businessmen, dockworkers, truck drivers, construction workers, and machine operators (to name but a few professions). Only a minority were members of the Nazi party, and only a few belonged to the SS. During their stay in Poland they participated in the shootings, or transport to the Treblinka gas chambers, of at least 83,000 Jews.
Notable Event: The battalion's first engagement with mass murder occurred in 1942, when the men were sent to the Polish town of Józefów and ordered to round up Jewish men of working age to serve in labour camps and to shoot the women, children, the old, and the sick. The battalion's commander, Major Wilhelm Trapp, unhappy with the orders, made the offer that any man who did not feel up to the task could be excused. Only around a dozen men accepted this offer, although some more joined them once the shooting began and the full horror of their orders became apparent. Whatever their level of engagement, the men were silent, disturbed and distraught after engaging in this mass murder.

With this summary of Battalion 101 presented, we return to the work of Hannah Arendt, who made the following statement; '[T]he sad truth is that most evil is done by people who never make up their minds to be good or evil' (1981). So too, Browning (1992) stated that:

'These were men who had known political standards and moral norms other than those of the Nazis. Most came from Hamburg, by reputation one of the least Nazified cities in Germany, and the majority came from a social class that had been anti-Nazi in its political culture. These men would not seem to have been a very promising group from which to recruit mass murderers on behalf of the Nazi vision of a racial utopia free of Jews.' (Ibid, p. 48)

With this in mind, it is important to consider that there were a multitude of sentiments, motivations and justifications for the actions this police battalion engaged in — transcending the attenuate and limited constructs we often attribute to a word such as 'evil.'

During their interrogations in the 1960s, those battalion veterans who claimed to have stopped shooting at Józefów cited physical revulsion, in the main, as the reason. Such sentiments can be witnessed in the account from Georg Kageler, who was a tailor prior to being recruited into the battalion:

'After I had carried out the first shooting and at the unloading point was allotted a mother with daughter as victims for the next shooting, I began a conversation with them and learned that they were Germans from Kassel, and I took the decision not to participate further in the executions. The entire business was now so repugnant to me that I returned to my platoon leader and told him that I was still sick and asked for my release.' (Ibid, p. 67)

Kageler's request was granted, and he was then tasked with guarding a marketplace — facing no further consequences. Very few claimed to have had ethical misgivings as a reason. A few observed that they felt they were freer than others to withdraw from the killing process because they had no intention of remaining policemen after the war; their colleagues, though, had to think about their careers. Browning notes that Captain Hoffman — a high ranking officer within the battalion — was a classic example of a man driven by careerism:

'Crippled by stomach cramps — psychosomatically induced, at least in part, if not entirely, by the murderous actions of the battalion — he tenaciously tried to hide his illness from his superiors rather than use it [to] escape his situation. He risked his men's open suspicion of cowardice in a vain attempt to keep his company command.' (Ibid, p. 171)

For many, the pressure to conform to the group, and to not seem like cowards, played a role in their continuing to shoot. Browning draws attention to this, noting that 'the basic identification of men in uniform with their comrades and the strong urge not to separate themselves from the group by stepping out' (p. 71) was of significant importance. Browning expands on this theme:

> 'The act of stepping out that morning in Józefów meant leaving one's comrades and admitting that one was "too weak" or "cowardly." Who would have "dared", one policeman declared emphatically, to "lose face" before the assembled troops. "If the question is posed to me why I shot with the others in the first place" said another who subsequently asked to be excused after several rounds of killing, "I must answer that no one wants to be thought a coward".' (Ibid, p. 72)

Other members of the battalion found different ways in which to rationalise and justify their actions. For instance, one metalworker from Bremerhaven contented himself with the rationale that he would shoot only children, since if his partner shot the mother then the child would be unable to survive alone and killing it would be an act of mercy:

> 'I made the effort, and it was possible for me, to shoot only children. It so happened that the mothers led the children by the hand. My neighbour then shot the mother and I shot the child that belonged to her, because I reasoned with myself that after all without its mother the child could not live any longer. It was supposed to be, so to speak, soothing to my conscience to release children unable to live without their mothers.' (Ibid, p. 73)

For nearly all, the Jews were not in the same human family as members of the battalion were. Their commander, Major Trapp, had told them, in his initial speech, that all Jews were enemies who deserved to be killed, even their women and their children, because Germany's enemies were killing German women and children with bombs. Browning notes that, while it would seem that the men that comprised this particular battalion did not consciously adopt the anti-Semitic doctrines and propaganda of the Nazi regime, they had 'at least accepted the assimilation of the Jews into the image of the enemy' (Ibid).

Though Trapp and many of his men found their participation in the murder of Józefów Jews difficult, that difficulty diminished as the battalion continued its work. This, it would appear, was primarily due to the changes implemented towards the killing process itself:

'This time the men did not have to pair off with their victims face-to-face. The personal tie between victim and killer was severed. In sharp contrast to Józefów, only one policeman recalled the identity of a particular Jew he had shot. In addition to the depersonalisation of the killing process, through rapid rotation the men were spared the sense of unremitting, endless killing that had been so salient at Józefów…Habituation played a role as well. Having killed once already, the men did not experience such traumatic shock the second time. (Ibid, p. 85).

For a few members of the battalion, the initial horror was replaced by acts of sadism, in which Jews, totally naked, were forced to crawl in front of their intended graves and to sustain beatings with clubs before being shot:

'Even before the shooting began, First Lieutenant Gnade had personally picked some twenty to twenty-five elderly Jews. They were exclusively men with full beards. Gnade made the old men crawl on the ground before the grave. Before he gave them the order to crawl, they had to undress. While the totally naked Jews crawled, First Lieutenant Gnade screamed to those around, "Where are my non-commissioned officers? Don't you have any clubs yet?" The non-commissioned officers went to the edge of the forest, fetched themselves clubs, and vigorously beat the Jews with them.' (Ibid, pp. 82–83).

The aforementioned account demonstrates that there is far from being one answer that explains the actions of each officer assigned to the battalion. Browning, in his account, provides a multi-layered and multi-causal explanation as to why these men engaged in the actions that they did. It is evident that factors such as conformity, peer pressure, and deference to authority framed within the legitimising capacities of the Nazi government are all important variables to consider.

After the war, many members of the battalion returned to their earlier occupations. A large number continued their police careers. Between 1962 and 1967, 14 men of Battalion 101 were indicted by West German prosecutors. After appeals, one received a sentence of eight years' imprisonment, one of four and one of three-and-a-half. Of the many thousands of other German policemen involved in the Final Solution, West German prosecutors brought to trial only a few, and still fewer convictions were obtained.

In bringing this case study to a close, Browning states that, 'a combination of situational factors and ideological overlap that concurred on the enemy status and dehumanisation of the victims was sufficient to turn "ordinary men" into "willing executioners".' (Ibid, p. 216)

We will now move on to what is often considered the final stage in genocide: *denial* (Stanton, 1998). The perpetrators 'deny that they committed any crimes, and often blame what happened on the victims' (Stanton, 1998). The ways in which portrayals of genocide are constructed may contribute to creating 'zones of denial' (Shavit, 2005), that allow space for minimising the harsh realities of genocide in our collective understanding. Holocaust denial gained notoriety in the US and Europe by the 1980s and has spread to other parts of the world. Key denial assertions are that the murder of approximately six million Jews during World War II never occurred, that the Nazis had no official policy or intention to exterminate the Jews, and that the poison gas chambers in Auschwitz-Birkenau death camp never existed. While there have been numerous academics that have challenged Holocaust denial, it is important to keep in mind the words of Stanton (1998): 'The black hole of forgetting is the negative force that results in future genocides.'

Closing Comments

While Stanton's conceptual framework concerning the stages of genocide is highly influential, more recent examples of genocide, such as in Rwanda and Yugoslavia have captured scholars' attentions. From these more recent examinations of genocide, three contemporary perspectives have emerged. The first is rooted in the concept of ideology, with Weitz (2003) stating that genocide occurs when leaders seek to create a utopia. Similarly, Kiernan (2007) suggests that there are several ideological pathways to genocide, including race, religion, cults of past glory, and fear of biological contamination. The second is rooted in strategic aims of leaders and State interest. Valentino (2004) puts forth that leaders engage in mass killings when they believe it is the best way to achieve their political goals. The third is rooted in the context of long-term political development. Mann (2005) argues that 'murderous ethnic cleansing' is a perversion of a democratic ideal of rule by the people. He points to the role of nationalism and democratisation of ideologies that emerged largely in the middle of the nineteenth century in generating organic conceptions of the nation and the State. Nationalism entwined the *demos* with the dominant *ethnos*, leading to forms of democratic nation State-building that, according to Mann, produced wholesale inter-group violence. This he termed the 'dark side of democracy' (Mann, 2005). Specifically, Mann states that, 'Democracy has always carried with it the possibility that the majority might tyrannise minorities, and this possibility carries more ominous consequences in certain types of multi-ethnic environments.' (Ibid, p. 2).

While there are indeed numerous perspectives and theories as to why genocides and mass killings occur, it is important to consider that such events require time, and are rarely the product of spontaneity. So too, such forms of mass direct violence against a particular group are the end point of a process that involves — in various configurations and forms — both structural and cultural forms of violence, further demonstrating the entrenched inter-connectedness between these forms of violence. It is also important to consider that most of those involved in the extermination process are, as presented by Browning (1992), ordinary people. Apart from those select few that appear to gain some form of sadistic pleasure from such acts (Baumeister, 2002), most people come from various walks of life and professions and it is evident that, from the accounts provided in the case study, the very act itself clearly impacts people in different ways as they struggle to reconcile their actions with whatever morals and principles they adhere to. Charny (1986) observes,

'[T]he mass killers of humankind are largely everyday human beings — what we have called normal people according to currently accepted definitions by the mental health profession…Placed in comparable situations and similar social constituencies, you or I might also commit murderous ethnic cleansing.' (cited in Mann, 2005, p. 9)

And Holocaust survivor Primo Levi:

'Monsters exist, but they are too few in number to be truly dangerous. More dangerous are the common men, the functionaries ready to believe and to act without asking questions.'

Questions to consider:
- How do structural forms of violence contribute to acts of genocide?
- In what way is cultural violence important leading up to and during acts of genocide?
- Why is it difficult to successfully prevent acts of genocide?
- Do acts of genocide necessarily have to resort to acts of murder?
- Are there other ways groups can be targeted?
- How prevalent is genocide in human history?
- What are the practical difficulties to understanding this aspect of our past (or present)?

References

Anderton, C. H. and Brauer, J. (2016), *Economic Aspects of Genocides, Other Mass Atrocities, and Their Prevention*, Oxford: Oxford University Press.

Arendt, H. (1963), *Eichmann in Jerusalem: A Report on the Banality of Evil*, London: Penguin Books.

Arendt, H. (1978), *The Life of the Mind*, London: Harcourt Brace Jovanovich.

Baumeister, R. (2002), 'The Holocaust and the Four Roots of Evil', in L. S. Newman and R. Erber (eds.), *Understanding Genocide: The Social psychology of the Holocaust*, Oxford: Oxford University Press, pp. 241–258.

Bessel, R. (1995), *Germany After the First World War*, London: Clarendon Press.

Bourdieu, P. (1979), 'Symbolic Power,' *Critique of Anthropology*, 4(13–14), pp. 77–85.

Browning, C. (1992), *Ordinary Men: Reserve Police Battalion 101 and the Final Solution in Poland*, London: HarperCollins.

Burnet, J. E. (2012), *Genocide Lives in Us: Women, Memory, and Silence in Rwanda*, Wisconsin: Wisconsin Press.

Charny, I. (1986), 'Genocide and Mass destruction: Doing Harm to Others as a Missing Dimension in Psychopathology,' *Psychiatry*, 49(2), pp. 144–157.

Clare, J. D. 'Hyperinflation' (n.d.) https://www.johndclare.net/Weimar_hyperinflation.htm

Courthoys, A. and Docker, J. (2008), 'Defining Genocide,' in Stone, D. (ed.), *The Historiography of Genocide*, London: Palgrave Macmillan.

Esteban, M., Morelli, M. and Rohner, D. (2010), 'Strategic Mass Killings,' Institute for Empirical Research in Economics, University of Zurich Working Paper No. 486: http://ssrn.com/abstract=1615375

Fein, H. (1979), *Accounting for Genocide,* New York: Free Press.

Fergusson, A. (1975), *When Money Dies — Nightmare of the Weimar Collapse*, Sainte Croix du Mont: Tradibooks.

Galtung, J. (1990), 'Cultural Violence,' *Journal of Peace Research*, 27(3), pp. 291–305.

Genocide Watch (2019), 'Countries at Risk,' http://genocidewatch.net/

Gomes, L. (2010), *German Reparations, 1919–1932: A Historical Survey*, London: Palgrave Macmillan.

Guttmann, W. and Meehan, P. (1976), *The Great Inflation: Germany 1919–23,* London: Gordon and Cremonesi Limited.

Harff. B. (1996), 'Reviewed Work(s): Death by Government by R. J. Rummel,' *Journal of Interdisciplinary History*, 27(1), pp. 117–119.

Haven, C. (2010). 'Stalin killed millions. A Stanford historian answers the question, was it genocide?', *Stanford News*, September 23rd: https://news.stanford.edu/2010/09/23/naimark-stalin-genocide-092310/

Hayes, P. (2015), *How Was It Possible?: A Holocaust Reader*, Nebraska: University of Nebraska Press.

Henig, R. (2002), *The Weimar Republic 1919–1933*, London: Routledge.

Jewkes, Y. (2004), *Media and Crime*, London: Sage.

Kallis, A. (2005), *Nazi Propaganda and the Second World War*, London: Palgrave Macmillan.

Kiernan, B. (2007), *Blood and Soil: A World History of Genocide and Extermination from Sparta to Darfur*, New Haven: Yale University Press.

Keynes, (2007), *The Economic Consequences of the Peace*, Hampshire: Harriman House Ltd.

Klein, M. (2003), *Rainbow's End: The Crash of 1929*, Oxford: Oxford University Press.

Lemkin, R. (2008), *Axis Rule in Occupied Europe: Laws of Occupation, Analysis of Government, Proposals for Redress* (2nd edn.), London: Lawbook Exchange Ltd.

Majer, D. (2003), *'Non-Germans' Under the Third Reich*, London: Johns Hopkins University Press.

Mann. M. (2005), *The Dark Side of Democracy. Explaining Ethnic Cleansing*, Cambridge: Cambridge University Press.

Neiberg, M. S. (2019), *The Treaty of Versailles: A Very Short Introduction*, Oxford: Oxford University Press.

NPR News (2011), '"Less than Human": The Psychology of Cruelty,' March 29: https://www.npr.org/2011/03/29/134956180/criminals-see-their-victims-as-less-than-human

Prichard, M. C. (1958), *The Origins of the 'War Guilt Clause' in the Treaty of Versailles*, Kentucky: University of Kentucky.

Rees, L. (2012), *The Holocaust: A New History*, London: Penguin Books.

Rummel, R. J. (1994), *Death by Government: Genocide and Mass Murder in the Twentieth Century*, New Jersey: Transaction.

Sharp, A. (2008), *The Versailles Settlement: Peace-making After the First World War, 1919–1923*. London: Palgrave Macmillan.

Sharpe, V. (2011). *Politicide*, lulu.com

Shavit, Z. (2005), *A Past without Shadow: Constructing the Past in German Books for Children*, London: Routledge.

Smith, D. L. (2012), *Less than Human*, New York: St. Martin's Press.

Stanton, G. H. (1998), 'The Seven Stages of Genocide', Paper presented at the Genocide Program Seminar, February 12.

Trunk, I. (1996), *Judenrat: The Jewish Councils in Eastern Europe under Nazi Occupation*, Lincoln: University of Nebraska Press.

United Nations. (1948), Convention on the Prevention and Punishment of the Crime of Genocide: https://www.ohchr.org/en/professionalinterest/pages/crimeofgenocide.aspx

United Nations. (1948), Universal Declaration of Human Rights: https://www.un.org/en/universal-declaration-human-rights/

Valentino, B. A. (2004), *Final Solutions: Mass Killing and Genocide in the Twentieth Century*, Ithaca: Cornell University Press.

Waite, R. (1993), *The Psychopathic God: Adolph Hitler*, London: Hachette Books.

Wawro, G. (2018), *Sons of Freedom: The Forgotten American Soldiers Who Defeated Germany in World War I*, London: Basic Books.

Weiss-Wendt A. (2008), 'Problems in Comparative Genocide Scholarship,' in Stone D. (ed.), *The Historiography of Genocide*, London: Palgrave Macmillan.

Weitz, E. D. (2003), *A Century of Genocide Utopias of Race and Nation*, Princeton: Princeton University Press.

Wilson, D., Tolputt, H., Howe, N. and Kemp, D. (2010), 'When Serial Killers Go Unseen: The Case of Trevor Joseph Hardy,' *Crime, Media, Culture*, 6, pp. 153–167.

Worth, R. (2005), *Heinrich Himmler: Murderous Architect of the Holocaust*, London: Enslow.

Zabecki, D. T. (2015), *World War II in Europe: An Encyclopaedia* (2nd edn.), London: Routledge.

CHAPTER 7

Death at the Hands of the State

'But what then is capital punishment but the most premeditated of murders, to which no criminal's deed, however calculated it may be, can be compared? For there to be equivalence, the death penalty would have to punish a criminal who had warned his victim of the date at which he would inflict a horrible death on him and who, from that moment onward, had confined him at his mercy for months. Such a monster is not encountered in private life.'

Albert Camus, French philosopher

Introduction

We have so far covered various forms of homicide including serial and spree murder, yet despite the multitude of differences between these various types of homicide they all share one key trait: they were committed by a clearly identifiable agent or agents. These individuals are almost universally met with condemnation for their 'violent' and 'immoral' acts, and the Criminal Justice System generally responds with severe retributive punishments in the form of a life sentence or, depending on the country, the death penalty. With this in mind, this chapter introduces a re-orientation of sorts, in which we will now be examining the role of the State—often considered as being the source for a country's moral, ethical and legal framework by which all citizens should abide—including in relation to homicide. This discussion first critically examines how the State conceptualises and operationalises various modes of punishment—namely of the death penalty—in the name of law, order, and justice. Discussions then move on to another form of seemingly 'justified' or 'excusable' form of homicide in the name of maintaining a safe and law-abiding society: police killings. Given the nature of these discussions, attention will shift between historic and contemporary examples, as well as national and international illustrations. Lastly, it is worth reminding readers here of the crime of genocide dealt with in *Chapter 6,* arguably the most heinous form of death at the hand of the State, into which State killings can progress.

The Death Penalty in England and Wales: A Bloody History

The death penalty provides perhaps the most suitable looking-glass to observe how a country's culture, politics, economics and Criminal Justice System shape citizens' understanding of what constitutes morally 'righteous' or 'evil' forms of homicide. Echoing the theme of cultural violence introduced earlier in this book and the words of Galtung (1990), one way cultural violence works is by changing the moral colour of an act from red/wrong to green/right or at least to yellow/acceptable. One historic (within the context of the UK) and contemporary (for example, China, Iran and certain States in North America) example is that of the death penalty.

Capital punishment in the United Kingdom was used as a form of punishment all the way until the second half of the twentieth century. The last executions in the United Kingdom were by hanging, and took place in 1964, prior to capital punishment being abolished for murder. Historically, that punishment was often made into a public spectacle, with members of the public being able to witness executions. The primary reason for such public displays was that they would act as an effective deterrent to others. This rationale behind the use of public executions as a form of general deterrence (Hood and Hoyle, 2015) is perhaps best illustrated during the period often referred to as that of the 'Bloody Code' between the years 1723 and 1820. In 1688 there were 50 crimes for which a person could be put to death, but by 1765 this had risen to about 160 and to 222 by 1810 (Glyn-Jones, 2000). It is important to note here that many of these crimes punishable by death were associated with theft of some kind. For example, an individual could be sentenced to death for stealing goods worth more than five shillings (today around 25p) (in even earlier times for stealing goods worth just 12 old pence), taking goods from a shipwreck, and pilfering from a naval dockyard. The Bloody Code was, in essence, a response from rich landowners and affluent citizens who were scared at the thought of others — mainly those within the lower echelons of society — stealing their goods.

Whilst arguments in support of the death penalty were deteriorating by the early-twentieth century, it was a series of high profile wrongful executions that played a major part in the abolition of capital punishment in the United Kingdom via its suspension in 1965 and permanent abolition in 1969. This became the entrenched position in 2006 when the UK belatedly signed up to the Sixth (now Thirteenth) Protocol to the European Convention for the Protection of Human Rights and Fundamental Freedoms Concerning the Abolition of the Death Penalty.

One UK victim of wrongful execution was Welshman Timothy John Evans, who was charged and convicted of murdering his wife and infant daughter in 1949. With the police sure that Evans killed his wife and child they proceeded to interrogate him, and when asked if he had killed them he replied that he did murder them (Potas and Walker, 1992). It was later revealed that much of his confession was actually dictated to him by police investigators and there was an almost total absence of forensic evidence. His trial lasted three days and the jury took only 40 minutes to return a guilty verdict — Evans was hanged on 9 March 1950. Three years later police uncovered a number of bodies at 10 Rillington Place, the location where Evans and his family stayed when his alleged murders took place. It transpired that Evans' wife and child, along with at least six other women, were the victims of serial murderer John Reginald Christie, who was Evan's landlord (though Christie never admitted to killing the child). Christie was a war-time constable who also let out rooms at 10 Rillington Place — including to Evans and his family (Jenkins, 1988). Whilst Christie would also be hanged for his crimes, the case of Timothy Evans was one of several that eventually contributed to the abolition of capital punishment in Britain.

The Death Penalty in the USA: An Unjust System?

While the death penalty was abolished in the UK in 1969 for murder and 1998 for acts of treason (Frankis, 2019), such a form of punishment is still practised around the world today. Such State-sanctioned penalties for criminal acts provide a fascinating looking-glass into how structural violence can result in particular groups being disproportionately subjected to such punishments. For instance, in the US, people of colour are disproportionately sentenced to death, in comparison to those who are white. According to research published by the Bureau of Justice Statistics, of the 2,979 people on death row (as of December 31, 2013), 1,248 were black and 1,663 were white (US Department of Justice, 2014, p. 9). Proportionally, this means that approximately 41.89 per cent of individuals on death row were black and 55.82 per cent were white. These ratios are immensely unrepresentative of the US population in 2013, which was approximately 13.17 per cent black and 77.66 per cent white (US Census Bureau, 2014).

A recent report from the Texas Coalition to Abolish the Death Penalty (TCADP) determined that, between 2014 and 2018, Texas handed down 28 death sentences, and 20 of the defendants belonged to a minority race. This example from just one State is indicative of the US's historic application of the death penalty, and that race and capital punishment there have always been inseparable. This brings us to this chapter's case study—that of 14-year-old George Stinney.

Case Study: George Stinney

The Victims: Two young white girls, eleven-year-old Betty June Binnicker and seven-year-old Mary Emma Thames, were found dead in the company mill town of Alcolu, South Carolina, in March 1944, after they had failed to return home the night before.

The Suspect: When law enforcement officers learned from a witness that Betty and Mary were last seen talking to 14-year-old African-American, George Stinney, they went to his home. There, Stinney was handcuffed and taken to the Sumter County Jail, where he was interrogated for hours in a locked room with no witnesses or attorney.

The Trial: A month after the murders, Stinney's trial began in a Clarendon County courtroom, where a white court-appointed defence attorney Charles Plowden did little to defend his client. During the two-hour trial, Plowden failed to call witnesses to the stand or present any evidence that would cast doubt on the prosecution's case. The most significant piece of evidence presented against Stinney was his alleged confession, but there was no written record of the teenager admitting to the murders. Following ten-minutes deliberation, the all-white jury found Stinney guilty of first-degree murder. That same day, the judge sentenced the youngster to death by the electric chair.

The Execution: Standing five feet one inch tall and weighing just over 40 kilogrammes, Stinney was so small compared to the usual adult prisoners that law officers had difficulty securing him to the frame holding the electrodes. Stinney was made to sit on a bible in order to fit properly into the chair. The state's adult-sized facemask also did not fit him, and slipped off after the first surge of electricity hit him. Stinney was declared dead within four minutes of the initial electrocution. From the time of the murders until Stinney's execution, just 83 days had passed.

Whilst the execution of George Stinney took place over 70 years ago, some of the elements outlined in the case study can be witnessed to this day. According to the Washington-based Death Penalty Information Centre (DPIC), 56 per cent of death row inmates are black or Hispanic. However, although racial minorities comprise half of all murder victims nationwide, a far greater proportion (77 per cent) of the victims in capital convictions were white. The racial identity of the murder victim is thus a leading factor in determining who receives a death sentence in America. Amnesty International also reports that all-white juries convicted 20 per cent of African-Americans nationwide. Here we return to the work of Johan Galtung, who coined the term structural violence. According to Galtung (1996), one of the key defining feature of structural violence is the exploitation of particular groups that lack economic and/or cultural capital. According to him, such disempowered groups can be so 'disadvantaged that they die ... from it ... [T]his happens within complex structures and at the end of long, highly ramified causal chains and cycles' (1996, p. 198). Whilst this can be readily applied to cases in which such groups lack basic necessities including food and clean water, there are perhaps other causal chains that result in death that are arguably hidden or justified in the narrative of criminal justice proceedings.

One example of exploitation against ethnic minorities in capital punishment becomes apparent in observing sentencing patterns by the race of the victim. Identifying and confirming patterns of bias with regards to the handing down of the death sentence was, historically, thwart with difficulties. Justice Potter Stewart in *Furman v. Georgia* (1972) illustrated such difficulty in the following statement:

> 'These death sentences are cruel and unusual in the same way that being struck by lightning is cruel and unusual. For, of all people convicted of rapes and murders in 1967 and 1968, many just as reprehensible as these, the petitioners are among a capriciously selected random handful upon whom the sentence of death has been imposed. My concurring brothers have demonstrated that, if any basis can be discerned for the selection of those few to be sentenced to die, it is the constitutionally impermissible basis of race. But racial discrimination has not be proved, and I put it to one side.'
> (*Furman v. Georgia*, 1972, p. 238 cited in Thomson, 1997, p. 65)

Some researchers at first upheld the notion that the racial disparities stemmed from the discernibly higher homicide rates among African-Americans (Kleck, 1981), until it became clear that a significant majority of the homicides committed by African-Americans were intra-racial but that most death sentences dispensed to African-Americans involved inter-racial homicides (Thompson,

1997). These findings were reaffirmed by the US General Accounting Office, which stated that the 'race of [the] victim was found to influence the likelihood of being charged with capital murder or receiving the death penalty, i.e. those who murdered whites were more likely to be sentenced to death than those who murdered blacks'(1997, p. 271). Taking this into account, the degree of sentence severity that a capital case receives is largely dependent on the race of the victim. Racial composition of juries in death penalty cases is yet another example of exploitation in the capital punishment system. Prejean (2005) discusses the issue of racial discrimination in the selection of jury members:

'Many prosecuting attorneys have been able to eliminate most or all people of colour from juries in capital trials without fear of reversal by higher courts. Although the Supreme Court has outlawed such practices in Batson v. Kentucky (1986), prosecutors have been able to circumvent the law by offering reasons other than race for eliminating each black juror' (p. 215).

The lack of racial diversity on juries unarguably disadvantages defendants from ethnic minorities. A racially homogenous jury pool can have a damaging impact on the public's perception of the justice system. Undeniably, a jury pool's make-up can raise serious questions regarding the US's overall commitment to racial equality. A system in which non-diverse juries are almost uniformly deciding the fate of minority criminal defendants is inherently contrary to the US declared dedication to achieving and maintaining equality. Tehranian (2000) notes that one of the consequences of this lack of racial diversity is that ethnic minority defendants are coerced into disavowing their own cultural identity in order to reproduce and replicate those values held by the predominantly white jury in an effort to appeal to these individuals.

There have also been high-profile cases in which African-American defendants were not provided with the necessary information or legal counsel expected in such trials involving murder charges. Jackson et al (2001) discuss the case of Brian Baldwin, which perfectly exemplifies these deficiencies in legal proceedings. Baldwin and another African-American teenager, Edmund Horsley, got a ride as hitchhikers from North Carolina to Alabama with a white teenager, Naomi Rolon. Upon arriving in Alabama, Baldwin and Horsley went separate ways, with Horsley continuing to ride with Rolon. When Rolon's body was found, Baldwin and Horsley were both arrested for murdering her. The two teenagers were convicted in separate trials. Prior to Baldwin's trial, his attorney met with him for a total of 20 minutes. Furthermore, the attorney (it is alleged) neglected to conduct an investigation and presented no witnesses at the trial. Consequently, Baldwin was left unprepared for the trial that would ultimately result in a death sentence. Most alarming about this was the abundance of evidence that could have been presented to save Baldwin's life, had his attorney improved Baldwin's understanding of and role in the trial, thus giving Baldwin a more comprehensive and holistic view of what was going on:

> 'The jury never learned that police had repeatedly beaten Baldwin and tortured him with a cattle prod until he confessed. The jury never learned that Baldwin's "confession" named the wrong weapon and the wrong method for Rolon's killing. The jury never learned that Horsley's statement, pointing to Baldwin as the killer, did describe her killing accurately. The jury never learned that forensics showed Naomi Rolon's killing to be the work of a left-handed assailant—and Horsley, not Baldwin, was left-handed. The jury never learned that Horsley's clothes were stained with blood and Baldwin's clothing tested negative for any blood at all. Baldwin was sentenced to die in Alabama's electric chair.' (Jackson et al 2001, pp. 56–57)

All of the aforementioned evidence could easily have been presented or verified by Baldwin himself, had his understanding of and role in his own sentencing proceedings been enhanced. However, he was given only a very partial view of what was going on in his own trial. Thus, Baldwin was executed largely as a result of being provided with incomplete information.

Another key facet of structural violence is the prevention and omission of particular groups from positions of power and authority within society. Within the capital punishment system, there is an evident omission of people of colour from positions of power. As noted by Barak et al (2010), the death penalty is a symbol of State control over ethnic minorities. In his keynote address to the American Bar association in 2000, Anthony Amsterdam stated that:

> 'The death penalty is accepted, even popular, in precisely the way that big-league baseball and football are accepted and popular: as a spectator sport to

the fans, and a competitive *agon* to the players, and a logo of the American way to everybody.' (Anthony Amsterdam, Keynote address to the American Bar Association, 12 October 2000: cited in Garland, 2002)

Garland (2002) builds upon this entrenched acceptance of the death penalty, noting that such a form of punishment now seems to be acutely imprinted in the American political cognisance. It is, very much, a largely accepted and rarely questioned component of political existence. Garland (2002) takes these sentiments further, stating that the death penalty is 'an American institution, to which political officials solemnly swear allegiance, particularly when they are running for elective office' (Ibid, p. 460). Such sentiments towards the death penalty at the hands of elected individuals of Government could be witnessed in 2019, with the Donald Trump administration ordering the first set of federal executions since 2003. Trump, during his 2016 campaign for the presidency of the US, adopted what we would consider a right-realist perspective on crime and punishment.

Key Terms: Left and Right-Realism
- Right-realism, also known as neo-classicism, considers the phenomenon of crime from the perspective of political conservatism and states that it takes a more realistic assessment on the causes of crime and deviance.
- Due to this position, right-realism argues that it is best suited at identifying the most appropriate mechanisms for its control.
- Whilst right-realists posit that crime has little to nothing to do with social inequality, left-realists argue that living in a capitalistic society, a society where private corporations control trade and industry instead of the State, is one of the central and significant causes of crime.

In one of his many media interviews Donald Trump was quoted as saying the following in relation to his stance of crime and punishment:

'First of all, Secretary Clinton doesn't want to use a couple of words, and that's law and order. And we need law and order. If we don't have it, we're not going to have a country…We have a situation where we have our inner cities, African-Americans, Hispanics are living in hell because it's so dangerous. You walk down the street, you get shot.' (Mark, 2016)

Not only can we see Trump's right-realist position on crime and punishment, but we can also witness how certain groups and ethnic minorities are embroiled in the overall narrative presented. The symbolic significance of cultural violence (Galtung, 1990) with regard to the over-representation of African-Americans on death row is only further compounded when we consider how particular media and even politicians, as depicted by Trump's remarks, describe such individuals. Smiley and Fakunle (2016) state that 'over the last several years, the term "thug" has become a way to describe Black males who reject or do not rise to the standard of White America' (p. 350). They also state that, while historically in America explicit and overt forms of racist language were socially acceptable, 'there has been a cultural shift of social intolerance to this blatant racist behaviour' (Ibid, p. 354). It is important to consider that this does not mean that racism or prejudiced actions have been eliminated but rather pushed beneath the surface and re-orientated and re-configured as coded language, gestures, signs, and symbols to highlight and designate difference. Smiley and Fakunle demonstrate this re-arrangement as follows:

'Terms such as "thug," "ghetto," "hood," "sketchy," and "shady" are all examples of coded language that are used to refer to or speak of Blackness without overtly sounding racially prejudiced. Fraternities on college campuses throw "Pimps and Hos" parties, where stereotypes of Black people as pimps or prostitutes, exemplifying characters from the film *Superfly* (1972), also lack the language of race but show in physical gesture and imagery the racism encoded in the details.' (Ibid, p. 354).

Such attitudes appear to be only further compounded when we consider the words used by President Trump regarding particular areas of the US. For instance, he has been known to use the word 'infested' when discussing those areas often characterised by extreme inequality and home to various ethnic minorities. In July of 2019, Trump criticised Representative Elijah Cummings, who chairs the House Committee on Oversight and Reform, and his home district of West Baltimore. In doing so Trump called the district a 'rat and rodent infested mess' where 'no human being would want to live' (Miller, 2019). There also appears to be popular support for the death penalty in the US, with the Death Penalty Information Centre determining that approximately 55 per cent of Americans were in favour of it in 2018. This support, along with the symbolic demonisation of African-American males has resulted in such individuals being handed the death penalty by the overwhelming advocacy of middle-aged white, male prosecutors (Barak, et al 2010, p. 272). In addition, in 2017, 71 per cent of district court judges were white, while only 14 per cent were African-American and ten per cent Hispanic (Duffin, 2019). Taking these points into consideration, it is difficult to argue that there is such a thing as race-neutral decision-making in the US Criminal Justice System, especially when we consider the impact such decisions have on people from ethnic minorities when their voice is not part of the discussion leading to such finite and lethal decisions (Barak et al 2010, p. 272).

Galtung (1996) discusses how another key component of structural violence is the dismantling of social bonds and the sense of collective identity. This, as we have previously witnessed, can be in the form of separating particular groups from 'mainstream' society, including positions of power and authority. Such actions can also be witnessed in a multitude of ways within a societal context including, for instance, the systematic segregation and isolation of African-Americans in the form of inner-city housing while white people were positioned in more affluent suburbs via mortgage policies.

Richard Rothstein's book, *The Colour of Law* (2017), examined the local, State and federal housing policies that mandated segregation. He notes that the Federal Housing Administration (FHA), which was established in 1934, furthered the segregation efforts by refusing to insure mortgages in and near African-American neighbourhoods—a policy known as 'redlining.' At the same time, the FHA was subsidising builders who were mass-producing entire subdivisions for white people. This came with the requirement that none of the homes be sold to African-Americans. Not only can this dismantling of social bonds be witnessed in relation to the erosion of collective identity amongst various groups that make up a society, but also in the corrosion of bonds within a particular group itself. We can perhaps witness this dismantling of collective identity in the over-representation of African-Americans in North America's penal complexes and—further still—the isolated living conditions and harsh lived realities of those on death row Johnson (1979).

What we must acknowledge here is that the final act of execution is the end product consisting of structural forms of violence identified above, which is seemingly normalised via the means and production of cultural violence in the shape of the demonisation of African-American males from various forms of media and, at times, politicians. As Galtung (1990) states, 'The culture preaches, teaches, admonishes, eggs on, and dulls us into seeing exploitation and/or repression as normal and natural, or into not seeing them (particularly not exploitation) at all' (p. 295). While there may be debates regarding the implementation of such a form of punishment, it is evident that this examination into the death penalty provides a 'periscope' through which we can witness how those individuals lacking agency and who are marginalised via a plethora of ways appear to be disproportionately targeted by the State.

While we have so far examined the structural and cultural factors that result in the disproportionate targeting and executions of those lacking in cultural and economic capital, it is also important to critique the death penalty more broadly within the context of the US. The public and political demand for the death penalty for crimes such as murder functions on the attitude of externalising the problem of gross inequality, biased law enforcement policies (such as, for instance, the War on Drugs), poor education and employment opportunities (Mong and Roscigno, 2010), a history of social exclusion including biased housing policies (Rothstein, 2017), and negative stereotypes represented within the media (Oliver, 2003). In the State's role in punishing and executing individuals within the context of law and order, it in essence pushes aside such factors and instead locates the 'real' issues within the individual actor. While this chapter is not attempting to remove responsibility and role of the identifiable agent, it is worth stressing here that the aforementioned structural variables are often omitted entirely, and the intense inter-relationship between structural and direct forms of violence is routinely underacknowledged. This is only further compounded when we consider that demands for the death penalty are rarely made if the perpetrators are from socially and politically powerful backgrounds and often experience State exemption. Convicted of a murder he did not commit, Ndume Olatushani spent 20 years on death row in Tennessee and stated that, '[A]ll that time, I never met a rich person sitting on death row' ('Death Row

Reserved for the Poor,' United Nations Human Rights, 2018). Philip Alston, the UN independent expert on poverty and human rights, said that:

'The death penalty is reserved for those who cannot buy themselves out of arrest, cannot afford legal representation, cannot afford a decent appeal, and carry no weight in the eyes of the government.' (Ibid)

It is much easier to demand and call for a death sentence on those individuals coming from already marginalised backgrounds that struggle to challenge the mainstream and normative narrative of the State and those holding privileged positions. Within the context of the death penalty, it completely changes the frame of reference in which we understand the problem of crime itself (in particular murder cases) and allows it to be defined in terms of only punishment rather than positioning such actions within a milieu characterised by oppression, inequality, institutional biases, and social exclusion. This kind of emphasis on punishment seen within the Criminal Justice System and relevant mainstream media also increases the discourse and legitimacy of more targeted policing and control of environments which such individuals come from and live within. Such points are indicative of Žižek's concepts of subjective violence and objective violence, and the important distinctions between them. For instance, subjective violence (within this example those crimes that result in being sentenced with the death penalty) is experienced as such against a background of a non-violent zero-level, and is therefore seen as a disturbance of the 'normal' and peaceful state of things (Žižek, 2008). This disruption of 'normality' is precisely what Criminal Justice Systems, acting on behalf of the State, fixate on — attempting to address such disturbances with punishments up to and including the death penalty. Objective violence, on the other hand (including the structural factors previously mentioned), is the violence inherent within this 'normal' state of things. It is therefore invisible since it sustains the very zero-level standard against which we perceive something as subjectively violent (Ibid). Due to the invisible nature of objective violence, the State's reaction (including the media and general public) is targeted towards the more visible forms of subjective violence — never addressing the underlying and systemic forms of violence that are undoubtedly integral to instances of direct violence including that of murder. As Žižek (ibid) states:

'We should learn to step back, to disentangle ourselves from the fascinating lure of this directly visible "subjective" violence, violence performed by a clearly identifiable agent. We need to perceive the contours of the background which generates such outbursts. A step back enables us to identify a violence that sustains our very efforts to fight violence and promote tolerance.' (Ibid, p. 1)

It is also worth stressing that the state's approach to addressing structural forms of violence via the means of execution is evidently misplaced, with the structural inequalities that lead to individuals committing criminal acts not being addressed or considered when designing punishments and subsequently carrying them out on, as discussed, society's most disadvantaged and marginalised groups. With this in mind, whilst such forms of violence are ignored, those without a voice or lacking necessary economic or cultural capital will continue to be subject to the state's harshest punishments in the name of 'justice.'

Police Killings in the United Kingdom: An Overview

In the UK, the number of people whose lives are lost following police contact each year is a matter of public record (National Statistics, 2016). Shootings which result in a fatality are carefully scrutinised, not only by academics and the public but also by the media and the Independent Police Complaints Commission (IPCC). This response and process is, as will be discussed later in this chapter, different in the US. In the UK, it is primarily the responsibility of the IPCC to investigate all police fatal shootings and their legitimacy and context (IPCC, 2017). The organization has not been without controversy, and allegations of 'insensitivity' from relatives of some of those killed led it to 'review its own practice' in 2014 (Shaw, 2014). Nevertheless, the IPCC has reinvestigated cases at the request of relatives, has been instrumental in seeking legal redress following fatalities, and has referred cases to the Crown Court (IPCC, 2016). The Home Office collates information from the IPCC and makes these reports available to the public via its own website (National Statistics, 2016).

This abundance of information is in stark contrast to analysis of such incidents in the US. As we will touch upon further into this chapter, there is a marked difference in the historical tradition of police cultures in the UK and US, although British attitudes do appear to be evolving in the face of perceived challenges and threats to security. The concept of 'suicide by cop' is a well-established American phenomenon (Patton and Fremouw, 2016). However, there is evidence that this method of self-destruction has become more prevalent in the UK in recent decades, although still not as common as in the US (Best et al, 2004).

Key Term: 'Suicide by Cop'
- Suicide by cop (or suicide by police) is a suicide method in which a suicidal individual intentionally behaves in an aggressive or intimidating manner, with the motivation to incite a lethal reaction from a law enforcement officer.

Taking this cross-Atlantic comparison further, British police differ from their American counterparts in their traditional lack of weaponry. For instance, the application and use of CS gas and Tasers by police generated intense debate and disagreement regarding how the police should be shaped in order to meet twenty-first century challenges (Tyler and King, 2000). Yet concomitantly, a point of contention is the apparent lack of power that British police possess in comparison to their transatlantic equivalents. Given relatively recent high-profile events such as the Manchester Arena bombings and the terrorist attacks that took place in Paris in 2015, there has been some critical commentary towards the perceived deficit in UK policing (Dodd, 2018). Specifically, then Prime Minister David Cameron awarded £143 million to boost national capability following the 2015 massacres carried out by Isis militants in Paris (Dearden, 2018). However, according to a survey by the Police Federation, while a slight majority of British police are prepared to be armed with guns, it is only a 55 per cent majority and the routine carrying of firearms remains extremely contentious (Donald, 2017). Perhaps one reason for this absence of enthusiasm is the scrutiny to which British police are held if they discharge a firearm—an accountability that is more lacking in the US (Riley, 2019). Despite the comparative rarity of police shootings in the UK, researchers still, and rightly so, scrutinise the use of deadly force, and there remains a tension between security and the principles of liberty and police accountability when police use lethal force (Kennison and Loumansky, 2007).

What is important for us to consider is that, when the life of a citizen is taken—whether by accident or design—by a representative of the State, without a trial and with no access to due process, it can have far-reaching implications and consequences for society. In some cases, extensive press coverage, furious protests and lengthy court cases can ensue. As previously mentioned, there is greater transparency in the UK, though this does not mean that when the police shoot someone dead there is little impact on community relations. The anger and increased scrutiny towards the State in response to a police-shooting can, under particular circumstances, provide the catalyst for large swathes of the population who feel marginalised to some degree or frustrated by continual perceived injustices at the hands of the State, to protest or riot. For instance, such sentiments can be witnessed with regards to the police fatal shooting of Mark Duggan, which acted as the prelude to the English riots of 2011.

Police Killings in the United States and the Qualified Immunity Doctrine

In the United States police officers, at the authorisation of the State, may use deadly force to stop or apprehend a fleeing felon, but only if the suspect is armed or has committed a crime that involved the infliction, or threatened infliction, of serious injury or death. With regards to the use of reasonable force, police in the US are under mounting pressure in relation to unlawful killings, in particular with regard to those of members of ethnic minorities. In recent years, fatal shootings of unarmed African-American males across the US have sparked outrage and apprehensions over police use of deadly force. Despite several high-profile cases and increased video evidence, convictions of police officers have been rare (Park, 2018). There have even been cases whereby an individual police officer who shot and killed an innocent civilian was fired and then re-hired in order to gain access to their pension. For example, Philip Brailsford, 28, killed 26-year-old Daniel Shaver in the hallway of an Arizona hotel in early 2016. He was fired and charged with murder, but he was acquitted at trial in 2017. Bodycam footage of the incident, released after Brailsford was acquitted, displayed Shaver on his knees asking officers not to shoot him. Despite these pleas he was shot five times whilst he crawled towards the officers. At the trial, lawyers contended that Brailsford had responded appropriately and in accordance with his training when Shaver reached towards his waistband. Brailsford apparently opened fire due to believing that there was a concealed firearm, which Shaver was reaching for. No weapon was found on the body. It was later revealed that he was briefly re-hired in 2018 — two years after the fatal incident — so he could apply for a lifetime pension worth more than $2,500 (£2,000) a month. Brailsford is now retired from the force with a tax-free pension worth $31,000 a year for life. His attorney also confirmed that the settlement was a result of him suffering from post-traumatic stress disorder due to the shooting involving Shaver (Ortiz, 2019).

The issue of fatal shootings at the hands of the police has only intensified through the arrival of new technologies that have been used to capture incidents of police violence, including the death of Eric Garner in 2014.

Case Study: The Death of Eric Garner

The Victim: Eric Garner (September 15, 1970 - July 17, 2014) was an African-American man. Garner, who was married, has been described by his friends as a 'neighbourhood peacemaker' and a generous, congenial person (BBC News, 2014). He was the father of six children, had three grandchildren, and at the time of his death had a three-month-old child. Garner had been arrested by the New York Police Department (NYPD) more than 30 times since 1980 on charges such as assault, resisting arrest, and grand larceny. According to an article in the *New York Times* many of these arrests had been for allegedly selling unlicensed cigarettes (Baker et al, 2015). It is important to note here that significant attention focused on Garner's history with the police, and as noted in another article for the *New York Times* he was often referred to by the police as a 'condition,' 'a nettlesome sign of disorder well-known in the 120th Precinct' (Ibid).

The Police Officer: Daniel Pantaleo was a 29-year-old NYPD officer living in Eltingville, Staten Island. He joined the NYPD in 2006 after graduating from Monsignor Farrell High School, and with a bachelor's degree from the College of Staten Island. Pantaleo was the subject of two civil rights lawsuits in 2013 where plaintiffs accused him of falsely arresting them and abusing them. In one of the cases, he and other officers allegedly ordered two African-American men to strip naked on the street for a search and the charges against the men were dismissed.

Case Summary: Police officers approached Garner on July 17, 2014 on suspicion of selling single cigarettes from packs without tax stamps. Garner told the police that he was tired of being harassed, reportedly stating 'I'm tired of it' and 'It stops today' (Capelouto, 2014). When Pantaleo placed his hands on Garner, Garner pulled his arms away. Pantaleo then placed his arm around Garner's neck and wrestled him to the ground. With multiple officers pinning him down, Garner repeated the words, 'I can't breathe' eleven times while lying face down on the sidewalk. After Garner lost consciousness, he remained lying on the sidewalk for seven minutes while the officers waited for an ambulance to arrive. Garner was pronounced dead at an area hospital approximately one hour later.

Aftermath: Daniel Pantaleo was fired over the death of Eric Garner, whose dying words, 'I can't breathe' became a rallying cry for protests against police brutality. It is important to note here that a State grand jury declined to press criminal charges. After a lengthy civil rights investigation, federal prosecutors said they would bring no charges (BBC News, 2015). In explaining his decision, NYPD Commissioner James O'Neill said mobile phone video of Garner's death clearly shows the officer used a chokehold, which is banned by the NYPD.

It is important to stress in the above case study the importance of the recording of this homicide, and the increased use of video-recording technology in an effort to bring attention and greater visibility to such incidents. Without the video of his final struggle, Eric Garner's death may have attracted little notice and, as a result, less public attention and calls for change. Without seeing it, the world would not have known exactly how he died. So too, as reported by the *New York Times*, 'We didn't know anything about a chokehold or hands to the neck until the video came out,' said a former senior police official with direct knowledge of the investigation, who spoke on the condition of anonymity to protect his access to confidential department information. 'We found out when everyone else did' (Baker et al, 2015).

Without the use of recording technology, the officers' narratives of events would be difficult to question, and nuances and realities behind such incidents would be omitted. For instance, for years such cigarettes as Eric Garner sold were common around Bay Street and the park, an area often characterised as poor and working-class whose 'population swells each day with those bound for the welfare office across the street' (Ibid). Due to these economic conditions, some individuals preferred to buy cigarettes individually at $1 or less, rather than a whole pack for ten times that (Ibid). Eric Garner was among a handful of men, mostly middle-aged and African-American or Hispanic, who sold near the park. He used the money to help support his wife and their six children (Ibid). Whilst the activities Eric was engaged in sheds light into how structural factors can lead someone into criminal behaviour, it also brings into question the problematic nature of the processes of criminalisation. In particular, it raises questions concerned with how criminalisation is often at the hands of those with much more political and economic capital than those who the activity labelled as criminal usually impacts. The very activity Eric Garner was accused of engaging in appears to also be criminalised not due to the harm or threat it causes, but is more concerned with implications for tax. Without such video documentation of the events that transpired, such narratives would be omitted, and instead such violence at the hands of police would be reduced to operating in the name and protection of law and order. The inherent problematic nature of operating under such an explanation would therefore be absent. Compounding this, it is important to consider the orthodox narrative presented and maintained by the State and mainstream media prior to the recording of such incidents. For instance, Professor Douglas Flowe stated, '[T]here has been a habit of explaining black death at the hands of police officers as tragic, but necessary to keep the public safe' (ITV News, 2020). This is unfortunately the traditional narrative presented prior to and, to an extent, after, the death of Eric Garner. For instance, in 1992, four officers were found not guilty in the beating of Rodney King (Sastry and Bates, 2017), and no officer has been charged in relation to the death of Eric Garner.

The death of Andrew Finch is another modern example of the State's ability to alter narratives and exercise its power of definitions of criminality. For Finch, a law-abiding citizen who lost his life in a swatting incident (deceiving emergency services by calling them to someone else's premises), the chain of events starting over a $1.50 bet disagreement in the video game Call of Duty: WWII (Lefler, 2019). Twenty-eight-year-old Tyler Barriss made a call to Wichita City Hall and was transferred to 911 dispatch, claiming that he had shot his father in the head, was holding his mother and brother hostage and planning to commit suicide. Before he hung up the phone, Barriss provided the address of Finch (Gagliardo-Silver, 2019). Shortly after the arrival of the police, Finch walked outside his home on West McCormick Street and was fatally shot on his front porch by a single round to the heart fired by a police officer (Lefler, 2019). Once the shooting had ceased, the police officers realised that this was a hoax and Finch was a target and victim of swatting. Consequently, the police — following the protocols set out and established by the FBI — initiated a search for the individual who made the initial 911 call and who ultimately directed police to Finch's home. The investigation subsequently led the police to Barriss, who was charged with domestic terrorism and given 20 years in prison (Dellinger, 2019).

With regard to the officer who shot Finch, the department — echoing similar sentiment to that in the case of officer Brailsford — claimed that their officer acted within protocol and no charges were brought against him (Johnson,

2018). In essence, Andrew Finch's death was presented as another example of a 'tragic incident' in order to protect the public.

To understand how the events leading to how Eric Garner, Andrew Finch, and many others' deaths transpired, it is important to look towards the increasing militarisation of this organization at the behest of the State. The events of 9/11 had far reaching consequences on the US's approach to policing. Specifically, the increased perceived threat of terrorism resulted in police departments being armed with military-style weaponry and equipment (Kraska, 2007). Moreover, these military strategies and approaches became further embedded into the day-to-day realities and lived experiences of policing. For instance, as noted by Campbell and Campbell (2014), the rise of international terrorism has shaped a mutual environment for the military and the police, as both pursue counter-measures appropriate to their responsibilities. The authors elaborate further, stating that, 'Counter-terrorism strategies have also pushed the police and the military together with exchanges of tactics and equipment and with the need for similarity in skills (if not in attitudes and orientations)' (Ibid, p. 350). Events such as 9/11 built upon the already aggressive rhetoric of the War on Drugs, and have served to blur traditional domestic/foreign divisions, resulting in increased military/police imitation.

However, this blurring of the divisions between the military and the police has resulted in numerous deaths and this has brought the police, and its use of lethal force, into question. Specifically, in 2017, 1,147 individuals were killed by the police as a consequence of the mentality of 'shoot first, ask questions later' (Police Violence Report, 2017). This number increased in the subsequent year, with 1,164 people being killed (Mapping Police Violence, 2018). This mentality of militarisation and 'us vs them' can perhaps be best illustrated by an extract from an article written by a former police officer recalling a confrontation with a potential suspect:

'At that point, my adrenaline was in control, and my training had me thinking that this would be where I would get shot. The man bent slightly and was digging for something from his waistband. I immediately drew my gun and shouted for him to stop moving and show me his hands. When he turned to face me, I saw a flash of silver in his hands. I began to squeeze the trigger of my gun; at the same time, he dropped what he was holding and threw his hands in the air. I didn't shoot him, but I came really close. The other officer came chugging to where we were and helped me take the man into custody. I noticed the man had an open fanny pack on his waist, and when I checked the ground, I found the silver object he had been holding. It was a radar detector about the size of a cell phone. I'd almost shot a man for holding a radar detector.' (Smith, 2018)

This author continued by stating that the 2016 killing of five police officers at the hands of Micah Johnson at a protest for the deaths of Alton Sterling and Philando Castile at the hands of the police created far reaching fear in his department, and that training quickly became centred on such scenarios. So too, this event lead to a stronger emphasis on first aid in order to 'stay in the fight' but, as Smith notes, 'The narrative in all this was saving ourselves and other cops — but not citizens' (Ibid). The author summarised his experiences as a police officer, affirming that:

'In all the training I had, officers were trained to fear even the average citizen — to beware that someone will take your gun and use it on you, to be on alert for ambushes, to be ready to fix yourself up if shot so you can keep going.' (Ibid)

While the author does state that he cannot, and does not, speak for every police officer, such a mentality may assist in providing some explanations for the aforementioned statistics. It is also important to contextualise the training received in the US compared to other nations. In Germany, for instance, police recruits are mandated to spend two-and-a-half to four years in basic training to become an officer, with the opportunity to undertake the equivalent of a bachelor's or master's degree in policing. In contrast to this extensive level of preparation, basic training in the US can take as little as 21 weeks (or 33.5 weeks, with field training). 'The less time recruits have to train, the less time is afforded for guidance on crisis intervention or de-escalation' (Serhan, 2020).

It is also important to acknowledge that many victims of police shootings are from BAME backgrounds. For example, in 2017 African-Americans comprised 25 per cent of those killed despite being only 13 per cent of the population (Police Violence Report, 2017). There is also another, much less well-documented feature of police violence: the prevalence of disabled people and, in particular, those with mental difficulties, who are victims. A Massachusetts-based disability rights non-profit organization — the Ruderman Family Foundation — published a paper in which it estimated that a third to half of all people killed by police in the US have a disability (O'Hara, 2016). The authors of the said paper stated that, 'media coverage of police violence fails to recognise or report the disability element when Americans are injured or killed by law enforcement, resulting in their stories being segregated from the issue in the media' (Ibid). This is even more startling when we frame this discussion around international law, where it is stated that police officers are to only use lethal force as a last resort in order to protect themselves or others from death or serious injury:

> 'If the force is unavoidable it must be no more than is necessary and proportionate to achieve the objective, and law enforcement must use it in a manner designed to minimise damage or injury, must respect and preserve human life and ensure medical aid [is] provided as soon as possible to those injured or affected.' (Amnesty International, 2015, p. 1)

In the cases of both Eric Garner and Andrew Finch, the force used was not necessary or proportionate as they did not pose an immediate threat. Andrew Finch was unarmed and the single shot aimed at him was not intended to minimise damage, as it was a direct shot to his heart, therefore using force that may cost the life of a person cannot be justified as acting according to protocol (Amnesty International, 2015). So too, Eric Garner was not armed, and the level of force used to arrest him was not designed to minimise damage or injury. However, the authorities used Tylor Barriss as an example for the consequences of swatting in order to avoid discussions around police use of violence, and there have been many commentators attempting to blame Eric Garner for his death. For instance, New York representative Peter King stated that, 'you had a 350lb (159kg) person who was resisting arrest. The police were trying to bring him down as quickly as possible ... If he had not had asthma and a heart condition and was so obese, almost definitely he would not have died' (BBC News, 2014). Indirectly, these two cases created the examples through which we can witness how the State legitimises certain forms of violence and death.

Such legitimisation can be witnessed in how police officers in America are protected through the qualified immunity doctrine (QID). The doctrine specifies that, '[W]hen government officials are sued in their individual capacity, they generally are shielded from civil damages as long as their conduct does not violate clearly established rights in which a reasonable person would have known' (Jeffries, 2010). It is in place to protect police officers from lawsuits brought against them. In theory this doctrine is constructive, as it would allow such individuals employed within a law enforcement capacity to protect the public without the anxiety and fear of persecution or legal responsibility. It is also important to stress here that the following discussions are relevant to only a small number of officers, with most carrying out their duties with utmost professionalism. Nevertheless, it has been demonstrated that such a doctrine has been used as an effort to deprive the private civil rights of victims of police violence and their family members. Such family members can be considered as being related victims, often defined as those victims who were, at the time of the violent crime, a close family member of a deceased primary victim; was a dependant of a deceased primary victim; or had an intimate personal relationship with a deceased primary victim (Victims of Crime Assistance Tribunal, 2016). Another significant consequence of such a doctrine is that it has evidently weakened the civil courts' capacity to deter police violence (Stefan, 2016). Only by implementing sweeping reforms of the QID can these aforementioned statistics of police violence see significant reductions and, possibly, increased trust and confidence in the police (Stefan, 2016).

According to a study by Mesic et al (2018), African-Americans are approximately five times more likely to be fatally shot by law enforcement. The racial disparity in police shootings is, according to the authors of this particular study, not a reflection of increased crime in communities of colour. Rather, police shooting disparities are amplified by residential segregation and the resulting racial biases. These statistics are only further compounded when we consider the very low conviction rates of such instances. Since 2005, 98 non-federal law enforcement officers have been arrested in connection with fatal, on-duty shootings, according to the Police Integrity Research Group's data. To date, only 35 of these officers have been convicted of a crime, often a lesser offence such as manslaughter or negligent homicide, rather than murder. Only three officers have been convicted of murder during this period and seen their convictions stand. Another 22 officers were acquitted in a jury trial and nine were acquitted during a bench trial decided by a judge. Ten other cases were dismissed by a judge or a prosecutor, and in one instance no true bill was returned from a grand jury. Philip Stinson, an associate professor at Bowling Green State University's Criminal Justice Program and the university's lead for the Police Integrity Research Group, stated that:

> 'None of these cases, cases involving police shootings, is ever easy or exactly the same…But today, an officer gets on the stand and says "I feared for my life," and that's usually all…No conviction, more often than that, no charges at all.' (cited in Ross, 2019)

An important consideration here is the purpose of such violence in the affirmation and reinforcement of the role such institutions play in the protection of the general public. Specifically, such organizations and institutions 'disavow' such actions to protect national security—especially within a post 9/11 context.

Key Term: Fetishistic Disavowal

'Disavowal' or, more specifically, fetishist disavowal, which Žižek summarises as, 'I know, but I don't want to know that I know, so I don't know' (2010) is a process of denial, the denial of one's position in the world relative to others. He argues that life functions on the basis of such denials. Žižek, in his seminal work, *Violence* (2008) discusses the treatment of animals so that large swathes of the population can eat meat, and how such people are indeed aware but do not want to ponder or consider the actualities of the conditions these animals find themselves in before being cut-up, packaged, and then sold and bought for our convenience.

With reference to cultural violence, both the State and mainstream media tend to gravitate towards offenders, focusing on their individual actions, behaviours and subsequent punishment at the hands of the Criminal Justice System. The primary consequence of such narratives results in violence at the hands of the State being pushed aside or hidden from view and thus attention. Through this myopic representation of the individual offender and his or her actions (in the case of Andrew Finch being Tyler Barriss and in the case of Eric Garner his own past behaviour and health factors), the State's application and displays of violence are thus both disavowed and legitimatised. This is only further reinforced when we consider the rarity of convictions and, up until relatively recently, a general lack of critical and nuanced media coverage of such instances. Police killings are therefore a demonstration of power and a fundamental practice of the killing State (Williams, 2015).

Whilst we have, to an extent, examined the role and significance of the increasing militarisation of the police in the US, Williams (2015) further elucidates the role of the police in the exercising of power at the hands of the State. Specifically, Williams highlights that even the 'kinder, friendlier face of law enforcement (community policing) works to conscript civilians and "helping" institutions into the project of social control, while serving as the stick that continues to enforce the "order" that serves existing power relations in the United States' (p. 2). This is only further compounded when we consider that, in 2005, the US Supreme Court ruled that the police did not have a constitutional duty to protect a person from harm, 'even a woman who had obtained a court-issued protective order against a violent husband making an arrest mandatory for a violation' (Greenhouse, 2005). This pivotal ruling only further support notions that the primary role of the police in North America is to support and maintain the interests of both the State and capital. Such institutional imperatives related to the maintenance of State control and capitalist ideology can be traced throughout the history of the police there. For example, there have been documented cases of police killing individuals involved in labour disputes who were seeking better pay and standards of living and working conditions. Such incidents include the Lattimer massacre of 1897 where 19 unarmed workers were shot and killed whilst being forced to disperse from a peaceful march (Shackel, 2019), and in 1927, during a coal strike in Colorado, State police and mine guards fired pistols, rifles and a machine gun into a group of 500 striking miners and their wives in what came to be called the Columbine Mine Massacre (Libcom, 2006). So too, we can witness recent protests related to police violence being met with the use of tear gas, batons, vehicles and pepper spray (Gabbatt, 2020). Foucault (1978) refers to the State as the final arbiter of life and death, and the State produces and demonstrates its power through its killable subjects. Foucault argues that, unlike particular moments in history where those in power had total control over their subjects, as time progressed it was no longer considered that this power of the sovereign over his or her subjects could be exercised in an absolute and unconditional way. Within the modern landscape, Foucault suggests that power no longer asserts itself in this manner. The primary interest of power now is in life, and how to secure, extend, and improve it. Wars are still waged (with far greater numbers of casualties) in the face of external or internal threats but they are not waged on behalf of the 'right of death' of some sovereign lord, but rather to secure a better way of life for all. Power is now exercised exclusively over life, and is exercised either to foster life or to disallow it.

In the case of the US, the already militarised approach to the 'War on Drugs' was only further entrenched after the events of 9/11 — the external and internal enemies were 'revealed' and established in the eyes of the State. These deaths as a result of police shootings are, through the lens of the State, casualties in a 'war' designed to protect the lives of others. With this in mind, the State maintains a militarised model of policing that creates fear and uses lethal force to maintain State control and the capitalist interests of those with significant political and economic power. In doing so it also protects such individuals who operate and work for the State under the QID.

The cases of Eric Garner and Andrew Finch created a periscope into how the State's success functions on the detriment of others. Although practices of police violence are authorised and legitimised by federal institutions such as the courts, they have not been subjected to a process of counting and quantitative research and are consequently not part of national statistics. In contrast, the government has produced detailed research on murders by the wider public. This is another example of the way the State is trying to disavow the issue and prevent such discussions concerning deaths caused by police shootings from transcending the narrative of security, law, and order. Nonetheless, the Black Lives Matter movement has assisted in transforming these statistics by naming the victims of police brutality and putting in motion the acts of more media outlets to take it upon themselves to look into the issue of how certain police officers are misusing their discretionary powers (King, 2018). So too, at the time of writing, the death of George Floyd in May 2020 has sparked significant public reaction and condemnation both nationally and internationally. Due to this public response, the officer who was recorded placing his knee on Floyd's neck and thus cutting blood flow to his brain and restricting his ability to breathe (Furber et al, 2020) faces eleven charges, including murder and aggravated assault with a deadly weapon (BBC News, 2020). There have also been renewed debates from both sides of the political spectrum with regard to the abolition of the QID, though this has been met with some scepticism with regard to the actuality of deterring officers from resorting to violence (see, for instance, Epps, 2020). Despite these raised considerations, eliminating the QID is one of the most practical, promising ways to encourage police to conform their behaviour to constitutional limitations. Alongside these practical factors, it is important to consider the symbolic significance of the removal of such a doctrine—an important signifier that certain individuals are not above the law.

Closing Comments

It is important to acknowledge and keep in mind that the Criminal Justice System is oriented around the individual offender who, equipped with *mens rea*, chooses to engage in criminal behaviour. Under such stipulations, the individual, depending on the severity of their actions, is then sentenced from a range of punishments in order for the 'scales of justice' to be brought back into balance. Of note is that such scales are usually held by Lady Justice, who also wears a blindfold. This symbolises that justice is 'blind'—in other words, it is supposed to be objective, without bias; never favouring the strong nor the weak, the rich nor the poor, the righteous nor the wicked.

This chapter has sought to reveal that this blindfold is, depending on the accused, occasionally removed and this objectivity is brought into question. Consequently, harms caused by the State under the premise of safety, security and justice—including deaths—are rarely put on trial. As a result, the rich and powerful, and those associated with or working for them have a far different experience with the State than those who are, for a variety of reasons, marginalised and silenced.

Questions to consider:
- In what way does cultural violence normalise deaths caused by the hands of the State?
- What are some of the other ways the State's actions lead to deaths of citizens?
- Does the death penalty reduce or prevent crime?
- What type of crimes, other than murder, is the death penalty applied to around the world?
- What are the consequences of police killings in the US?
- What are some ways police killings could be reduced in the US?

References

Baker, A., Goodman, D and Mueller, B. (2015), 'Beyond the Chokehold: The Path to Eric Garner's Death,' *New York Times*, 13 June: https://www.nytimes.com/2015/06/14/nyregion/eric-garner-police-chokehold-staten-island.html

Barak, G., Leighton, P., and Flavin, J. (2010), *Class, Race, Gender, and Crime: The Social Realities of Justice in America* (3rd edn.), Lanham, MD: Rowman & Littlefield.

BBC News (2014), 'Eric Garner: NY officer in "I can't breathe" death fired,' 19 August: https://www.bbc.co.uk/news/world-us-canada-49399302

BBC News (2014), 'Profile: Eric Garner,' 5 December: https://www.bbc.co.uk/news/world-us-canada-30350648

BBC News (2014), 'Viewpoint: Why Eric Garner was blamed for dying,' 8 December: https://www.bbc.co.uk/news/magazine-30340632

BBC News (2020), 'George Floyd: What we know about the officers charged over his death,' 8 June: https://www.bbc.co.uk/news/world-us-canada-52969205

Campbell, D. J. and Campbell, K. M. (2014), 'Police/Military Convergence in the USA as Organisational Mimicry,' *International Journal of Research and Policy*, 26(3), pp. 332–353.

Capelouto, S. (2014). 'Eric Garner: The haunting last words of a dying man,' *CNN*, 9 December: https://edition.cnn.com/2014/12/04/us/garner-last-words/index.html

Cunningham, M. D. and Vigen, M. P. (2002), 'Death Row Inmate Characteristics, Adjustment, and Confinement: A Critical Review of the Literature,' *Behavioural Sciences and the Law*, 20, pp. 191–210.

Dearden, L. (2018), 'British police could be "routinely armed" to respond to terror threat in rural areas,' *Independent*, 17 May: https://www.independent.co.uk/news/uk/home-news/police-armed-routine-uk-terror-attacks-target-missed-recruitment-a8354926.html

Death Penalty Information Centre (2019), 'Facts about the Death Penalty': https://files.deathpenaltyinfo.org/documents/pdf/FactSheet.f1562867044.pdf

Dellinger, A. (2019), '"Call of Duty" swatter to serve 20 years in prison,' *Engadget*, 29 March: https://www.engadget.com/2019/03/29/tyler-barriss-20-year-prison-sentence-swatting

Demme, J. (Dir), 'The Silence of the Lambs' (1991), USA: Strong Heart/Demme Production.

Dodd, V. (2018), 'UK police chiefs discuss officers routinely carrying guns,' *Guardian*, 17 May.

Donald, C. (2017), 'To be armed or not be armed, that was the question,' Police Federation: http://www.polfed.org/newsroom/Blogs.aspx?item=129

Duffin, E. (2019). 'Percentage of active US district court judges as of August 2017, by race and Hispanic origin,' *Statistica*: https://www.statista.com/statistics/408483/percentage-of-us-district-court-judges-by-race/

Epps, D. (2020), 'Abolishing Qualified Immunity Is Unlikely to Alter Police Behaviour,' *New York Times*, 16 June: https://www.nytimes.com/2020/06/16/opinion/police-qualified-immunity.html

Foucault, M. (1978), *The History of Sexuality. 1: The Will to Know*, London: Penguin.

Frankis, D. (2019). 'FACT 2: Capital punishment in the UK was abolished in 1965, but the Death Penalty was a legally defined punishment until 1998,' in J. Treadwell and A. Lynes (eds.), *50 Facts Everyone Should Know About Crime and Punishment in Britain*, Bristol: Policy Press, pp. 17–21.

Furber, M., Burch, A. D. S. and Robles, F. (2020), 'George Floyd Worked with Officer Charged in His Death,' *New York Times*, 30 May: https://www.nytimes.com/2020/05/29/us/derek-chauvin-george-floyd-worked-together.html

Gabbatt, A. (2020), 'Protests about police brutality are met with wave of police brutality across US,' *Guardian*, 6 June: https://www.theguardian.com/us-news/2020/jun/06/police-violence-protests-us-george-floyd

Gagliardo-Silver, V. (2019), 'California man pleads guilty to 51 charges in fatal "swatting" prank case,' *Independent*, 29 March: https://www.independent.co.uk/news/world/

americas/swatting-tyler-barris-guilty-california-prank-andrew-finch-death-call-of-duty-a8845836.html

Galtung, J. (1973), *Theories of Conflict: Definitions, Dimensions, Negations, Formations*: https://www.transcend.org/files/Galtung_Book_Theories_Of_ Conflict_single.pdf

Galtung, J. (1990), 'Cultural Violence,' *Journal of Peace Research*, 27(3), pp. 291–305.

Galtung, J. (1996), *Peace by Peaceful Means: Peace and Conflict, Development and Civilization*, Oslo: International Peace Research Institute.

Garland, D. (2002), 'The Cultural Uses of Capital Punishment,' *Punishment and Society*, Vol. 4(4), pp. 459–487.

Glyn-Jones, A. (2000), *Holding Up a Mirror: How Civilizations Decline* (2nd edn.), Exeter: Imprint Academic.

Greenhouse, L. (2005), 'Justices Rule Police Do Not Have a Constitutional Duty to Protect Someone,' *New York Times*, 28 June: https://archive.is/gHlb4#selection-1801.0-1801.73

Hall, S. (2012), *Theorizing Crime and Deviance: A New Perspective*, London: Sage.

Hood, R. and Hoyle, C. (2015), *The Death Penalty: A Worldwide Perspective* (5th edn.), Oxford: Oxford University Press.

IPCC (2016), 'IPCC refers James Herbert investigation to Crown Prosecution Service,' Independent Police Complaints Commission.

IPCC (2017), 'Deaths in police custody stable but sharp increase in pursuit-related deaths and fatal shootings, figures released by IPCC show,' Independent Police Complaints Commission.

ITV News (2020), 'The History of Police Brutality against Black People in America,' 7 June: https://www.itv.com/news/2020-06-09/george-floyd-history-of-police-brutality-against-black-people-in-america

Jackson, Sr., J.L., Jackson, Jr., J.L, and Shapiro, B. (2001), *Legal Lynching: The Death Penalty and America's Future*, New York, NY: New Press.

Jeffries, J. C. (2010), 'What's Wrong with Qualified Immunity?' *Florida Law Review*, 62(4).

Jenkins, P. (1988), 'Serial Murder in England, 1940–1985,' *Journal of Criminal Justice*, 16, pp. 1–15.

Johnson R. (1979), 'Under Sentence of Death: The Psychology of Death Row Confinement,' *Law and Psychology Review*, 5, pp. 141–192.

Kennison, P. and Loumansky, A. (2007), 'Shoot to Kill—Understanding Police Use of Force in Combatting Suicide Terrorism,' *Crime, Law and Social Change,* 47(3), pp. 151–168.

King J. (2018). 'How Black Lives Matter Has Changed US Politics,' *New Internationalist,* 5 March: https://newint.org/features/2018/03/01/black-lives-matter-changed-politics

Kleck, G. (1981), 'Racial Discrimination in Criminal Sentencing,' *American Sociological Review,* 46, pp. 783–805.

Kraska, P. B. (2007), 'Militarization and Policing—It's Relevance to 21st Century Police,' *Policing: A Journal of Policy and Practice,* 1(4), pp. 501–513.

Lefler, D. (2019). 'Tragedy again strikes the family of swatting victim Andrew Finch,' *The Wichita Eagle,* January 10: https://www.kansas.com/news/local/article224258200.html

Libcom.org (2006), 'Colorado miners' strike and Columbine mine massacre, 1927,' 10 November: https://libcom.org/history/1927-colorado-miners-strike-and-columbine-mine-massacre

Mapping Police Violence (2018): https://mappingpoliceviolence.org/

Mark, M. (2016), 'Where Donald Trump stands on criminal justice,' *Business Insider,* October 8: https://www.businessinsider.com/where-donald-trump-stands-on-criminal-justice-2016-10?r=USandIR=T

McLeod, M. S. (2016), 'Does the Death Penalty Require Death Row? The Harm of Legislative Silence," *Ohio State Law Journal,* 77(3), pp. 526–592.

Mesic, A., Franklin, L., Cansever, A., Potter, F., Sharma, A., Knopov, A. and Siegel, M. (2018), 'The Relationship between Structural Racism and Black-white Disparities in Fatal Police Shootings at the State Level,' *Journal of the National Medical Association,* 110(2), pp. 106–116.

Miller, C. (2019), 'CNN anchor tears up in powerful on-air response to Trump's racist description of his hometown as "rodent infested",' *Independent,* 28 July: https://www.independent.co.uk/news/world/americas/us-politics/trump-cnn-anchor-victor-blackwell-racist-hometown-rodent-infested-a9023911.html

Mong, S. N. and Roscigno, V. J. (2010), 'African American Men and the Experience of Employment Discrimination,' *Qualitative Sociology,* Vol. 33, pp. 1–21.

National Statistics, 'Deaths during or following police contact in England and Wales: 2015 to 2016' (2016), GOV.UK: https://www.gov.uk/government/statistics/deaths-during-or-following-police-contact-in-england-and-wales-2015-to-2016

O'Hara, M. (2016), 'Up to half of people killed by US police are disabled,' *Guardian*, March 29: https://archive.is/gE0iI#selection-1435.1-1435.54

Oliver, M. B. (2003), 'African American Men as "Criminal and Dangerous": Implications of Media Portrayals of Crime on the "Criminalization" of African American Men,' *Journal of African American Studies*, Vol. 7, pp. 3–18.

Ortiz, E. (2019), 'Police officer who fatally shot sobbing man temporarily rehired to apply for pension,' NBC News, 12 July: https://www.nbcnews.com/news/us-news/police-officer-who-fatally-shot-sobbing-man-temporarily-rehired-apply-n1028981

Park, M. (2018), 'Police shootings: Trials, convictions are rare for officers,' CNN, 3 October: https://edition.cnn.com/2017/05/18/us/police-involved-shooting-cases/index.html

Police Violence Report (2017): https://policeviolencereport.org/

Potas, I and Walker, J. (1987), 'Capital Punishment' in P. R. Wilson (ed.), *Issues in Crime Morality and Justice*, Canberra: Australian Institute of Criminology.

Prejean, H. (2005), *The Death of Innocents: An Eyewitness Account of Wrongful Executions*, New York, NY: Random House.

Riley, L. (2019), 'Between 2004 and 2017, 33 people were fatally shot by the police in England and Wales,' in J. Treadwell and A. Lynes (eds.), *50 Facts Everybody Should Know About Crime and Punishment in Britian*, Bristol: Policy Press, pp. 70–74.

Ross, J. (2019), 'NBCBLK Police officers convicted for fatal shootings are the exception, not the rule,' NBC News, 14 March: https://www.nbcnews.com/news/nbcblk/police-officers-convicted-fatal-shootings-are-exception-not-rule-n982741

Rothstein, R. (2017), *The Colour of Law: A Forgotten History of How Our Government Segregated America*, New York, NY: Boni & Liveright.

Sastry, A. and Bates, K. G. (2017), 'When LA Erupted in Anger: A Look Back at the Rodney King Riots,' NPR, 26 April: https://www.npr.org/2017/04/26/524744989/when-la-erupted-in-anger-a-look-back-at-the-rodney-king-riots

Serhan, Y. (2020), 'What the World Could Teach America About Policing,' *The Atlantic*, 10 June: https://www.theatlantic.com/international/archive/2020/06/america-police-violence-germany-georgia-britain/612820/

Shaw, D. (2014), 'Independent Police Complaints Commission plans overhaul after review,' BBC News: http://www.bbc.co.uk/news/uk-26602773

Shackel, P. A. (2019), 'How an 1897 Massacre of Pennsylvania Coal Miners Morphed From a Galvanizing Crisis to Forgotten History,' *Smithsonian Magazine*, 13 March: https://www.smithsonianmag.com/history/

how-1897-massacre-pennsylvania-coal-miners-morphed-galvanizing-crisis-forgotten-history-180971695/

Smiley, C. and Fakunle, D. (2016), 'From "Brute" to "Thug": The Demonization and Criminalization of Unarmed Black Male Victims in America,' *Journal of Human Behaviour in the Social Environment*, 26(3–4), pp. 350–366.

Smith, L. (2018), 'Police are Trained to Fear,' *Medium: Justice*, 27 November: https://medium.com/s/story/fearing-for-our-lives-82ad7eb7d75f

Stefan, L. (2016), '"No Man is Above the Law and No Man is Below it": How Qualified Immunity Reform Could Create Accountability and Curb Widespread Police Misconduct,' 47 *Seton Hall L Rev* 543: https://heinonline.org/HOL/LandingPage?handle=hein.journals/shlr47anddiv=18andid=andpage=

Tehranian, J. (2000), 'Performing Whiteness: Naturalization Litigation and the Construction of Racial Identity in America,' *Yale Law Journal*, 109(4), pp. 817–848.

Thomson, E. (1997), 'Discrimination and the Death Penalty in Arizona,' *Criminal Justice Review*, 22(1), pp. 65–76.

Tyler, L. and King, L. (2000), 'Arming a Traditionally Disarmed Police: An Examination of Police Use of CS gas in the UK,' *Policing: An International Journal of Police Strategies and Management*, 23(3), pp. 390–400.

United Nations Human Rights: Office of the High Commissioner (2018), 'Death Row Reserved for the Poor,' 16 October: https://www.ohchr.org/en/newsevents/pages/deathpenaltyisabane.aspx

United States Department of Justice (2014), 'Capital Punishment, 2013 — Statistical Tables': http://www.bjs.gov/content/pub/pdf/cp13st.pdf

United States General Accounting Office (1997), *Death Penalty Sentencing: Research Indicates Pattern of Racial Disparities*, New York: Oxford University Press.

US Census Bureau (2014), 'Race and Ethnicity': https://www.census.gov/mso/www/training/pdf/race-ethnicity-onepager.pdf

Victims of Crime Assistance Tribunal (2016), 'Related Victim': https://www.vocat.vic.gov.au/assistance-available/types-victims/related-victim

Williams, K. (2015), *Our Enemies in Blue: Police and Power in America* (3rd edn.), Edinburgh: AK Press.

Žižek, S. (2008), *Violence*, London: Profile Books.

Žižek, S. (2010), *Living in the End Times*, London: Verso.

CHAPTER 8

The Business of Homicide

'A basic principle of modern state capitalism is that costs and risks are socialised to the extent possible, while profit is privatised'

Noam Chomsky, Linguist, philosopher and activist

Introduction

We have so far examined various forms of homicide and acts of murder whereby
it is generally easy to determine the identifiable agent responsible for the act(s)
committed. Be it a case of domestic violence, a serial murderer who kills repeatedly over an extended period of time, or a mass murderer who kills numerous
individuals in one incident—the process of determining responsibility and
mens rea is a relatively straightforward exercise. These direct forms of violence
dominate our media landscape and this is one of the primary reasons why many
in society hold a rather narrow and myopic understanding of violence and the
processes that can result in death.

In this chapter we examine how 'corporate killings' challenges these orthodox perceptions of violence, and how the logic of the market entwined with
the deregulated processes of neo-liberalism have created a myriad of structural
harms in which death can occur. We will first attempt to define what we mean
by 'corporate killing' as—similar to other forms of homicide—the concept is
fraught with conceptual ambiguity. We then explore how the process of neoliberal ideology has created opportunities for such forms of homicide to occur
with very little in the way of effective deterrence mechanisms. Next we explore
one of the most tragic historic examples of deaths caused by a corporation in
what is often referred to as the Bhopal disaster. Finally, we look to the present

day and the future with regard to how the emergence of the 'gig economy' has created new challenges so far under-recognised and discussed.

Defining 'Corporate Killing'

In attempting to define 'corporate killing' we come across some conceptual challenges. For instance, laws concerning such actions are centred on gross negligence which results in an individual's death. Current conceptualisation of these killings revolves around notions of manslaughter and as a consequence fails to identify other work-related factors that may result in death. In the UK, corporate manslaughter is a relatively novel criminal offence. It became law in 2008 when the Corporate Manslaughter and Corporate Homicide Act 2007 came into force. Section 1 of this Act states that an organization is guilty of manslaughter, 'if the way in which its activities are managed or organized causes a person's death.' This new conceptualisation is designed to make companies accountable in criminal law where they fall far below what can be expected in the circumstances. The statutory (and suggested) penalty for such forms of homicide is an unlimited fine and a remedial order to correct the original cause of the accident. Directors of such companies might also be liable for disqualification. There are a number of perceived advantages to this. Firstly, such changes may assist in changing people's perception of the serious nature of offences committed by employers who kill their own employees in a business context. This issue of the public's perception of corporate manslaughter is that such instances are more an example of breaches of health and safety law, and less a 'real' crime in comparison to theft or physical assault (Wells, 2001).

Another key development came in 2010, whereby it is now possible to order companies to take out advertisements publicising the fact they have been convicted. This change in public perception, along with unlimited fines and the risk of public embarrassment and shaming may serve as a greater deterrent to corporations, and potentially prevent such crimes from occurring in the future.

There are also a number of challenges that categorisation of this particular form of homicide faces. For instance, there is the significant issue of resource allocation in investigating such offences. Estimates of Health and Safety Executive (HSE) inspector time involved in a manslaughter investigations indicate around two-to-three months per case, with many such cases requiring lengthy and time-consuming preliminary investigations before it can be determined whether or not there is a case for prosecution. Given the sheer quantity of evidence that would need to be examined, resource needs could be a potentially significant issue. There are also potential issues in differing approaches to investigating: for example, the HSE's underlying objective is its enforcement procedures in the improvement of health and safety in the workplace, along with prevention of further instances occurring. On the other hand, the police approach is understandably more concerned with arrests and convictions for everyday homicide offences. There is also the difficulty in defining director responsibility in such instances. This particular offence is, so far as the 2007 Act matters, concerned with corporate liability and does not apply to directors or other individuals who have a senior role in the company or organization. This particular category of homicide does not necessarily ensure real accountability at a director level of a company and may thus allow flexibility for directors to remove themselves from responsibility. While there have been a growing number of critics arguing against such laws with regard to the economic costs they may have on organizations, Clarkson (1996) has identified four valuable characteristics of criminal prosecution:

'Stronger procedural protection of corporations, such as proof beyond reasonable doubt; more powerful enforcement agencies, such as the Health and Safety Executive in the UK; the Stigma and censure that follow from conviction; and the symbolic role of criminal law that "sends a message" to society.' (Ibid, p. 557)

It is important to consider that, at a political level, corporations are seen as a source of economic progress and social good, no matter what their failings are (Tombs and Whyte, 2015). The corporation is portrayed as the 'single best way of organizing the production and distribution of goods and services' and has a dominant status in a capitalist society (Ibid, p. 92). Thus, the harmful effects of such organizations are described as peripheral, when the reality is they are inherent consequences of corporate activity (Ibid). As corporations are argued to be benevolent institutions, when illegality occurs they are expected to reform themselves (Ibid). Only in the event that corporate social responsibility fails should governments intervene to regulate corporate crime (Ibid). As a result of these views, corporate crime is often neglected within academic, legal, political and media discourse.

Perpetual Pursuit of Profit in a Deregulated Economy

We are in, according to Jock Young, an *exclusive* society. One plagued by a myriad of structural harms that have evaporated notions of social cohesiveness, collectivity, and equality that were once a staple of Britain's society. For many, an *inclusive* society may appear as nothing more than a pipe dream—a dream that is simply not practical. This is primarily due to notions of capitalist realism: so pervasive has neo-liberalism become that we seldom even recognise it as an ideology. While we may struggle to recognise that neo-liberal ideology is not absolute nor unavoidable, Wilson (2009), in his examination into the history of British serial killing highlights that there were no serial murderers active during the inter-World War II period. In examining public documents on murder in 1935, he explains:

> 'Of the forty-seven people who faced a criminal trial: three were discharged; one died while on remand in prison; six were found to be insane; six were acquitted; fourteen were found guilty but insane; eight were executed; seven had their death sentences commuted to life imprisonment; one was sent to Broadmoor; and the final defendant had his conviction quashed at the Court of Appeal.' (Wilson, 2009, p. 86)

Wilson expands, stating that 'these statistics give an appearance of certainty, finality and order' (Ibid, p. 86) in Britain at that time. While Wilson entertains the possibility that many cases of reported suicide during the inter-war period may have actually been murders, the socio-economic climate and Home Office records suggest that 'any serial killer active at the time would not have escaped detection for long' (Ibid, p. 92). The significance of this finding is predicated on the notion that this particular period of history is characterised by a strong sense of collective working towards a shared goal.

This period, which placed great emphasis on community, locality and employment was, according to Jock Young, irrevocably changed during the 1980s when Thatcherism's antisocial welfare policies de-emphasised these very principles. As a result of the more 'exclusive' society, which emphasised materialistic consumption, individualism, anonymity, and less about 'traditionalities of community and family' (Young, 1999, p. 6) certain groups became increasingly marginalised in society.

Government policies have, over time, weakened the economic and social protection of the elderly, gay men, runaways and throwaways, children, and women involved in prostitution (Wilson, 2007). While we can witness how such ideology has resulted in structural forms of violence that created vulnerabilities that serial murderers within the UK exploited, we can also begin to see how the patterns of community disintegration and the collapse of social welfare in the name of profit has provided intense motivation for companies to operate with minimal regard for the lives of others.

At its crux, neo-liberal ideology works on the basis of intense competition at both the individual level and that of an organization such as a corporate entity. Neo-liberalism sees competition as the defining and most significant characteristic of human relations. It re-orientates individuals as consumers, whose democratic choices are best exercised by buying and selling, a process that rewards merit and punishes ineffectiveness. It maintains that 'the market' delivers benefits that could never otherwise be achieved—especially by a State which takes a more proactive and regulatory role in its economy. Attempts to limit competition are treated as hostile to liberty. Tax and regulation should be minimised, and public services such as the prison sector or health service should be privatised. The organization of labour and collective bargaining by trade unions are portrayed as market distortions that obstruct and hinder the development of a natural hierarchy of 'winners' and 'losers.' This, we can see, was one of the lasting legacies of then Prime Minister Margaret Thatcher, who weakened the power of unions in the 1980s (Young, 1999). In one of neo-liberalism's greatest trappings, inequality is reorganized and packaged as virtuous—a reward for utility and a generator of wealth. Such a powerful narrative is indeed one of the (many) reasons why many individuals who are marginalised or socially excluded are unable to truly articulate and determine the structural forces that harm them (Treadwell et al, 2013).

Within this context, corporations are now untethered by less regulation and comprised of motivated individuals who pursue profit. Notions of neo-liberalism can be traced back to the ideals of Adam Smith to whom is often attributed the concept of the 'invisible hand.'

> **Key Term: The Invisible Hand**
> - The invisible hand describes the unintended social benefits of an individual's self-interested actions, a concept that was first introduced by Adam Smith in *The Theory of Moral Sentiments*, written in 1759, invoking it in reference to income distribution.

One of the primary criticisms towards the 'invisible hand' is that it fails to truly comprehend the powerful cultural messages of the potential (consumer) rewards of individual and self-interested competition. Another key criticism is of the idea that individuals and corporations will regulate themselves, and that regulation from the State is unwarranted and counterproductive. What such a view fails to consider is that enforced self-regulation with little in the way of governmental oversight provides an exploitative space which companies use in order to cut corners in the perpetual pursuit of profit. It is in this cutting of corners that negligence in workers' (and in some cases members of the public's) safety manifests itself.

So too, as we will come to see later in this chapter, this pursuit of profit in an age of receding worker's rights has resulted in immense pressures that may manifest in severe accidents, deaths (for example, same or next day delivery drivers who cause such incidents as they hastily rush to meet their targets) and even suicides (for example, some factory workers in China whereby suicide nets are now installed due to the high number of employees attempting to end their lives).

To summarise, neo-liberal ideology along with consumer culture is transmitted and embedded in all levels of capitalist society, and has eroded informal networks of support by converting collectives into markets, public services into privatised corporate opportunities and people into consumers (Hayward and Smith, 2017). Alongside this, market logic and consumer values have a significant psychological impact, shaping individual consciousness by propagating insatiable wants and desires and promoting a culture that exalts atomised individual competition over all other social considerations (Ibid). Taking this into consideration, we now explore a number of case examples that demonstrates how a deregulated economy that values monetary gain above all else generates the space in which deaths at the hands of corporations can occur.

The Bhopal Disaster

One of the worst industrial disasters and example of deaths caused by a corporation's negligence can be traced to the 1980s; a period characterised by the adoption of neo-liberal ideology in both North America and the UK. Specifically, both then US President Ronald Reagan and UK Prime Minister Margaret Thatcher championed the notion that deregulated markets were the only way in which economies could truly grow. A hallmark of this period was the intense growth and development of international trade as a result of the relaxing of borders and the reduction of tariffs—a process often referred to as globalisation.

Key Term: Globalisation
- Globalisation is a process by which economies and cultures have been drawn deeper together and have become more inter-connected through global networks of trade, capital flow, and the spread of technology and global media.
- As a complex and multi-faceted phenomenon, globalisation is considered by some as a form of capitalist expansion which entails the integration of local and national economies into a global, unregulated market economy.

There are naturally those that support the process of globalisation, who put forward the argument that such a process creates the ability to tap into a wider talent pool, promotes cultural diversity, improves information-sharing between countries, and increases overall standards of living (Metz, 2013). While there may be truth in some of these arguments, less discussed is the issue of power and how that can seriously affect, influence and manipulate trade for certain interests. For instance, in 2018 it was reported that 42 people hold the same wealth as the 3.7 billion poorest of the global population (Oxfam, 2018). The

Oxfam report added that 82 per cent of the global wealth generated in 2017 went to the wealthiest one per cent — demonstrating a significant disparity between the 'haves' and the 'have nots.' So too, and perhaps most importantly given the case study we are about to examine, is the hollowing-out of work and industry in countries such as the US and UK in order to seek cheaper production costs in the developing world. This is exactly why Union Carbide Corporation (UCC) set up a pesticide plant in Bhopal, Madhya Pradesh, India.

One of the world's worst industrial disasters ever took place in Bhopal on December 2, 1984, when lethal methyl isocyanate gas from a Union Carbide pesticide plant blanketed the city, killing 16,000 to 30,000 people and injuring 500,000 others (Matilal and Höpfl, 2009). Union Carbide was one of the first American companies to invest in India due to the lack of regulations and cheaper labour costs. They set-up the Bhopal factory in 1980 to produce the pesticide Sevin and 'help the country's agricultural sector increase its productivity and contribute more significantly to meeting the food needs of one of the world's most heavily populated regions' ('History of Union Carbide India Limited,' Union Carbide Corporation, n.d.).

It is important to note here that the company, due to poor profit reports, were looking for avenues to cut costs and 'improve' efficiency. Due to such motivations, between 1980 and 1984 the workforce in Bhopal was halved. The crew responsible for the dangerous gases used to create pesticides was also halved from 12 to six. In the control room a single operator had to monitor up to 70 panels, indicators and controls, all outdated and some even defective (Sinha, 2009). Alongside these cuts to staffing and potentially dangerous and old controls, safety training was reduced from six months to two weeks. To further compound a myriad of issues, much of this training was provided in the form of written signs and directions that were dotted around the facility. These slogans, it was revealed, were in English and many of the staff could not read them. Such issues were routinely brought to the attention of management who swiftly ignored such concerns, and the alarm siren that repeatedly went off due to the number of small leaks was eventually turned off altogether as it was seen as simply a nuisance (McFadden, 1984).

In 1982, a safety audit conducted by US engineers had inspected and recorded the dirty, mistreated status of the facility and identified 61 hazards, 30 of which were critical (BBC News, 2004). It is interesting to note here that, upon receiving such reports, such gases were kept at minimal levels and concentrations in order to avoid potential incidents at a similar facility in West Virginia, USA. Such considerations and implementations of standards were evidently not kept in Bhopal, where a series of accidents had occurred along with one fatality prior to the 1984 explosion. Despite these series of events and tragedies, nothing was done to improve conditions and repeated warnings and pleas from local workers were ignored and disavowed. For those that tried in vain to get the attention of management and State officials, their worst fears were realised on the night of December 2, 1984:

> 'As night fell...none of the factory's safety systems was working. The vent gas scrubber lay in pieces. The flare tower was undersized. The siren stayed silent...From Union Carbide's factory, a thin plume of white vapour began streaming from a high structure. Caught by the wind, it became a haze and blew downwards to mingle with smoke coming from somewhere nearer the ground. A dense fog formed. Nudged by the wind, it rolled across the road and into the alleys on the other side.' (Sinha, 2009)

Twenty-seven tons of methyl isocyanate gas (used to make pesticides) leaked out of a large storage tank after an explosion and drifted over Bhopal neighbourhoods near the factory while people were sleeping. It was reported that people woke from their sleep gasping and choking on their own body fluids (Ibid). It was later revealed that the tank was around 90 per cent full, despite safety regulations asserting that this should never be more that 50 per cent at any given moment. Some residents died in their sleep and others were crushed to death as others tried desperately to escape the toxic fumes when the surrounding neighbourhoods were covered by the toxic gas. In one horrific account, one man described seeing a ball of gas bouncing down a road and watching it envelop his wife and children, killing them instantly. At least 8,000 people died that night, along with approximately half-a-million who were injured from either the gas or in the attempt to escape. In the years since, as more people died of their injuries and illnesses caused by inhaling the gas, the death toll has risen above 20,000.

Thirty-five years later, Union Carbide and its owner, the Dow Chemical Company, which acquired it in 2001, have repeatedly refused to publish the results of studies into the negative effects of methyl isocyanate gas. Despite failed attempts to secure publication, it is evident that the corporate mentality of cutting corners in order to save money resulted in the mass exposure to such devastating gas. For the residents of Bhopal, who have been subjected to years of physical and emotional pain that has destroyed families and entire communities, they were the victims of a political economy that valued profits over their lives and well-being.

While we will explore some of the challenges in prosecuting corporate killings later in this chapter, it is worth noting here the importance of structural violence with regards to such forms of homicide. It is clear that there were a range of factors, individuals and agencies behind this tragic event, which makes locating an identifiable agent a complex task. Corporate killings and the Bhopal disaster specifically, highlight how the logic of the global market perpetuates and preys upon individuals within less developed countries in the name of profits and cuts to spending. For the people of Bhopal, these tragic events represent only the tip of the 'violence iceberg.' Long before the catastrophic gas tank explosion, the residents of Bhopal were seen as cheap labour who had little economic and cultural capital to challenge working conditions or seek alternative employment. In essence, their individual agency was limited such that they had little opportunity to seek better and safer forms of employment. So too, these structural forms of harm can be witnessed with a perceived indifference and lack of serious attention towards the survivors, who to this day are seeking justice for the tragic events that occurred almost four decades ago.

A Look to the Future: Corporate Killing in the Age of the Gig Economy

As discussed previously in this chapter, while there have been some attempts at creating stronger and more robust policies relating to the prosecution of corporate killings, there are still a myriad of issues that need to be addressed; especially when we consider how the nature of work has gone through a relatively recent seismic shift in the UK and other western countries. Specifically, it is important to consider whether the relatively recent UK corporate manslaughter laws are sufficient when we consider the rapidly changing nature of work in the wake of a shift from a production centric to a service economy—otherwise known as a 'gig economy.'

> **Key Term: Gig economy**
> - In a gig economy, temporary, flexible jobs are commonplace and companies tend toward hiring independent contractors and free-lancers instead of full-time employees.
> - A gig economy undermines the traditional economy of full-time workers, i.e. those who rarely change positions and instead focus on a lifelong career.

How people live, work and spend their money has changed dramatically over the past decade, especially with the introduction of smartphone technology. Being constantly connected via social networks has increased communication, and given birth to different ways to make and spend money. This has generated new incentives for corporations who are seeking to offer services that provide incredibly quick deliveries for a range of consumer goods and items. We are in the age where we are encouraged to give in to desires for instant gratification and pursue our every want and need (Hayward and Smith, 2017), and of companies offering quick delivery of food or, in some instances, items delivered to us within the space of two hours from purchasing via an online website or app, which is very attractive for consumers. So too, there is a general perception towards the positive possibilities such an industry—facilitated via digital technologies—provides in relation to flexible employment.

For many, picking up a 'gig' (as a temporary work commitment is often referred to) is seen as being quick, easy and most of all able to be tailored around an individual's lifestyle. Finding and selecting a gig is facilitated via internet and smartphone applications, and as such gig employees can work remotely. While contract gig workers seemingly enjoy greater scheduling flexibility and extra income, they also suffer from relatively low pay, lack of benefits, and increased stress. Gig economy workers also risk longer-term financial insecurity as many are not subject to pension auto-enrolment rules. They therefore do not have access to workplace pensions or benefits from employer contributions to long-term saving. While this new age of the gig economy may appear, at least on the surface, as simply 'changing with the times,' such an economic approach provides immense power to corporations while reducing the agency of employees by the erosion of workers' rights. This, as we have come to see, can be interpreted as a form of structural violence whereby, in the mission to find faster and more convenient ways to provide goods to consumers, new harms have been generated. This is, of course, normalised (a key reason why such harms are often neglected) due to the powerful and deeply embedded cultural message of consumerism:

> 'A good life is a life in which we have tasted extreme indulgence, a life in which we have denied ourselves nothing and exposed ourselves constantly to the thrill of the new; a life of sexual adventure, global travel and committed consumerism, in which we forge our own path and blithely ignore decaying conservative accounts of frugality, commitment, obligation and work.' (Winlow and Hall, 2013, p. 121)

Through the advent and rapid evolution of computer technology and smartphone apps, it has never been easier for consumers to fulfil this powerful cultural message of giving in to desires and fulfilling the need for instant gratification. For corporate entities — the provider of these consumer goods — such digital technologies provide fruitful avenues for expansion and consequently more profit.

With reference to this gig economy, one of the fastest growing industries is the courier service sector, which includes jobs with those such as: UberEATS; Deliveroo; JustEat; Amazon Prime; DPD; Instacart; DoorDash; and Drizly. England and Wales currently have laws in place with regard to vehicle-related homicide, e.g. causing death by dangerous driving, causing death by careless or inconsiderate driving and causing death by driving whilst unlicensed, disqualified or uninsured (these latter varieties attracting controversy because, e.g. of the lack of any real or logical connection between not having insurance and the homicidal event). While such laws capture a range of behaviours and scenarios related to vehicular homicides, this shift to zero hours contract transient work, which operates under a 'payment by number of deliveries' (Morrell, 2016), poses serious questions with regard to responsibility and culpability. For instance, let's take the death of Telesfora Escamilla, who was struck down and killed in 2016 by a delivery driver as she attempted to cross a street in Chicago (Ward,

2016). While this is an example that took place in the US, it is important to acknowledge that, in 2018, the Bureau of Labour Statistics reported that 55 million people there are gig workers, which is more than 35 per cent of the US workforce. That number is projected to jump to 43 per cent by 2020 (Forbes, 2019). At first, the mainstream media narrative framed the death of Telesfora Escamilla around individual responsibility, stating that:

> 'A witness told ABC7 that the driver drove around a car in front of him and made a left, hitting Escamilla, who was in the crosswalk. He knew he did something. He was just screaming: "I can't believe I did this! I can't believe I did this!"' (Ward, 2016)

The driver was later arrested and charged with vehicular homicide but, while such a conviction may appear justified, it is important to consider how this move to a gig economy is slowly removing corporate responsibility. For instance, an undercover investigation by the BBC into conditions as a delivery driver showed that those working for one of the many agencies supplying drivers can earn less than the minimum wage and face significant levels of stress in getting their deliveries done in time. It also found incidents of drivers speeding to meet their deadlines and even going to the toilet in their vans simply because they were so under pressure to get their deliveries done in the time expected. So too, drivers routinely did eleven hour shifts and were expected to be available at least six days a week. The undercover reporter was also paid the equivalent actual pay of £2.59 per hour in his first week and £4.76 in his second (Morrell, 2016).

Since 2016 there have been numerous injuries caused by workers within the courier service sector, and the general response from corporations is one of ambiguity. Take for instance one response to the death of Telesfora:

> '[They are not our employees], and the company hires independent contractors to handle most deliveries … logistics is made up of small and medium sized businesses who employ hundreds of local drivers to deliver packages to …… customers. We have high standards for our delivery service partners and investigate claims made about inappropriate driver behaviour and take the appropriate actions, which may include no longer delivering for [our company].' (Savini, 2018)

In attempting to explain this 'distancing' at the hands of corporate entities with regard to vehicle manslaughter in the age of the gig economy, it is important to consider the significance of the previously introduced concept of special liberty.

When we consider the precarious nature of the gig economy—an economy built upon neo-liberal ideology at the cost of workers' rights—it is evident that corporations are further receding from responsibility and culpability. While, as stated earlier, there is a range of vehicle-related homicides, they are invariably centred on the individual behind the wheel and fail to acknowledge and address how the rapidly changing work environment creates pressures that may negatively impact the safety of both the driver and pedestrians. While such questions are beyond the remit of this chapter, this conundrum related to individual culpability within the context of the courier service sector demonstrates how society's conceptualisation and understanding of homicide is ever shifting in the face of technological, cultural, political and economic changes. Such discussions centred on perceptions of homicide now takes us to the topic of punishing corporate killings.

Punishing Corporate Killing

As previously discussed in this chapter, corporate entities are seen as a source of economic progress and social good, no matter their failings or perceived deficiencies (Clough, 2007). The corporate body is depicted as the most efficient method of organizing, producing and distributing goods and services, and as a result holds a dominant and privileged position in a capitalist society (Tombs and Whyte, 2015, p. 92). Consequently, the damaging effects of such businesses are labelled as marginal, when, in actuality, they are inherent consequences of corporate activity (Tombs and Whyte, 2015). Within a neo-liberal political economy, corporations are claimed to be benevolent institutions and, when illegality does transpire, such organizations are expected to improve and reform their operations (Ibid).

As a result of these economic and cultural perceptions, corporate crime is often neglected within media, political and academic discussions. Specifically, criminological inquiry is often by powerful interests (Muncie, 2000), and as a result has become essentially submissive to State and corporate interests. Subsequently, this has provided a myopic understanding of 'crime' by neglecting harmful actions committed by the powerful. Criminology, as a discipline, has been criticised for being too orientated around those actions codified in criminal law. As noted by Hillyard and Tombs:

'Criminologists, like other criminal justice actors, have largely accepted a definition of crime as a violation of the criminal law, hence leaving the discipline hostage to a system that has criminalised individual behaviours … but largely not the harms generated through corporate activities.' (Hillyard and Tombs, 2017, p. 285)

This has generated considerable debate and many scholars have both accepted and endeavoured to move beyond the fundamentally limited State-based definitions of crime. For critical criminologists, it is argued that the focus should lie in a disciplinary approach which concentrates on the concept of social harm such as, for instance, Zemiology.

Key Term: Zemiology
- Zemiology is often considered as the social harm approach, and provides an alternative line of enquiry that goes beyond Criminology in concentrating on harm rather than crime.
- Zemiology argues that any activity, process or set of circumstances that is harmful or damaging is a potentially important focus of analysis, whether or not it happens to be against the law (Hillyard and Tombs, 2007).

Established via the limited State-based definitions of crime, the Criminal Justice System has an extremely myopic understanding of harmful activity, which results in an overall disavowal of broader and more complex forms of violence and the subsequent harms caused. Within this context of narrow legalistic conceptualisations of crime, numerous harms are unevenly and ideologically criminalised (Hall, 2012). The State, along with criminological orthodox accounts affiliated with both left and right wing ideologies, tends to orientate their attention towards direct and interpersonal forms of violence whereby an identifiable agent is detectable:

> 'For right-wing liberals, the individual is essentially a rational and self-interested hedonist who can be encouraged to make the right choices by a functional social order and the core institutions of a minimal state. Others see the self simply as an object created and directed by the immediate social environment...while still others position the individual as a flexible agent periodically transformed, oppressed or liberated by "narratives," "discourse," and the vicissitudes of power and language.' (Winlow and Hall, 2019, p. 27)

With a legal (often) academic discourse related to the individual agent, it is arguable the State deliberately chooses to ignore and thus conceal the often-normalised forms of systemic (structural) violence. Systemic violence is defined as, 'the difference between actively killing and passively letting die' (Tyner, 2015, p. 110). This obscured type of violence is essentially a core component of capitalism, whereby violence becomes 'limitless and hegemonic' (Pawlett, 2013, p. 119). Consequently, individuals or groups become victims and are fundamentally disposable in the perpetual pursuit for profit. So too, the very nature of globalisation and living as a 'global society' has logistically made transnational corporate crime easier to commit (Mooney and Evans, 2007). This is because corporations can exploit globalisation and their economic power to move around freely. As a result, Norman (2014) has stated that through opening the borders the floodgates to crime have been opened as it is now something that can operate transnationally, as well as domestically. It also likely puts developing nations at risk as powerful corporations are given the opportunity to exploit the powerless. This is due to the fact that corporations can seek nations and jurisdictions with the least regulations and punishments, where the workers are relatively inexpensive, and where they have protection from liability (Gilbert and Russell, 2002).

Referring back to our earlier case study, Union Carbide are a prime example of what is described in the last paragraph above as they did not transport the same level of health and safety standards to their power plant in Bhopal as they adopted in the US, whilst also opting to use more dangerous substances to reduce costs (Walters, 2009). It was also likely known by Union Carbide that the Indian judicial system would have been unable to prosecute them due to the complexities associated with transnational crime; had the incident taken place in America specialist legal professionals would likely have been able to close down the company (Sherrill, 1988).

Along with these issues with the global regulation of transnational corporate crime, there are also significant challenges related to media representation of such activities. For instance, there is a general tendency to perceive and thus represent such forms of criminality as completely separate from traditional notions of crime, despite the fact that it is more costly to the American economy (Vold et al, 2002). Wright et al (1995) remind us that corporate wrongdoing, including homicide, is largely ignored by the mainstream media due to such actions not being considered 'newsworthy' enough. So too, Sherrill (1988) stresses that another significant factor is that legislators appear to respect businessmen, a respect not afforded to those from a lower economic strata, and associated with more 'conventional' forms of criminality. It is also important to consider those examples of corporate related homicide that technically did not fall under recognised and codified criminal law such as the Ford Pinto case. Ford, the well-known car manufacturing company based within the US, designed and manufactured the Ford Pinto in 1971. Before producing this model, Ford crash-tested various prototypes in order to test if they met a safety standard proposed by the National Highway Traffic Safety Administration (NHTSA) to reduce fires from traffic collisions. This standard would have required that by 1972 all new autos be able to withstand a rear end impact of 20 mph without fuel loss, and that by 1973 an impact of 30 mph. The prototypes all failed the 20 mph test. With this information, Ford knew that the Pinto signified a severe fire threat when hit from the rear, even in low speed collisions. Ford officials faced a decision. Should they go ahead with the existing design, thereby meeting the production timetable but possibly jeopardising consumer safety? Or should they delay production of the Pinto by reforming the gas tank to make it safer and consequently accept 'another year of subcompact dominance to foreign companies?' (*Business Ethics*, ND). Ford not only pushed ahead with the original design but stuck to it for the next six years. As a result of this decision — fuelled by the perpetual pursuit of profit — 27 to 180 deaths were reported as a result of rear impact-related fuel tank fires (Wojdyla, 2011). In the face of a public backlash and mounting pressure, the Ford Motor

Company defended itself by contending that it used a risk/benefit analysis. Ford stated that its reason for using such analysis was that the NHTSA required them to do so. The risk/benefit approach excuses a defendant if the monetary costs of making a production change are greater than the 'societal benefits' of that change. The philosophy behind risk/benefit analysis promotes the goal of allocative efficiency. The problem that arose in the Ford Pinto case (and many other similar cases) highlights the human and emotional circumstances behind the numbers which are not factored into risk/benefit analysis. There were no criminal charges brought and no-one faced any form of punishment, due the fact that they were technically following standards set by the NHTSA.

These instances emphasise the fact that corporate crime does not conform to the traditional notion of criminality and is disavowed by society, pushing it outside the boundaries of the legal system where corporations, at times, can escape prosecution. It is not in the economic interests of the media or those involved in the Criminal Justice System to challenge corporate killings — especially when linked to big businesses that employ a large number of workers and that contribute to the wealth of a nation. Žižek (2008) goes further to suggest that the fake sense of urgency surrounding traditional notions and understandings of crime is another important reason as to why there is little political will to prosecute corporate criminality and killings.

In relation to Bhopal, the American press were more likely to call the incident a 'disaster,' whereas the Indian press named Union Carbide as 'negligent and irresponsible' (Coleman, 2001, p. 172). This demonstrates how corporate crime is socially constructed and can be perceived differently in both severity and culpability by different countries. Taking this into consideration, attempting to prosecute corporate wrongdoing (including deaths that are in some way caused by corporate activity) has continually been perceived as unfeasible and, perhaps more significantly, undesirable from the point of view of the State (Alvesalo and Lähteenmäki, 2016).

With this in mind, the State exercises its 'special liberty' (Hall, 2012) when choosing which behaviours or activities will be considered criminal and therefore capable of being prosecuted. Corporations, both national and international, are perceived as the most feasible and sustainable sources of employment, tax, and investment. Within the neo-liberal narrative that promotes deregulation as a powerful motivating force for individuals to seek increasing profits, corporations are endowed in ways that permit them to cause harms through a myriad of legal, ideological and political processes (Tombs and Whyte, 2015). Within a neo-liberal State (such as the UK), which is strongly defined by consumer capitalism, the perpetual pursuit for profit supersedes the morality or legality of conduct (Tudor, 2018) and ultimately results in an overall disavowal towards largescale corporate harms, including deaths. This disavowal is defined by a form of exceptionalism where both the State and corporations perceive themselves as 'being above external forms of regulation' (Tudor, 2018, p. 8).

While we are repeatedly told that the law is impartial and objective, that it treats all citizens equally, the law is a social process and its complexity lies in its ultimate goal of preserving the existing social order (Bittle, 2012). In order to demonstrate this, one only has to look at current statistics related to class within the custodial environment, in which the working-class and those characterised by minimal economic and social capital are over-represented in prisons (Newburn, 2016). Newburn elaborates further, stating that:

'The Surveying Prisoner Crime Reduction (SPCR) study, a longitudinal cohort study which tracks the progress of newly sentenced adult (18+ years) prisoners in England and Wales, found 24 per cent of prisoners to have lived with foster parents or in an institution (Williams et al, 2012). In terms of living circumstances, SCPR found 16 per cent of prisoners reported having been homeless (either sleeping rough or in temporary accommodation) immediately prior to their incarceration.' (Newburn, 2016, p. 8)

Such statistics and observations towards the punishment of those who do not occupy positions within the upper strata of society is by no means a new phenomenon. For instance, in 1979 Jeffrey Reiman wrote *The Rich Get Richer and the Poor Get Prison*. Though the title was 'intentionally provocative, it nevertheless spoke to a number of criminological truths' (Newburn, 2016, p. 8). Such truths extend to corporations so that, despite the relatively recent changes to legislation concerning corporate killings, very few are ever faced with significant legal repercussions.

It is important to note that the State has, at times, prosecuted much smaller corporate entities. An example of this specific targeting of smaller companies can be found in the successful prosecution of OLL Ltd. This particular company provided customers with kayaking activities and on 22 March 1993 a group of eight schoolchildren and their teacher from Southway Community College, Plymouth were accompanied by two instructors from an outdoor centre on a kayak trip across Lyme Bay, Dorset. Due to a series of circumstances, four students drowned (Johnson, 2008). The ensuing investigation resulted in the owner of the activity centre being convicted of gross negligence manslaughter. This was the only successful conviction involving a corporation for this offence in the UK and the owner was jailed for three years. Due to the small size of the organization, determining the 'controlling mind' was a relatively easy procedure (Tombs, 2018).

However, larger companies still represent a challenge to prosecutors (Hsiao, 2009). The primary reason for this is that smaller companies tend to contribute far less in terms of revenue, along with being comprised of less individuals and lacking in economic power. It is also important to consider that the Corporate Manslaughter and Corporate Homicide Act 2007 appears to reduce the emphasis on individual responsibility. Section 18 of the Act states, 'no individual liability' — thus preventing individuals from being prosecuted under that Act. This section states that '[a]n individual cannot be guilty of aiding, abetting, counselling or procuring the commission of an offence of corporate manslaughter.' This has been severely criticised, and it has been perceived by many as unsatisfactory and 'a serious watering down of the proposed legislation' (Tombs, 2018, p. 490).

While the offence of gross negligence manslaughter is still in place as a mechanism to hold individuals responsible, this arguably provides little deterrence if individuals — especially within larger organizations — know they will not be subject to prosecution as an accessory to corporate manslaughter. Some have suggested that this process is designed for companies to agree towards a corporate manslaughter charge, by arguing that it provides an attractive alternative for senior managers or directors who may be facing a custodial sentence if they are found guilty of gross negligence manslaughter (Mears-White, 2012, p. 1).

This symbolic exercise and display of authority of the State towards small corporate entities serves as a means to satisfy those opposed to the perceived exemption of corporations, and as a result quells any potential discontent. Despite this attempt to focus almost exclusively on these smaller symbolic 'sacrifices,' the Law Commission has stated that it is prejudicial that small corporations are more susceptible to being found guilty, and that larger businesses should be just as liable to prosecution by the State (Hsiao, 2009). Whilst it has been argued that the 2007 Act needs to be properly used against all corporations and not just smaller targets, the reliance of such entities to bolster the State's economy—along with the autonomy provided via deregulation—serves as a strong rationale to not seek justice in all instances related to corporate killings.

Conclusion

In bringing this chapter to a close, it is important to acknowledge that the exercise in defining, identifying and punishing corporate killings is fraught with difficulties. At a conceptual level, corporate killings tend to challenge prevailing orthodoxies within the Criminal Justice System that is predominantly focused upon individual acts of direct violence with a clearly identifiable agent who is responsible. Within a CJS that places great emphasis on *mens rea,* and a media that sees news value with direct and more familiar forms of violence, corporations (especially in their larger and transnational forms) tend to be omitted or treated far differently to those that commit more 'conventional' forms of criminality. In comparison to the vast majority of individuals who are prosecuted in the courts, corporations are made up of individuals with (generally speaking) far more economic and social capital. Alongside this, the UK, US and other developed nations have adopted a politico-economic model designed to deregulate and relax legislation that supposedly stifled innovation and money-making potential, providing a climate in which, in the words of Enron's CEO Jeff Skilling, '[T]he rules were not quite clear' (Léautier, 2018).

While acts of corporate killing may not appear as visceral or shocking in comparison to acts of serial murder or terrorism (that tend to occupy news headlines and other forms of media), it is quite clear that this form of systemic violence—inherent in the day-to-day running of capitalist systems—has the capacity to inflict far greater harm. In many respects, acts of corporate killing are a symptom of a system that places particular emphasis on money and the value of consumerism. As witnessed across this chapter, the perpetual pursuit of profit results in the lives of others being perceived as secondary to this goal and, while such institutions may not actively seek to kill, their negligence and irreverence for others has, and will continue to have, tragic consequences.

Questions to consider:
- What is the significance of neo-liberalism with regard to the existence and prevalence of corporate killings?
- Why is Zemiology important in the effort to understand and capture the range of harms caused by corporations?
- In what ways do corporate killings differ from conventional notions of crime and, more specifically, homicide?
- What could be done to more successfully deter corporations from committing such actions?

References

Alvesalo-Kuusi, A. and Lähteenmäki, L. (2016), 'Legislating for Corporate Criminal Liability in Finland: 22-Year Long Debate Revisited,' *Journal of Scandinavian Studies in Criminology and Crime Prevention*, 17(1), pp. 53–69.

BBC News (2004), 'US Firm "Knew of Dangers" at Bhopal Plant,' 2 December: http://news.bbc.co.uk/1/hi/programmes/file_on_4/4062611.stm

Bittle, S. (2012), *Still Dying for a Living: Corporate Criminal Liability After the Westray Mine Disaster*, Vancouver: UBC Press.

Business Ethics (n.d.), 'Case: The Ford Pinto': https://philosophia.uncg.edu/phi361-matteson/module-1-why-does-business-need-ethics/case-the-ford-pinto/

Clarkson, C. M. V. (1996), 'Kicking Corporate Bodies and Damning their Souls,' *Modern Law Review*, 59(4), p. 557.

Clough, J. (2007). 'Bridging the Theoretical Gap: The Search for a Realist Model of Corporate Criminal Liability,' *Criminal Law Forum*, 18(3), pp. 267–300.

Coleman, J. W. (2001). *The Criminal Elite — Understanding White Collar Crime*, New York: Worth Publishers.

Forbes (2019), 'What Are the Pros and Cons of the Gig Economy?' 8 January: https://www.forbes.com/sites/quora/2019/01/08/what-are-the-pros-and-cons-of-the-gig-economy/#39878b9a1388

Gilbert, M. J. and Russell, S. (2002), 'Globalization of Criminal Justice in the Corporate Context,' *Crime, Law and Social Change*, 38(3), pp. 211–238.

Hall. S. (2012), *Theorising Crime and Deviance: A New Perspective*, London: Sage.

Hall, S. (2015), 'What is Criminology About? The Study of Harm, Special Liberty and Pseudo-Pacification in Late-Capitalism's Libidinal Economy,' in Crew, D. and Lippens, R. (eds.), *What is Criminology About? Philosophical Reflections*, London: Routledge.

Hall, S. and Winlow, S. (2018), 'Ultra-realism,' in Dekeseredy, W. S. and Dragiewicz, M. (eds.) *Routledge Handbook of Critical Criminology*, London: Routledge.

Hayward, K. and Smith, O. (2017), 'Crime and Consumer Culture,' in A. Liebling, S. Maruna and L. McAra (eds.), *The Oxford Handbook of Criminology* (6th edn.). Oxford: Oxford University Press, pp. 320–326.

Hillyard, P. and Tombs, S. (2017), 'Social Harm and Zemiology,' in: Liebling, A., Maruna, S. and McAra, L. (eds.), *Oxford Handbook of Criminology*, Oxford: Oxford University Press.

'History of Union Carbide India Limited' (n.d), *Union Carbide Corporation*: http://www.bhopal.com/History-of-UC-India-Limited

Hsiao, M.W. (2009), 'Abandonment of the Doctrine of Attribution for Gross Negligent Test on the Corporate Manslaughter and Corporate Homicide Act 2007,' *Company Lawyer*, 30(4), pp. 110–112.

Johnson, C.W. (2008), 'Ten Contentions of Corporate Manslaughter Legislation: Public Policy and the Legal Response to Workplace Accidents,' *Safety Science*, 46(3), pp. 349–370.

Léautier, T. O. (2018), *Imperfect Markets and Imperfect Regulation*, London: MIT Press.

Matilal, S. and Höpfl, H. (2009), 'Accounting for the Bhopal Disaster: Footnotes and Photographs,' *Accounting, Auditing and Accountability Journal*, 22(6), pp. 953–972.

McFadden, R. D. (1984), 'India Disaster: Chronicle of a Nightmare,' *New York Times*, 10 December: https://www.nytimes.com/1984/12/10/world/india-disaster-chronicle-of-a-nightmare.html

Mears-White, T. (2012), 'Lion Steel: Lessons from the third corporate manslaughter prosecution,' *DWF View Point*, 31 August: www.dwf.co.uk/insight/view-point/lion-steel-lessonsfrom-the-third-corporate-manslaughter-prosecution

Metz, F. (2013), *Globalization. Advantages and Disadvantages*, Norderstedt: GRIN.

Mooney, A. and Evans, B. (2007), *Globalization: The Key Concepts*, Oxford: Routledge.

Morrell, L. (2016), 'Amazon comes under fire for stress placed on its delivery drivers,' *eDelivery*, 11 November: https://edelivery.net/2016/11/amazon-comes-fire-stress-placed-delivery-drivers/

Muncie, J. (2000), 'Decriminalising Criminology,' *British Criminology Conference: Selected Proceedings 3*, British Society of Criminology: britsoccrim.org/volume3/010.pdf

Newburn, T. (2016), 'Social Disadvantage, Crime, and Punishment,' in Dean, H. and Platt, L. (eds.), *Social Advantage and Disadvantage*, Oxford: Oxford University Press.

Norman, M. (2014), 'Has Globalisation Rendered the State Paradigm in Controlling Crimes, Anachronistic?,' *Journal of Financial Crime*, 21(4), pp. 381–399.

Oxfam International (2018), 'Richest 1 percent bagged 82 percent of wealth created last year — poorest half of humanity got nothing,' 22 January: https://www.oxfam.org/en/press-releases/richest-1-percent-bagged-82-percent-wealth-created-last-year-poorest-half-humanity

Pawlett, W. (2013), *Violence, Society, and Radical Theory: Bataille, Baudrillard and Contemporary Society*, Burlington: Ashgate.

Savini, D. (2018), 'Drivers Delivering Amazon Packages Accused of Devastating and Deadly Accidents, CBS Chicago, 15 May: https://chicago.cbslocal.com/2018/05/15/amazon-drivers-accused-deadly-accidents/

Sherrill, R. (1988), 'Corporate Crime and Violence: Big Business Power and the Abuse of the Public Trust,' *The Nation*, November 28: http://go.galegroup.com.ezproxy.bcu.ac.uk/ps/i.do?p=AONEandu=uceandid=GALE|A6824156andv=2.1andit=randsid=summon#

Sinha, I. (2009), 'Bhopal: 25 Years of Poison,' *Guardian*, 3 December: https://www.theguardian.com/environment/2009/dec/04/bhopal-25-years-indra-sinha

Tombs, S. and Whyte, D. (2015), *The Corporate Criminal: Why Corporations Must be Abolished*, London: Routledge.

Tombs, S. (2018), 'The UK's Corporate Killing Law: Un/Fit for Purpose?,' *Criminology and Criminal Justice*, 18(4), pp. 488–507.

Treadwell, J; Briggs, D, Winlow, S and Hall, S. (2013), 'Shopocalypse Now: Consumer Culture and the English Riots of 2011,' *British Journal of Criminology*, Volume 53(1), pp. 1–17.

Tudor, K. (2018), 'Toxic Sovereignty: Understanding Fraud as the Expression of Special Liberty within Late-Capitalism,' *Journal of Extreme Anthropology*, 2(2), pp. 7–21.

Tyner, J. (2015), *Violence in Capitalism: Devaluing Life in an Age of Responsibility*, Nebraska: University of Nebraska Press.

Vold, G. B., Bernard, T. J. and Snipes, J. B. (2002), *Theoretical Criminology* (5th edn.), New York, NY: Oxford University Press.

Walters, R. (2009), 'Bhopal, Corporate Crime and Harms of the Powerful,' *Global Social Policy*, 9(3), pp. 324–327.

Ward, J. (2016), '84-Year-Old Grandma Killed by Amazon Delivery Truck in Little Village,' *dnainfo*, 22 December: https://www.dnainfo.com/chicago/20161222/little-village/elderly-woman-struck-killed-by-truck-little-village-police-say/

Wells, C. (2001), *Corporations and Criminal Responsibility* (2nd edn.), Oxford: Oxford University Press.

Wilson, D. (2007), *Serial Killers: Hunting Britons and Their Victims 1960–2006*, Winchester: Waterside Press.

Wilson, D. (2009), *A History of British Serial Killing*, London: Sphere.

Winlow, S. and Hall, S. (2013), *Rethinking Social Exclusion: The End of the Social?*, London: Sage.

Winlow, S. and Hall, S. (2019), 'Shock and Awe: On Progressive Minimalism and Retreatism,' *Critical Criminology*, 27, pp. 21–36.

Wojdyla, B. (2011), 'The Top Automotive Engineering Failures: The Ford Pinto Fuel Tanks,' *Popular Mechanics*, 20 May: https://www.popularmechanics.com/cars/a6700/top-automotive-engineering-failures-ford-pinto-fuel-tanks/

Wright, J. P., Cullen, F. T. and Blankenship, M. B. (1995), 'The Social Construction of Corporate Violence: Media Coverage of the Imperial Food Products Fire,' *Crime and Delinquency*, 41(1), pp. 20–36.

Young, J. (1999), *The Exclusive Society: Social Exclusion, Crime and Difference in Late Modernity*, London: Sage Publications.

Žižek, S. (2008), *Violence*, London: Profile Books.

CHAPTER 9

Homicide and Consumer Society

'In many ways, serial killers are for adults what monster movies are for children — that is, scary fun!'

Scott Bonn, *Why We Love Serial Killers*

Introduction

Key arguments put forward in academic discourse concerning declining levels of violence stem from the influential works of Nobert Elias and Steven Pinker that we have referred to in previous chapters. German sociologist Elias first introduced the concept of the *civilising process* in 1939, arguing that humans, over the course of modern history, have progressively become more civil. This process essentially describes a notable change in human behaviour that led to the construction of modern society — as we know it today — in which humans tend to think rationally, they value education, good manners, they are considerate and they have strong restraints against potentially destructive impulses. It is these characteristics, according to Elias, that have enabled humans to live in conditions of relative peace.

Drawing upon this conceptual framework, American-Canadian cognitive psychologist Pinker published his critically acclaimed book *The Better Angels of Our Nature* in 2011. The primary aim of that book was to prove how we are nowadays living in the most peaceful time in the history of our species, as violence of all kinds has been decreasing. To support his thesis, Pinker gathered a considerable amount of statistical data, focusing on various domains, including war, homicide, genocide, animal cruelty and torture. Drawing upon comparative studies and considering the population of the planet in different historical periods, he showcased how, nowadays, there is a proportionately lower number of killings. He additionally highlighted how acknowledging and accounting for human rights have resulted in the decline of violence against women, children, homosexuals and ethnic minorities. Pinker's work has met with considerable critical acclaim for its informative content, its powerful ideas, its well-supported arguments and optimistic nature. It has been widely cited by academics, consistently acting as a point of reference in academic discourse and theorising around violence trends and rates. Critiques of his thesis have usually been concerned with the heavy focus upon physical and direct forms of violence that comes at the expense of considering in more depth other forms of violence — namely structural and cultural violence that we discussed in *Chapter 1* and elsewhere in this book. For instance, the work of ultra-realists Steve Hall and Simon Winlow describe a *pseudo-pacification* process instead; one that is located within the capitalist society of the West and involves the reduction of the more brutal and obvious forms of physical violence, that have given their place to the more hidden and insidious forms of structural violence.

Ultra-realists specifically describe a politico-legal and economic environment of atomised individualism, exploitative business practice, aggressive competition and conspicuous consumption that has resulted in widening inequalities, injustice, racism, social exclusion and environmental degradation — forms of violence that are very much normalised in the sense that we see them but we tend to tolerate them. The arguments of ultra-realists expand upon the work of Slovenian Philosopher Slavoj Žižek, who has persistently highlighted the consequences of our economic and political systems. Žižek argues that social harm is inherent in the pervasive conditions and values of global capitalism that have historically resulted in the creation of excluded individuals. His work has predominately focused on the systemic and anonymous violence of capitalism. Žižek has specifically drawn attention to the ways in which the overarching economic philosophy promotes profitability, being indifferent as to how this movement impacts upon social reality.

This chapter effectively draws upon the above arguments, as it considers the commodification of homicide in late-capitalist society and its potential social harms. Its main focus is placed upon the availability and sale of items associated with homicide events, a phenomenon known as *murderabilia*. Various definitions of this term will be critically discussed, before exploring the different forms the murderabilia industry has taken and the platforms used to facilitate its consumption. In turn, legal frameworks that have attempted to regulate murderabilia in the US will be considered, in order to highlight the controversial nature of the topic and the moral debates surrounding it. Further to this, particular attention should be given to murderabilia collectors and their enduring fascination with macabre commodities.

Murderabilia

Coined by victim advocate Andy Kahan, the term *murderabilia* constitutes an amalgam of the words *murder* and *memorabilia* (Bonn, 2014; Griffiths, 2013). It has been used to broadly describe the industry around collectibles that are perceived to be valuable due to their connection with violent crimes and offenders (Bonn, 2014; Hobbs, 2000). Literature around the phenomenon does not offer a unified definition, as scholars tend to construct the term in a loose manner, so as to serve the purposes of their research. According to Hurley (2009, p. 2), murderabilia 'refers to items associated with notorious criminals that have found a market on various internet sites that cater to serious collectors and to those with a macabre fascination for crime-related memorabilia.' Along similar lines, Chang (2005, p. 434) explains that the term 'encompasses the myriad of items … all of which can be linked to some notorious or infamous criminal or crime, all of which can be bought by anyone with access to cash and a computer'. Both definitions, importantly, place attention on the use of the internet that essentially provides an online platform for the murderabilia industry, thereby making items under sale easily accessible. It should be noted, however, that murderabilia collectibles can also be found and purchased traditionally in physical stores (Jarvis, 2007), an important fact that should be taken into account when defining the term. A more simplistic definition was provided by Mauro (2012, p. 323), according to whom 'murderabilia refers to items whose commercial value stems from their relation to a notorious crime or criminal.'

Interestingly, all of the above definitions refer to criminals rather than murderers, therefore significantly broadening the scope of the term that essentially encompasses every person that has been convicted of a crime and whose case has gained notoriety. The lack of an agreed-upon definition that could potentially be applied across jurisdictions and contribute to public understanding highlights the primitive stage of academic discourse and theorising around the phenomenon. Indeed, murderabilia has predominately been explored in terms of legality and morality (Chang, 2005).

In the US various legal frameworks have chronically been established in order to regulate the circulation of murderabilia collectibles. Specifically, Son of Sam Laws aim at preventing such convicted criminals as David Berkowitz from profiting from the publicity of their crimes (Bonn, 2014; Hurley, 2009). In addition, eight US States have 'notoriety-for-profit' laws which specifically oppose murderabilia and aim at preventing criminals from profiting from the sale of personal items (Kealy, 2000; Mauro, 2012). However, the US Supreme Court has determined Son of Sam Laws to be unconstitutional on the grounds that they violate the First Amendment right to free speech, as the laws essentially regulated speech based on their content. Despite victims re-living their victimisation being viewed as a compelling interest, it did not constitute sufficient reason to suppress the right of prisoners to express themselves through artwork and the public display of collectibles (Hurley, 2009). Further to this, Son of Sam Laws were found over-inclusive as they targeted any expressive activity of any person convicted of a crime, subsequently subjecting a considerable volume of works to law enforcement. As a result, several States tried to amend their respective laws regulating murderabilia so that they did not abridge freedom of speech (Loss, 1987; Mauro, 2012).

Along similar lines, scholars attempted to address these inconsistencies by putting forward recommendations as to how laws could effectively deal with murderabilia whilst being consistent with First Amendment principles. For instance, Mauro (2012) highlighted how child pornography receives no First Amendment protection as this would encourage others to commit child abuse and would additionally harm victims, who would be forced to re-live their traumatic experiences. He then argued that murderabilia, much like child pornography, has similar consequences, as it essentially encourages people to commit crimes that they could eventually profit from, thus resulting in harm to primary and secondary victims.

Another Bill, entitled 'Stop the Sale of Murderabilia to Protect the Dignity of Crime Victims' was introduced in May 2007 by Senator John Cornyn of Texas, aimed at avoiding First Amendment violations by targeting the delivery of items rather than their content (Hurley, 2009). The Bill specifically outlined that it would be illegal for prisoners to deposit items for delivery with the intention to place them in commerce. Despite avoiding the content-based element of the aforementioned Son of Sam law, critiques of the Bill referred to its over-inclusiveness, as it encompassed all prisoners irrespective of the specific circumstances surrounding their convictions (Hurley, 2009). The Bill did not reach a vote, a fact further indicating the controversial nature of the sale and distribution of murderabilia.

The topic has indeed sparked considerable ethical debate amongst academics, legislators and victims' rights advocates (Schmid, 2004). On the one hand, opponents of murderabilia, such as rights advocate Andy Kahan pay particular attention to the harm murderabilia inflicts on victims of crime. In homicide cases especially, secondary victims that are those who are personally affected by the death of primary victims, such as close family members and friends (Condry, 2010), are thought to be forced to re-live their victimisation (Bonn, 2014; Hobbs, 2000). The argument put forward is that not only do they suffer from the killing of their loved one, but also from the way in which their loss essentially turns into a commodity that murderabilia merchants profit from (Bonn, 2014; Chang, 2005; Hobbs, 2000; Kealy, 2000; Nelson and Prendergast, 2009; Mauro; 2012). This raises further questions as to whether free trade policies, prevalent in neo-liberal, capitalist societies encourage individualism and profiting even at the expense of others (Hall, 2012; Hall and Winlow, 2015).

Jarvis (2007) has addressed the commodification of homicide, explaining how we have essentially become a society that celebrates death and gore. This has further implications for the public image of the Criminal Justice System that is argued to be failing victims by allowing the commercialisation of crimes (Kealy, 2000). On the other hand, murderabilia advocates argue that restrictions to its sale and distribution can have implications as far as academic freedom is concerned, in the sense that items related to violent crimes can provide valuable insights for law enforcement officials, sociologists and criminologists (Nelson and Prendergast, 2009). Specifically, the availability of such items is thought to facilitate understanding of criminal behaviour, criminal profiling and potentially the apprehension of other criminals (Kealy, 2000). In that sense, it is important to provide an economic incentive to convicted criminals so that they share such items and disclose relevant information. Additionally, it is argued that prisoners should have the right to produce, publicly display and profit from their art, an approach viewed as both therapeutic and humane (Chang, 2005).

Engagement with art-based interventions has indeed been proven to result in psychological changes amongst inmates, who showcase lower levels of anger, depression and self-harming behaviour, higher levels of confidence, communication and self-esteem, as well as a shift in the way in which they view themselves, reconstructing their identities from criminals to artists, which is thought to be having a positive impact in terms of their desistance (Yardley and Rusu, 2018). Further to the rehabilitating effects of engaging prisoners in artistic endeavours, profiting from their art is perceived to be resulting in positive economic impact considering the costs of housing inmates (Hammit, 2011).

A final argument put forward is that convicted criminals themselves rarely profit from the sale of murderabilia, thus making bans unnecessary (Hobbs, 2000). However, it should be noted that it is still legal for sellers to send criminals money or gifts whilst the recipient is in prison in exchange for their cooperation, thereby providing them with an economic incentive (Bonn, 2014).

In summary, legislation in the US regulating the circulation of murderabilia is quite inconsistent and has been the subject of considerable debate and controversy. Consequently, application of existing legislation has been inconsistent as well. For instance, in May 2001 eBay banned the sale of murderabilia collectibles which only resulted in the industry moving elsewhere, specifically to such websites as Murder Auction, Supernaught, Serial Killers Ink and The Crime Auction House (Bonn, 2014; Ng, 2011). Despite these websites being easily accessible in the UK, there is still no dedicated legal framework to regulate the sale and distribution of murderabilia collectibles. However, the UK Proceeds of Crime Act 2002 arguably impacts to a certain if as yet unsettled extent. For example regional crime squads charged with enforcing court orders under the 2002 Act are reported to have sought to recover royalties from books written by offenders or earnings from art by purporting to classify such payments as crime proceeds that also, almost of necessity and by definition, involve criminal money laundering (personal information). On the other hand charitable organizations such as the Koestler Trust actively encourage all the arts in prisons and such bodies may help facilitate its sale (sometimes anonymously).

Despite there being limited academic work directly exploring murderabilia, cultural studies have provided valuable insights that help contextualise the phenomenon by placing particular focus on the human desire to acquire possessions (Pearce 1994, 1995), the concept of commodification (Root, 1996), the psychology of consuming in capitalist society (Baudrillard 1968; 1998) and the normalisation of collecting in modern times (Dillon, 2019). Belk (1995) has provided an overview of the historical development of consumer society, addressing why and how individuals and institutions collect. Key conditions for collecting include individuals having sufficient means, the cultural acceptance of collecting, consuming via trade and an evaluation of self and others based on consumption (Belk, 1995; Rassuli and Hollander, 1985). In terms of motivations, drawing upon psycho-analytical studies, Dillon (2019) summarises that multiple factors motivate collecting such as childhood trauma, deprivation, identity creation, self-presentation and thrill-seeking. The most influential typology, however, stems from the work of Formanek (1991) who argued that collecting is motivated by a range of diverse factors, such as acquiring knowledge, preserving history, socialising with fellow collectors, financial investment and addiction. All five categories proposed by Formanek are underpinned by a genuine passion for the object collected. Whilst the proposed typology provides useful insights and a solid basis upon which to build, it is considerably broad and therefore not necessarily applicable to collecting crime-related memorabilia that remains a very unique form of collecting (Griffiths, 2013). Indeed, very limited research has been conducted with regard to the reasons why murderabilia collectors are fascinated with acquiring and possessing these objects (Denham, 2019). According to Bonn (2014) potential inner drives involve low self-esteem, a need for attention, curiosity to get inside the minds of perpetrators and the intention to develop a closer relationship with them. Collecting murderabilia has also been viewed as a derivative of the wider fascination these individuals appear to have with violent crimes, most notably serial homicide considering the extensive market around it (Jarvis, 2007).

Public Fascination with Serial Homicide

David Berkowitz, Ted Bundy, Dennis Rader, Richard Ramirez, Jack the Ripper, Peter Sutcliffe, Ian Brady and Myra Hindley are only a few examples of serial homicide offenders who have been elevated to some sort of celebrity status, with items related to their notorious cases remaining amongst the most popular choices for murderabilia collectors (Bonn, 2014). Baudrillard (1998) has argued that it is consumption rather than production around which capitalist societies are organized, with mass media and advertising playing an important role in the process. In terms of murderabilia consumption specifically, representation, branding and marketing are integral elements to being viewed as a celebrity criminal (Denham, 2016; Valentine, 2015).

There is a considerable volume of academic literature examining media representations of serial homicide and their re-construction of serial killers into popular celebrities (Bonn, 2014; Cettl, 2003; Denham, 2016; Duclos, 1998; Hodgkison et al, 2016; Jarvis, 2007; Jenkins, 2014; Knox, 2014; MacDonald, 2013; Presdee, 2001; Seltzer, 1997; Wiest, 2016). News media have been heavily reporting and recycling serial homicide cases (Bonn, 2014) as these usually meet newsworthiness criteria of threshold, risk, individualism, simplification, sex and violence (Jewkes, 2004). Media representations tend to be sensationalist and stereotypical (Hodgkinson et al, 2015), as serial killers are usually portrayed as either celebrities or monsters, constructed in such a way as to make their cases more appealing to the public (Duclos, 1998). Research conducted by Wiest (2016) examined media representations of serial killers in US and UK contexts based on the observation that serial homicide cases have become a frequent subject of media coverage. The primary aim of this research was to compare mediated representations of both nations and to highlight the points of agreement and collision between them. In order to do so, the researchers conducted a qualitative content analysis of a sample of 80 news media articles about serial homicide. Amongst the key findings were that UK representations of serial killers present them as traditional monsters, in the sense that they are portrayed as savage animals who target vulnerable victims. This is attributed to a wider effort of marginalising the perpetrator from the wider community, a notion indicative of a society that values the community over the individual. Conversely, US representations portray perpetrators as fantastic monsters with exceptional skills, a fact which elevates them to celebrity status in public consciousness, therefore indicating a culture that promotes individualism. The valuable insights of this research essentially illustrate how media representations of serial homicide across nations are constructed in such a way as to reflect cultural values and beliefs, thus making the subject familiar and therefore appealing to the masses.

Further considering media representations of serial homicide offenders, extreme vocabulary (monster, bad, evil, and devil) is used to describe their personalities (Bonn, 2014) which effectively results in mediated transformations into larger-than-life creatures. Similarly, websites such as Monsterpedia.com, which is known as an extensive encyclopaedia of the subject, includes summaries of the lives and crimes of serial killers, further highlighting the monstrous depictions of these individuals within the realm of mass media.

Let us consider the case of Aileen Wuornos, for instance, one of the most prominent female serial killers, who was found to be responsible for the deaths of six men in Florida between 1989 and 1990. Her case provides interesting insights with regards to the tendency of mass media to sensationalise serial homicide offenders. Much of the media representations of Aileen Wuornos refer to her as a 'monster' and she was heavily portrayed as an evil woman who killed like a man (Bonn, 2014). A 2003 film entitled 'Monster' depicts her crimes, exclusively focusing on the time-period of her life when she committed them. The film is clearly aimed at perpetuating a stereotypical representation, as no space was given to the traumatic early life experiences of Wuornos that involved physical, emotional and sexual abuse, incest, neglect, poverty, and prostitution — risk factors which have had a direct impact upon her mental health and offending behaviour. The masses had simply learnt to demonise and hate her for her crimes, so a theatrical release of her life had to cater for these feelings. The word *monster*, in particular, has become a synonym of her identity, essentially highlighting the inability of society to accept the notion of a female serial killer who deviates from the gendered roles that women are *supposed* to occupy. As of today, Aileen Wuornos' identity as a woman who killed repeatedly is overshadowed by the media-constructed brand of a monster.

According to Denham (2016), persistent media representations eventually result in consumers recalling these criminals with a *selective memory*, shifting the focus of attention from their violent acts to the brand created. He specifically explains that the concept of selective memory denotes 'a trend towards romanticising and remembering criminals for their more attractive, charismatic or intelligent qualities' (Denham, 2016, p. 3). Further to this, within the realm of the media also lie numerous films, shows and documentaries on serial homicide that have embedded and to an extent normalised the phenomenon in public consciousness (Duclos, 1998; Jenkins, 1994; MacDonald, 2013). The

217

lines between reality and fantasy, fact and fiction, have become considerably blurred (Seltzer, 1997; Denham, 2016). Serial homicide has established its own place within popular culture, as experiences of shock, pain and trauma have chronically drawn the public. This is what Seltzer (1998) defined as *wound culture*. In this context, serial homicide offenders are viewed as the embodiment of exhibitions of atrocity, violence and senseless death, resulting in their cases becoming a gathering point for the public and being experienced in a collective manner. Expanding upon this theoretical framework and considering public desire for violent experiences, Denham (2016) argues that murderabilia is perceived to be the most authentic way to consume crime, as it essentially provides the ground for collectors to engage with the dead (Foltyn, 2008; 2016).

Key Term: Wound Culture
- Seltzer (1998, page 1) defined wound culture as 'the public fascination with torn and open bodies and torn and opened persons,' arguing that experiences of shock, pain and trauma have become a gathering point for the public that has been chronically attracted to the suffering of others.
- Seltzer specifically referred to a pathological public sphere, which can be understood as the space that is centred on and defined by shared exhibitions of atrocity, trauma and violence; one in which the lines between the mass and the individual, the public and the private have become blurred.
- Employing a sociological lens, he argued that the concept of sociality 'is bound to the excitations of the torn and opened body, the torn and exposed individual, as public spectacle' (Seltzer, 1998, p. 253), further highlighting the notion that spectacles of violence are viewed as a collective experience.
- He went on to say that in the context of wound culture, the natural body represents distorted concepts of crisis and disaster, serving as a referencing point for mass physical violence, whilst serial killers are viewed as the embodiment of senseless murder, serial brutality and compulsive violence—notions which give them some kind of celebrity status.

Finally, there appears to be theoretical coherence in literature that serial homicide has achieved ubiquity in popular culture. The popularisation of the phenomenon dates back to the 1970s with the emergence of well-known horror movies featuring serial killers, such as 'The Texas Chain Saw Massacre' and 'Halloween.' The positive commercial reception of contemporary films ('Friday the Thirteenth,' 'The Silence of the Lambs,' 'Seven,' 'Scream,' 'Bone Collector,' 'American Psycho,' 'Final Destination,' 'Monster,' 'Saw,' to name a few) and TV shows ('Criminal Minds,' 'CSI' (Crime Scene Investigation), 'Dexter,' 'American Horror Story,' 'Mindhunter') dealing with the subject are illustrative of the enduring fascination society has with this unique form of offending (MacDonald, 2013).

The act of a demented individual who repeatedly kills helpless victims in elaborate fashion has become a common spectacle and resulted in criminologists exploring the extent to which the consumption of serial homicide incidents has become very much normalised in public consciousness. Jarvis (2007) has addressed the issue of graphic depictions of death and violence in popular culture, arguing that they make serial homicide appear as a common, frequent phenomenon, drastically contributing to the fascination of a public that has learnt to consume whatever is marketed as a product to be consumed. Along similar lines, Presdee (2001) has also addressed the issue of the commodification of crime and violence through films, television, radio and the internet within the over-organized economical world. He argues that spectacles of violence, hurt and humiliation, which are produced especially for consumption, are perceived by the individuals who consume them as conduits through which they express their own pervasive emotions of oppression, hatred and revulsion.

Conclusion

This chapter has taken as its main focus the commodification of homicide in late-capitalist society, specifically using the murderabilia industry as a point of reference. Academic literature on murderabilia is considerably limited, largely stemming from the US and predominately focusing on issues of legality, morality and the controversy surrounding them. Conversely, the topic has not been explored to any significant extent by criminologists in the UK, despite its existing murderabilia industry and structurally embedded harms. Cultural studies have offered valuable insights with regards to the concepts of collecting, advertising and branding in consumer society, thereby providing a solid basis upon which to critically examine the topic at hand. Further to this, criminologists have addressed the impact of media representations of serial homicide that essentially fuel public fascination with this unique form of offending. A conclusive answer, however, as to why collectors are fascinated with crime-related memorabilia remains ambiguous. Future research on murderabilia should identify and critically evaluate the values, attitudes and beliefs that are inscribed by consumer capitalism and underpin the industry. Smith and Raymen (2016, p. 2) specifically describe 'activities that are often defended as being social goods or conduits for individual empowerment as inherently harmful.' It is therefore important that scholarship addresses theoretical and empirical gaps on murderabilia, as even the most culturally accepted forms of leisure might result in harm.

Questions to consider
- Is the murderabilia industry exploitative of the suffering of victims?
- Should legislation regulate the sale and distribution of murderabilia in England and Wales?
- Should homicide offenders be able to profit from their stories?
- Why is society fascinated with the subject of serial homicide?

References

Baudrillard, J. (1968), *The System of Objects*, London: Verso Books.

Baudrillard, J. (1998), *The Consumer Society*, London: Sage.

Belk, R. W. (1995), *Collecting in a Consumer Society*, New York: Routledge.

Bonn, S. (2014), *Why We Love Serial Killers: The Curious Appeal of the World's Most Savage Murderers*, New York: Skyhorse Publishing.

Cettl, R. (2003), *Serial Killer Cinema: An Analytical Filmography*, Jefferson, NC: McFarland & Company, Inc.

Chang, S. (2005), 'The Prodigal Son Returns: An Assessment of Current Son of Sam Laws and the Reality of the Online Murderabilia Marketplace,' 31 *Rutgers Computer and Technology Law Journal*, pp. 430–458.

Condry, R. (2010), 'Secondary Victims and Secondary Victimization,' in S. G. Shoham, P. Knepper, and M. Kett (eds.), *International handbook of Victimology*, pp. 219–249, Boca Raton, FL: CRC Press.

Denham, J. (2016), 'The Commodification of the Criminal Corpse: "Selective Memory" in Posthumous Representations of the Criminal,' *Mortality*, pp. 1–17.

Denham, J. (2019), 'Collecting the Dead: Art, Antique and Aura in Personal Collections of Murderabilia,' *Mortality*, pp. 1–16.

Dillon, A. (2019), 'Collecting as Human Routing Behaviour: Motivations for Identity and Control in the Material and Digital Word,' *Information and Culture*, 54(3), pp. 255–280.

Duclos, D. (1998), *The Werewolf Complex*, Oxford: Berg

Elias, N. (1939). *The Civilizing Process: Sociogenetic and Psychogenetic Investigations*, Cambridge, Mass: Blackwell.

Foltyn, J. (2008), 'Dead Famous and Dead Sexy: Popular Culture, Forensics, and the Rise of the Corpse,' *Mortality*, 13, pp. 153–173.

Foltyn, J. (2016), 'Bodies of Evidence: Criminalising the Celebrity Corpse,' *Mortality*, 21(3), pp. 246–262.

Formanek, R. (1991). 'Why They Collect: Collectors Reveal Their Motivations,' *Journal of Social Behavior and Personality*, 6(6), pp. 275–286.

Griffiths, M. (2013), 'Completing the "Killection": A Brief Look at "Murderabilia",' *WordPress.com*. No. 4: https://drmarkgriffiths.wordpress.com/2013/11/04/completing-the-killection-a-brief-look-at-murderabilia/ (Accessed 8 August 2020)

Hammit, L. (2011), 'What's Wrong With the Picture? Reviewing Prison Arts in America,' *Saint Louis University Public Law Review*, 30(2), pp. 575–616.

Hall, S. (2012), *Theorizing Crime and Deviance: A New Perspective*, London: Sage.

Hall, S. and Winlow, S. (2015), *Revitalizing Criminological Theory*, London: Routledge.

Hobbs, J. (2000), *Collectors*, Abject Films.

Hodgkinson, S., Prins, and H. Stuart-Bennett, J. (2016), 'Monsters, Madmen … and Myths: A Critical Review of the Serial Killing Literature,' *Aggression and Violent Behavior*.

Hurley, E. (2009), 'Overkill: An Exaggerated Response to the Sale of Murderabilia,' *Indiana Law Review*, 42(2), pp. 411–440.

Jarvis, B. (2007), 'Monsters Inc.: Serial Killers and Consumer Culture,' *Crime, Media, Culture*, 3(3), pp. 326–344.

Jenkins, P. (1994), *Using Murder: The Social Construction of Serial Homicide*, Oxfordshire: Routledge

Jewkes, Y. (2004), *Media and Crime*, London: Sage.

Kealy, S. (2000), 'A Proposal for a New Massachusetts Notoriety-for-Profit Law: The Grandson of Sam,' *Western New England Law Review*, 22(1), pp. 1–44.

Knox, S. (2004), 'A Gruesome Accounting: Mass, Serial and Spree Killing in the Mediated Public Sphere,' *Journal for Crime, Conflict and the Media*, 1(2), pp. 1–14.

Leavy, P. (2009). *Method Meets Art: Art-based Research Practice*, New York, NY: Guilford.

Loss, J. T. (1987), 'Criminals Selling Their Stories. The First Amendment Requires Legislative Re-examination,' *Cornell Law Review*, 72-(6), pp. 1331–1355.

MacDonald, A. (2013), *Murders and Acquisitions: Representations of the Serial Killer in Popular Culture*, London: Bloomsbury Academic.

Mauro, J. C. (2012), 'Rethinking Murderabilia: How States Can Restrict Some Depictions of Crime as They Restrict Child Pornography,' *Fordham Intellectual Property, Media and Entertainment Law Journal*, pp. 323–358.

Nelson, S. P. and Prendergast, C. (2009), 'Murderabilia Inc: Where the First Amendment Fails Academic Freedom,' *Academic Freedom*, 108(4).

Ng, C. (2011), 'The Business of "Murderabilia": Websites Selling Murder Memorabilia': http://abcnews.go.com/US/business-murderabilia-websites-selling-murder-memorabilia/story?id=14896607 (Accessed 7 August 2020).

Pearce, S. M. (1994), *Interpreting Objects and Collections*, London: Routledge.

Pearce, S. M. (1995), *On Collecting*, London: Routledge

Pinker, S. (2011), *The Better Angels of Our Nature*, London: Penguin Books.

Presdee, M. (2001), *Cultural Criminology and the Carnival of Crime*, London: Routledge.

Rassuli, K. and Hollander, S. (1986), 'Desire—Induced, Innate, Insatiable?,' *Journal of Macro-marketing*, 6, pp. 4–24

Root, D. (1996), *Art, Appropriation and the Commodification of Difference*, Boulder CO: Westview Press.

Schmid, D. (2004), 'Murderabilia: Consuming Fame,' *M/C Journal: A Journal of Media and Culture*, 7(5): http://journal.media-culture.org.au/0411/10-schmid.php

Seltzer, M. (1997), 'Wound Culture: Trauma in the Pathological Public Sphere,' *October*, 80, pp. 3–26.

Seltzer, M. (1998), *Serial Killers: Death and Life in America's Wound Culture,* New York, NY: Routledge.

Smith, O. and Raymen, T. (2016), 'Deviant Leisure: A Criminological Perspective,' *Theoretical Criminology*, pp. 1–20.

Valentine, C. (2015). *Flogging a Dead Corpse: The Sale of Human Remains* (Accessed October 14, 2015), Huffington Post: http://www.huffingtonpost.co.uk/carla-valentine/ Flogging-a-dead-corpse-th_b_8283974.html

Wiest, J. B. (2016). 'Casting Cultural Monsters: Representations of Serial Killers in US and UK News Media,' *Howard Journal of Communications*, 27(4), pp. 327–346.

Yardley, E. and Rusu, D. (2018), 'Edmund Clark's Artistic Residency at HMP Grendon: Exploring the Impact upon Residents,' *Prison Service Journal,* 239, pp. 50–57.

Žižek, S. (2008), *Violence*, London: Profile Books.

CHAPTER 10

Homicide Investigation — The Detective's Perspective

'Without fear or favour, go where the evidence takes you. Assume nothing, believe nobody and check everything'

The detective's philosophy

Introduction

Solving a murder (homicide) is frequently about details, it relies on thoroughness, persistence, and making sure that you are not taking things at face value (Innes, 2003). This chapter examines the reality of homicide investigation from the police perspective in England and Wales. It also involves analysis of the key fundamentals and reflective approaches within the lead detective's role, professionally referred to as the senior investigating officer (SIO).

Media Representations of the Investigative Process

The public seem to have a huge interest in homicide, deviant behaviour and major crime. An appetite that is served by a wide variety of sources, involving the mainstream media, social media and crime fiction, including film, television and literature. Indeed, in terms of books, crime fiction is currently the most popular genre of fiction in the UK with crime sales having increased by 19 per cent since 2015 (Hannah, 2018). There are many reasons for this growing popularity. Crime fiction, arguably, provides the reader with some release from an uncertain world. Crime novels put the balance back in life ... evil is punished, and the 'good guys' mostly win, after solving the puzzle (Ibid). There are certain norms that authors must conform to in order to ensure the genre's authenticity. For example, frequently the 'detective' appears as the SIO, the most senior police officer in overall command of the tactical direction, policy and conduct of the investigation. In fiction, he or she is often charismatic and driven, yet flawed and constantly conflicted. He or she also provides comparison and contrast to the killer's wickedness. The detective, often bitter and cynical is able to outsmart criminals, in part because they share elements of the same mindset (Rowe, 2014). Much crime fiction emphasises that central dynamic — the relationship between the detective and the killer. The pair enmeshed within a personal battle of wits.

Additional 'givens' within the genre commonly apply to close exchanges between the detective and an authoritative forensic pathologist and/or a typically worthy but more junior-ranking officer — often a detective sergeant — in an assisting role. Wider police and partnership teamwork is sometimes detailed, but referenced by minor characters, through which the writer moves the plot along. The genre also dictates that the SIO must be dedicated to one case at a time. This is deliberate and enables the audience to absorb and recall the narrative arc. The reality of operational policing is that SIOs often simultaneously investigate multiple and unrelated homicide incidents, generating substantial concerns for professional overload, welfare and resilience. In 2019, one SIO described having, 'Fourteen live homicide investigations — amongst those [were] three Cat As [see later in this chapter] — two child murders — a no body murder and two domestic violence and abuse murders ... my current case load is on my mind every waking moment' (Hines, 2019).

Furthermore, in crime fiction, plot lines habitually pivot and frequently climax around 'suspect interrogation scenes' where the SIO regularly presents as a practised and expert interviewer. Here, through superior cognitive processing and granular grasp of detail, he or she ultimately triumphs. Again, the reality is very different. Interviewing officers are likely to be detective constables, trained, accredited and professionally practised in the role. Police work and particularly effective homicide investigation requires industrial levels of teamwork and the investment of substantial human, technical and financial resources. The stereotypes presented through crime fiction have little to offer the contemporary policing doctrine of homicide investigation. It is simply undesirable for the SIO to work within the singularly close orbit of the 'side-kick' confidant. Even for the most apparently straightforward of matters, modern investigations can be highly complex and time-consuming. A wide range of leadership, political, economic, social, technological and legal skills are required at all levels to ensure that an effective investigation takes place. These requirements lock into an intrusive governance and policy-based legal framework where police accountability and professional conduct are constantly scrutinised.

Separating Myth from Reality

Specialisms within the homicide investigation team are skills-based and not affiliated to seniority or rank. Roles include those of officers who specialise in family liaison, witness and suspect interviewing, evidential disclosure, management of exhibits and house-to-house and CCTV enquiries. There are also non-warranted functions, i.e. those carried out by people who are not police officers as such, including forensic specialists, information communications technology (ICT) specialists, intelligence analysts, researchers and administrative staff. Scientific, forensic, medical, legal and other experts are also accessible to the SIO, either through formal policing structures or on a commissioning basis. All characterise critical elements within homicide investigation.

General external enquiry duties fall to specialist detective constables, usually working in pairs, under the direction and supervision of detective sergeants and action allocators, who detail specific actions and tasks, linked to the requirements of the SIO. The hub of the investigation is located within the 'Major Incident Room' (MIR) — the suite of police offices from where the investigation team works. The word 'investigation' comes from the Latin *vestigium* meaning 'trace' or 'footprint': investigation is the search for the trace or footprint and, if done professionally, demands commitment to enquire in detail, to observe carefully, and to examine systematically (Shepherd and Griffiths, 2013).

The core mechanisms, policies and practices of contemporary homicide investigation include:

- The investigation set-up, categorisation and the initial phases of the homicide investigation;
- Leadership and the police senior investigating officer (SIO) role;

- Resourcing, staffing specialist functions and responsibilities, including family liaison;
- The application of forensic science within homicide investigation, including the forensic *post-mortem*;
- Governance and review of homicide investigation; and
- The technological challenges and demands for investigators within a data rich environment.

Sudden and Suspicious Death, Primary Investigation and Homicide Incident Set-up

Dealing with the death of a person is a fundamental role within policing, which has over the years, brought much criticism to the police service in England and Wales (College of Policing, 2019). That fundamental role could vary from completing a simple report to the coroner, concerning a non-suspicious death, to the implementation of a largescale and complex homicide investigation. For every death in England and Wales, where a doctor does not certify the cause and issue a Medical Certificate of the Cause of Death (MCCD), an inquest to investigate the circumstances and determine the cause must be held by the coroner in whose jurisdiction the death occurred. In order to support this duty, it was formerly routine procedure for the police to attend all reports of sudden death where a doctor did not issue an MCCD. These were usually incidents taking place outside the context of a hospital or medical premises. Under supervision by more experienced officers, including a police coroner's officer, the attendance at and reporting on a sudden death was one of the very earliest tasks assigned to newly-appointed probationary or student constables. Partly seen as a 'rite of passage' during the formative part of a police career. This also developed investigative skills, empathy and humanity, particularly where family members and loved ones were present. On occasions, sudden death can be odorous, grisly and disturbing and attendance, as a matter of policy, was also set to test the new officer's stomach — sometimes literally — for the demands of police work.

Over recent years, most police force approaches have changed tack, both through the exponential demand for police services and the requirement for more proportionate police responses, based on threat, risk and public harm. For an elderly person dying at home, in non-suspicious circumstances, where an ambulance crew is at the scene and with family members present, most forces will not attend, even where the deceased's GP does not issue an MCCD. Matters are reported to the Coroner's Office (out-of-hours coverage is provided), the body removed, a coronial investigation commenced and a non-forensic *post-mortem* examination is usually held.

In suspicious or more unusual circumstances, there are substantial, professional, legal, moral and ethical duties for the police in attending and investigating sudden death. It is a fundamental responsibility of the police service to preserve life unless it is plainly obvious to a non-medically qualified person that the individual concerned is dead (College of Policing, 2019). Generally, no assumptions should be made about whether life is extinct, as countless examples point to human survival after the victim apparently suffered injuries incompatible with life. Although the emergency services frequently encounter incidents where injuries are incompatible with life, in law only a suitably qualified medical practitioner, including specially trained paramedics, can formally declare that life is extinct.

Numerous tasks present themselves in effectively assessing the scene of a sudden death. These include, public and personal safety—for example, there may be live electric circuits, escaping gas, road and building safety considerations and the potential for suspects to be at the scene or in close proximity. There is also the categoric identification of the deceased. Often this is straightforward through conventional means, for example a photo ID at the scene or formal identification by loved ones or friends. More complicated matters can be resolved through identification sciences, including fingerprint checks, DNA or dental records. There are also requirements to safeguard valuables and other property, as well as dealing sensitively and humanely with the bereaved. Care for the bereaved must always be balanced with effective investigation—particularly where parents are concerned. For example, in cases of sudden infant death syndrome (SIDS), the unexpected and unexplained death of an apparently well baby (College of Policing, 2014). These events are amongst the most challenging and difficult for professionals at all levels—from the police and forensic professionals to social care, local authorities and medical practitioners. There are extensively publicised examples where the police and partner agencies have implicated innocent parents and family members in the unexplained deaths of infants and children. Equally there have been cases where the authorities have not acted promptly enough to secure and preserve evidence in homicide incidents, where parents and carers have later been convicted. Careful and considered professional judgement is required in all instances of sudden death and much rests on the skills of the first police officers attending the scene.

The importance of the effectiveness of the initial police response to homicide was emphasised in a report published by the Forensic Science Regulator in 2015 (Forensic Pathology Unit of the Home Office, 2015) that highlighted the potential to 'miss' a homicide. In order to reduce the likelihood of such a miss, it is essential that the police service deals with death in a systematic and professional manner (College of Policing, 2019). Even for experienced police investigators, it can be professionally demanding distinguishing the differences between suspicious and non-suspicious circumstances. Suicide, for example, can take many forms and such deaths need to be investigated thoroughly due to the possibility of a disguised homicide (College of Policing, 2014). In addition, the presence of seemingly self-inflicted wounds could be interpreted as having been caused by a third party. Also, incidents where death has occurred through the process of illness, leading to internal haemorrhage, catastrophic external blood loss or through accidents can also make homicide assessment challenging. The scene might be severely contaminated with blood, tissue and other body fluids. There may or may not be signs of disruption at the scene. Premises and scenes can be so dishevelled that difficulties are created in establishing any signs of a struggle to indicate a physical attack. Some sudden deaths must await a forensic *post-mortem* examination to confirm whether or not foul play is at hand. The unequivocal necessity for careful and thorough investigation from the outset cannot be overstated.

Homicides in the United Kingdom remain comparatively rare events. For the year ending March 2018, there were 726 (murder, manslaughter and infanticide) in England and Wales (Elkin, 2019). Despite the recent increases in knife-related homicide, particularly involving young people as both victims and offenders, homicide rates for England and Wales remain reasonably stable at about 700 offences per year. This represents 12 offences of homicide per million of population and this compares as per a report released by the European Commission in 2019 to a homicide rate across the European Union, in 2015, of seven offences per million of population (European Commission, 2019). Rates in the USA are far higher, with 17,166 homicides reported in 2017, representing 52 offences per million.

A homicide in England and Wales is an atypical offence, i.e. distinctive in the extent to which it is subject to police attention (Rowe, 2014). Nevertheless, homicide occurs regularly enough to ensure that the skills and expertise of the relatively small cadre of investigating officers will be regularly required. Homicide does have a high clear-up rate when compared to other crimes — of 87 per cent up to March 2018 (Elkin, 2019). Arguably, this is due to a number of factors including the commitment of extensive police investigative and forensic assets, time and financial resources. Many incidents also involve victims and offenders known to each other and, additionally, homicide attracts wide public attention, stimulating the flow of information and intelligence.

Let us say that the police have identified an incident as homicide or suspected homicide and launch a major investigation. The term 'golden hour' is often used to describe the principle that effective early action can result in securing significant material that would otherwise be lost to the investigation (College of Policing, 2006). Whilst 'golden hour' should not be taken in a literal sense, it serves to emphasise that homicide events require expeditious and proactive investigation. Lost opportunities to secure and preserve evidence may never be recovered. That said, there is also a careful balance to be struck. The initial phases of a homicide investigation can be hectic and confusing and the SIO will also need to create 'slow time' or 'put their foot on the ball,' terms used to signify bringing some order (and prioritisation) to the many activities that others will have initiated during the initial response. If not brought under control, these activities run the risk of generating further confusion and, worse, the loss or contamination of material (College of Policing, 2006).

The police should establish as quickly as possible whether a suspect (or suspects) for the offence has (have) been identified — or through reasonable enquiries is/are readily identifiable. When homicide is suspected, the identification and arrest of the offender(s) must always be a priority (College of Policing, 2006). There are sound reasons for prioritising the detection components of a homicide investigation, particularly in the early stages of the enquiry. There is a pressing urgency for the police to secure and protect the scene and preserve evidence. The integrity of the scene might be highly vulnerable to interference.

Homicide crime scenes can be chaotic environments, including those within 'crowded places.' Some witnesses and onlookers may be intoxicated and/or fuelled with emotion, or simply just scared. Members of the public also have the capacity to record events on smartphones, including the police response and to upload or live-stream the action within seconds. In addition, mainstream media outlets can arrive at the scene during the early stages, reporting, questioning and speculating to degrees that might be unhelpful to the effective direction of the investigation. There are also many examples of suspects remaining at the location, through curiosity, audacity or the notion of 'hiding in plain sight.'

The police have much to think about in applying the numerous tasks and actions to effectively manage the scene of a homicide: establishing cordons (inner and outer) to prevent public access, commencing a crime scene log to record details of those attending and to 'freeze the scene,' securing witnesses, briefing, leadership and direction from supervisors and senior detectives, calling for forensic support, securing CCTV, searching adjacent areas for evidence, and making careful notes around initial attendance and actions. The list seems endless and, within all of that activity, officers can become overly 'task-orientated' and lose sight of the need to identify and arrest any suspect(s) as quickly as possible.

By the term 'suspect'—both in relation to the person(s) and any police suspicion—this does not mean to say that the police must be absolutely satisfied of someone's involvement. Police powers of arrest extend to having 'reasonable grounds to suspect' that a person is guilty of an offence (Police and Criminal Evidence Act 1984). This has the clear and obvious advantage of reducing the risks of loss, damage or disposal of evidence. Additionally, as a result of the MacPherson Enquiry into the racist murder of Stephen Lawrence in 1993—where, amongst other shortcomings, SIOs were criticised for not making early arrests of named suspects—SIOs now emphasise the tracing and arrest of suspects as quickly as possible. This also facilitates the use of further police powers, including searching of premises and vehicles, obtaining forensic samples, seizing clothing and mobile phones and securing other relevant evidence. Additional tactical benefits flow from this greater proactive approach, including methodologies around interviewing practice, where the suspect has limited time in which to absorb police activity and implement deception strategies. It also serves to reassure the public and fulfils the duty of the police to secure and preserve evidence that seeks to prove or disprove a person's involvement in crime. In the prompt elimination of an individual from enquiries, much time and effort can be saved in focusing on more productive lines of investigation.

Categorisation of Homicide Investigation

Professional homicide investigations can be categorised in three ways, i.e. as:
- self-solvers
- whodunits; and
- offences committed *in extremis* (Innes, 2003).

Self-solvers include homicide incidents, where the suspect(s) are readily identifiable and are subject to early arrest and charge, the police have little difficulty in securing and preserving evidence and meeting the Crown Prosecution Service's evidential sufficiency test. More complex, difficult or protracted investigations—whodunits or those comparatively rare but high-profile *in extremis* events—are subject to more intensive police attention, along with the allocation of substantial resources.

To further inform police approaches to homicide investigation, the National Police Chiefs' Council (NPCC) (previously the Association of Chief Police Officers (ACPO)) classifies offences as follows:
- Category A: Major incidents of the most severe public concern. For example, they will include homicide incidents involving child victims, multiple, serial and spree killings, as well as those involving police officers or victims of public significance.
- Category B: Major incidents of a more routine nature involving homicide where the suspect(s) is/are unknown.
- Category C: Major incidents where the suspect(s) is/are known and readily arrestable—largely less complex and protracted investigations than Category A or B incidents.

Category C investigations are commonly maintained through a 'manual' enquiry working system, where detectives gather and build a largely paper-based case file, although this also generally works through relevant force IT-based crime recording systems. Category A and B systems usually run to the full Major Incident Room Standardised Administrative Procedures (MIRSAP) (Centrex, 2005) protocol, including the application of the HOLMES 2, IT system (Home Office Large Major Enquiry System). This provides an automated, IT-based filing, retrieval, cross-referencing and intelligence tool that supports investigators in making sense of the scale of information and evidence gathered in a large and complex investigation.

Two key documents direct the authorised professional practice and tactical doctrine of homicide investigation: the *Murder Investigation Manual* (College of Policing, 2006) — that sets out the process of investigation and is aimed at the operational practice of SIOs and MIRSAP (Centrex, 2005) — that sets out the protocols for the implementation, practice and management of major incident rooms. These documents provide the operational doctrine and scaffolding around homicide investigation, whilst the continuing professional development and accreditation of investigators and senior investigators is governed through the College of Policing's Professionalising the Investigation Process (PIP) scheme. This ranges from PIP 1 — qualification at constable/basic practitioner level, PIP 2 — specialist investigator at detective constable and detective sergeant levels, PIP 3 — SIO at detective inspector and detective chief inspector, and PIP 4 — strategic management of major and critical crime, commonly detective superintendent and above. At all levels, officers must complete a rigorous training and development programme and demonstrate competency through mentoring, professional development and operational practice. Accreditation to perform at the level required can be withdrawn through lack of competency or due to insufficient operational deployments. These programmes are robust and demanding and would give any fictional detective pause for thought. In reality, the schemes largely produce capable and professional detectives.

Leadership and the Role of the SIO

Imagine for a moment, being the on-call, duty SIO woken by a phone call at 3 am. The voice is recognisable as a police colleague, perhaps it is the duty inspector or the force incident manager. The briefing you receive is earnest but edgy and immediately describes the discovery of a suspected homicide incident;

the scene location, the condition and position of the victim, the presence of any significant witnesses, actions tasked and resources committed, including the locations of police cordons and more besides.

The SIO has much information to immediately gather, interpret, make sense of and then must determine a course of action and allocate resources, which, even at this early stage, must be clear, precise and subject to ongoing review. Policing is amongst a few occupations where practitioners are required to make the most challenging of professional decisions and take actions in critical circumstances, at times when they are least well-disposed to do so. Further accountability mechanisms will follow, with formal briefings with senior officers from the force command team. Subject to individual police force policies, unsolved homicides also face regular and critical review to ensure all investigative opportunities are maximised. There is the intense and virtually immediate scrutiny of the media—both mainstream and social media—that influences public perceptions of the police and places further resilience demands on the SIO and investigation team. A lifetime of legal, moral and ethical accountability follows. The SIO knows that the propriety of any decision-making may be subject to intense public examination, months or years hence, under the exacting glare of the Crown Court and subjected to cross-examination by well-prepared advocates. Long and gruelling working hours also accompany homicide investigation, causing missed family events and other personal commitments. Accountability and scrutiny are essential elements of professional policing and the SIO must search for answers and provide for justice within the circumstances of the unlawful killing of another human being. This remains a unique and solemn duty.

Returning to the 3 am call, an experienced SIO will digest the broad details given by the caller, but should take a few moments to pause and organize his or her thoughts before dialling back—perhaps after washing and with a mug of coffee. The further conversation, before the SIO sets off to the scene of the incident—and the SIO should always visit and become orientated with the crime scene (Grieve, 2015)—is more granular, framing and agreeing a number of 'fast-track' actions for the police supervisor on the ground. These involve any investigative actions that, if pursued immediately, are likely to establish important facts, preserve evidence or lead to the early resolution of the investigation

(College of Policing, 2006). The circumstances of major investigations vary, but the principal fast-track actions should be considered, as follows:

    I.   Identify suspects

   II.   Intelligence opportunities

  III.   Scene forensics

  IV.   Crime scene assessment

   V.   Witness search

  VI.   Victim enquiries

 VII.   Possible motives

VIII.   Media

  IX.   *Post-mortem(s)*

   X.   Significant witness interviews

  XI.   Other critical actions

 XII.   Identify passive data opportunities

Source: *Murder Investigation Manual* (College of Policing, 2006).

Careful consideration must be given to any prevailing or adverse weather conditions, including forecasts, that might impact on scene management and forensic recovery, particularly if located outside. Lighting and tenting may be key requirements, balancing scene preservation with privacy and accesibility, whilst maintaining due dignity and respect for the victim.

Many SIOs will keep a 'grab bag' of essential equipment including an airwave police radio with spare batteries, torch, forensic suiting, overshoes and face-mask (to prevent DNA and other forensic cross-contamination and for health and safety reasons), as well as a phone charger and papers including the Major Incident Policy Document. The maintenance of this document applies to the police response for a range of major and critical incidents and investigations. In terms of homicide, its value is in the SIO recording and signing decisions that affect the functional or organizational features of the enquiry, along with showing clear reasoning for decisions.

Functional or organizational features involve details around the investigation set-up, including those initial decisions made at the scene(s) of the incident—this includes the SIO recording a 'keystone log' that effectively describes the investigation and outlines the known, initial facts. The policy document must also include any agreed terms of reference with senior officers, a clear definition of the scene(s), command and leadership structures and whether the investigation is to be placed onto the HOLMES 2 computer system or relies on a manual system. The success of any major investigation relies upon an organized and methodical approach.

Once the decision has been made to launch a homicide investigation and to engage the full MIRSAP set-up (see earlier and below), a range of police officer and police staff positions must be filled. Dedicated police accommodation generally houses the Major Incident Rooms (MIR), where the investigation team and information and communications technologies (ICT) systems are based. Material concerning the investigation is gathered and further enquiries directed. Information is documented and managed, using a set of administrative procedures, into a system used by the SIO to direct and control the course of the enquiry (Centrex, 2005).

The MIRSAP reforms were introduced as a result of Sir Lawrence Byford's report into the failings of the Yorkshire Ripper enquiry in 1981. Criticisms included shortcomings surrounding police inadequacy around information storage, retrieval and cross-force information-sharing and collaboration. Reforms sought to achieve national consistency and, where necessary, officers and staff can be deployed to other areas of the country and linked or series incidents addressed quickly and efficiently to maximise investigative opportunities.

All activity, including the entries made by the SIO within the policy document are detailed on the HOLMES system. The importance of adherence to MIRSAP and murder manual principles, including the deployment of sufficient staffing, resourcing and assets is essential. Any under-resourcing would amount to a disservice to the victim(s), their families and communities and seriously disadvantage the investigation. It may also attract criticism at court and be used by defence lawyers to undermine the prosecution case.

To illustrate the intensity of homicide investigation in terms of human resources, a Category B or Category A homicide incident will typically consist of the following roles and responsibilities:

- **Senior investigating officer (SIO):** Responsible for the control and direction of the enquiry.
- **Deputy senior investigating officer:** As above in the absence of the SIO. Often used for professional development, senior detective training and accreditation purposes.

- **Office manager:** Delegated responsibility for the efficient management of the MIR.
- **Finance manager:** Coordination and management of all financial and resourcing issues, including accommodation, overtime, expenses, vehicles and equipment.
- **Receiver:** Supervisory detective officer. Receives and reads all documents and information coming into the MIR—decides on actions, including raising fast-track actions for urgent enquiry.
- **Action manager:** Usually an experienced detective sergeant—allocates and reviews individual investigation tasks (actions), generated through the HOLMES system and in line with the enquiry policies set by the SIO. The SIO will also raise actions and allocate accordingly.
- **Document reader:** Proven investigator, reads in detail and assesses all documentation coming into the incident room and indicates how the information is to be stored on the HOLMES system.
- **Indexer/action writer/registrar:** Inputs information onto the HOLMES system, writes actions and allocates to team members according to workloads and instructions by enquiry team leaders.
- **Indexing team leader:** Leads and manages the above staff.
- **HOLMES 2 support manager:** Technical member of staff, available to deal with ICT issues.
- **Researcher:** Searches for and retrieves information and material in support of the investigation, compiles reports and briefings and presents to the SIO/incident room staff.
- **Analysts:** Including manager and lead analyst. Tactical advisor, responsible for evaluating and interpreting all information and material relating to the investigation and supporting the SIO in decision-making processes.
- **Intelligence research and development officer:** Investigator with experience in researching, gathering and disseminating material. Develops the means to generate the gathering of intelligence and information relevant to the investigation.

- **Graphics/briefing officer:** Prepares and gives briefings to incident room staff at all levels and maintains records of briefings and those present.
- **File preparation officer:** An officer with comprehensive knowledge of the case, identified at an early stage, from the outside enquiry teams, to prepare the case papers for prosecution at court in liaison with the SIO. Includes working with the CPS and prosecuting counsel.
- **Typist:** An essential role — documents and written material are required to be typed onto the HOLMES 2 system to allow searching for text contained within documents and assist the research capabilities of the investigation.
- **Admin/telephonist(s):** Take messages coming into the incident room, accurately submit information and support media appeals.
- **Exhibits officer:** Records property and evidence seized during the investigation, maintains it as appropriate in secure storage, ensures its evidential value and maximises investigative opportunities.
- **Disclosure officer:** In accordance with the Criminal Procedure and Investigations Act 1996, responsible for the scheduling and sharing of material with the CPS, including any unused, sensitive or non-sensitive material gathered by the incident room. The CPS has responsibility for the disclosure of material to the defence team in criminal proceedings. This is a principle consequent on Article 6 of the European Convention on Human Rights — the right to a fair trial — and to ensure 'equality of arms.'
- **House-to-house coordinator and enquiry officer:** Normally a police officer and supervisor, manages house-to-house enquiries within proximity to the scene(s) agreed by the SIO. Conducts resident interviews, identifies potential witnesses, details whereabouts at the time of the offence, including descriptions, clothing worn at the time and details of any vehicles owned or used.

Source: *Major Incident Room Standard Administration Procedures* (Centrex, 2005)

In addition to those officers and staff dedicated to working within the MIR, there are typically 16 detective constables, working 'outside' in pairs, under enquiry team supervisors. These officers do much of the 'legwork' of the investigation, in terms of taking statements, securing and preserving evidence, obtaining and viewing CCTV footage, gathering community information and intelligence, clarifying points raised by other actions and conducting enquiries at the discretion of the SIO. It is often from this pool that arrest and search teams and specialist witness and suspect interviewing officers are drawn. Their work is principally driven by the action manager.

Family Liaison

Specialist family liaison officers (FLOs) are also deployed, within the context of the investigation, to make key welfare and investigative links between the victim's family and the SIO/enquiry process. They provide support and information in a sensitive and compassionate manner, securing confidence and trust of families of victims of crime (primarily homicide), road fatality, mass disaster or other critical incidents, ensuring family members are given timely information in accordance with the needs of the investigation (College of Policing, 2019). FLOs are invaluable in gathering evidence and information from the family in order to assist the investigation and address any local and media speculation.

The FLO's role is highly challenging. A constant balance needs to be struck between addressing the understandable desire and need of the victim's family for information with the operational requirements of the investigation and in securing and preserving evidence with which to bring the offender(s) to justice. On occasions, the operational needs of the investigation may, for good reasons, contradict the duty of the police to provide the fullest information to the victim's family. For example, some information might be confidential or legally constrained, including restrictions under data protection legislation, or information that, if placed within the public domain, might prove advantageous to the offender(s). Therefore, given the importance of maintaining the trust and confidence of the victim's family and, by default, friends, associates and the wider community, FLOs must explain from the outset why they might not be able to disclose certain items of information about the case. There has to be the utmost clarity around briefings provided to FLOs by the SIO and other investigation leaders about what information can and cannot be disclosed. The SIO should be constantly vigilant in order to prevent inappropriate disclosures or breaches of professional and ethical standards.

Ensuring the support and welfare of FLOs is a key requirement for the SIO. In turn, FLOs should maintain their primary duty as investigators to act professionally and, furthermore, make careful notes, within an FLO policy file, concerning all interactions with family members — and disclose those notes for 'signing off' by supervising officers. FLOs should share with family members that they will make notes of conversations and interactions, for accountability and evidential purposes, but also as a reference document to assist clarification and to deal with any queries. This is particularly important for families as they move through the grieving process and begin to formulate questions not initially considered during the initial shock of losing a loved one in the circumstances of homicide.

The police must demonstrate patience, care and empathy in order to reduce the risks of any sense of procedural injustice on the part of families. This can particularly apply if communication is allowed to falter between the SIO/FLOs and the family. Perceptions can grow that the police are hiding facts or not making sufficient disclosures about the investigation. There are well-known examples of poor police practice within the realm of homicide investigation where families and the public have had cause to question police legitimacy. The investigation into the racially-motivated murder of Stephen Lawrence in 1992 and the subsequent MacPherson Enquiry proved to be a watershed in homicide (and major crime) investigation. Police treatment of the Lawrence family serves as a salutary lesson. Former Detective Chief Inspector Clive Driscoll, the SIO who in 2012 finally led the Metropolitan Police team in gaining convictions for Stephen's murder, powerfully described his parents' perspective in the following terms,

'Imagine being Neville and Doreen Lawrence. Not only have you lost your son but the attackers are still out there — gloating, a lot of people said … and the police force entrusted with bringing you justice has fallen short … Of course you're mad at the Met. Of course you think they're, at best, incompetent, at worst corrupt.' (Driscoll, 2015)

Under such circumstances, families have sought help from elsewhere, by instructing their own solicitors to provide legal advice and then to liaise with the police. These steps can, in turn, create apparent barriers for the SIO and enquiry team. The key for the SIO is to reflect and learn and to continuously question their own adaptability to changing circumstances (Adlam, 2003). Not to retreat into a defensive mind-set, but to demonstrate leadership and work with the family in the interests of an effective investigation. If policing by consent is to have any significance, the kinship of police leaders must include the public whom they serve (Ibid). The Lawrence case presents a powerful reminder to SIOs and police leaders, at all levels, to guard against hubris and become conscientious students of police history.

Attention is required on the part of the SIO around what and how much information should be disclosed to the family. Certainly, information about the case should not be publically released, especially for media circulation, without the family's knowledge (and also the reasons why). Dignity and respect for the family is paramount and out of courtesy—even though there is no legal requirement—the SIO should seek consent and cooperation in revealing information that might be in the interests of the investigation. The phrase commonly applied within policing, when there is no stated legal or procedural answer to an operational question is: 'It's a judgement call.' Ultimately, it is for the SIO to make the key tactical decisions around the conduct of a homicide enquiry, including the appropriate disclosure of information. In this regard, sagacity and accomplishment arrive through a combination of training, continuing professional development and experience.

Careful attention must be applied to the ethical consequences of exposing the victim's grieving family and friends to the mainstream media, often during the unfamiliar glare of the pre-planned press conference. Any approaches by the SIO for the victim's family and/or friends to consent to go before the media must be taken in consultation with FLOs.

Appeals for witnesses and information made by loved ones can be powerful and helpful to the police in generating lines of enquiry. Those who knew and loved the victim may also wish to publically acknowledge their personal feelings in seeking justice. The line of judgement for the police is a fine one. If families and friends aren't offered the opportunity to appeal to the public for assistance they may choose to approach the media independently. This can create difficulties and generate unhelpful tensions between the victim's family, their associates and the police. In addition the greater levels of disclosure concerning the incident provided to the family may inadvertently be revealed, risking the escape of an offender and loss or damage to evidence. In short, the aim of the SIO and police enquiry team is to manage messages and disclosure about the offence to the maximum benefit of the investigation, whilst maintaining a duty of care to the bereaved and simultaneously serving broader public interests.

There are some disadvantages of the press conference and public-facing approaches for family and friends. There have, sadly, been incidents where those concerned have been later convicted of the homicide incident in question. It seems that public attention can sometimes wear thin and relevant, authentic and heartfelt appeals by loved ones can become tainted through the cynicism of previous criminal manipulation. The contemporary nature of the media's thirst for round the clock information and news coverage, creates real and challenging ethical and technical issues for the police. All of this, adds to the sheer volume of information that the SIO and enquiry team must capture, sift and make sense of in order to effectively present it as evidence.

The Forensic Post-Mortem Examination

The purpose of the forensic *post-mortem* is to establish the cause of death, the extent of the victim's injuries, whether there is any natural disease and to make a factual record of the findings. Furthermore, the forensic pathologist can offer opinions concerning what may have happened at the scene and when death may have occurred (College of Policing, 2006).

The Home Office accredited forensic pathologist is therefore a pivotal figure within any homicide investigation and in implementing the SIO's forensic strategy and achieving these aims. To that end, it is imperative that the pathologist, if required by the SIO, attends the crime scene to examine the body in-situ and within the overall context of the incident. There is much to be emphasised around the pathologist and the SIO, with other forensic scene examiners, working in partnership to ensure that examination is orderly and chronological, to maximise evidential recovery and to enhance the effectiveness of the investigation. The process of 'orientation' is also key for the investigative process, with key personnel getting into investigation mode, not just geographically by walking the scene, but also conceptually—to understand the communities that live in the area. Re-visiting the scene at the relevant hour of the incident is also important and if possible during the relevant weather conditions (Grieve, 2015).

The SIO should also decide whether to attend the post-mortem examination. The *Murder Investigation Manual* indicates no technical requirement. However, attendance is usually best practice to ensure that the SIO is always involved where there are interpretational issues or findings that could significantly alter the course of the investigation (College of Policing, 2006). A full and comprehensive briefing must present the pathologist with the known details of the homicide incident under investigation. Other police officers and police staff specialists will also attend the *post-mortem*, in order to document, secure and preserve evidence, including the packaging of forensic material for laboratory submission. The SIO may want to explore the following issues with regard to the *post-mortem*:

- Cause of death
- Time of death
- Toxicology
- Level of attack
- Injury analysis
- Murder site
- Disguised cause of death [e.g. faking a suicide]
- Sexual evidence
- Weapon analysis
- Lifestyle
- Size and physique of the victim

Source: *Murder Investigation Manual* (College of Policing, 2006).

Photographing the examination takes place and, commonly, the pathologist will audio-record findings to assist in the completion of the *post-mortem* report. If appropriate, a video-recording will further assist the SIO and enquiry team in visualising and understanding crucial findings. Various tissue and blood samples obtained from the victim will support histological findings, i.e. blood toxicology to reveal the presence and levels of any toxins, alcohol and/or drugs. The *post-mortem* findings represent a vital ingredient of the crime scene assessment process. In addition to the forensic and pathology (hard science) elements to the *post-mortem*, the opportunity to collect the soft-science elements, i.e. the interpretive facts, for example by asking, 'What does this injury mean?' (College of Policing, 2006). In 'reading' the body and interpreting the patterns of the wounds, the pathologist contributes to police understanding of the fatal interaction (Innes, 2003). It then remains best practice for the SIO to see the role of the pathologist as not limited to the *post-mortem* examination. There may be a need for regular contact between the SIO and forensic pathologist throughout the investigation. This is particularly the case when evidence relevant to the injuries or cause of death becomes available from witnesses, scientists or the offender (Ibid).

In cases of homicide, whether or not a suspect is readily available, the coroner will direct the holding of a second forensic *post-mortem* examination. This provides for any second opinions and corroboration or otherwise, regarding the findings of the initial examination. Additionally, a further *post-mortem* examination may take place under the instruction of an accused person's defence team.

Enquiry Support Mechanisms, Parameters and Witness Considerations

There are also a range of other forensic, scientific, media, criminal behavioural, intelligence, technical support, ICT and legal specialists available to the SIO — depending on the scale, complexity and overall requirements of the investigation. A number of these functions are available 'in-house' within the relevant force and others can be sourced externally or commissioned through the College of Policing. For example, criminal psychologists, geographic profilers and other subject matter experts can be engaged on a bespoke basis, depending on the SIO's requirements. After the closure of the government owned Forensic Science Service, a number of forensic services have been contracted out to private sector providers. Staffing levels for homicide investigations can vary and fluctuate widely throughout the duration of the investigation. Areas of high demand tend to occur around the initial phases of the investigation and then at key action points. These include the search for witnesses and CCTV recordings, the searching of scenes, arrest actions and subsequent searches for evidence relating to suspects, premises and vehicles. The SIO has discretion to seek additional staff and role requirements as necessary.

Decisions and record-keeping around finance and administration are key items for the policy document and the SIO is expected to take day-to-day management responsibility for overtime spending, hours of duty for the enquiry teams, briefings, management meetings and any agreed media liaison policies. Individual homicide investigations are also commonly given a specific operational name and will include any crime reference number — for reasons of confidentiality, security and to provide a cost-centre code, against which overtime and other expenses can be budgeted for.

Homicide investigation is highly skilled and resource intensive. Therefore, for those police officers and staff who provide the skills, long working hours are often necessary. Significant overtime payments are seen as necessary, in order to deliver positive enquiry outcomes and to minimise further risks of harm. Force administration, governance and review systems are highly intrusive around spending and prudent financial and resource management skills are additional and essential requirements for an SIO. In 2018, the Home Office estimated the costs to police and criminal justice agencies as £812,940 per homicide, with the consequences of each incident — including social harm, lost output and other lost opportunity costs — as £2.3 million per homicide. The total annual cost of homicide offences (at 2015/16 levels) in England and Wales was placed at £1.8 billion (Heeks, 2018). Apart from making a strong case for the urgency of effective crime prevention and homicide suppression measures, this also serves to emphasise the importance of efficiency and cost-effectiveness within the management of homicide investigation. Even outside of the recent era of austerity forces often found the financing and resourcing of major enquiries to be highly challenging, frequently with the resultant impact on resources being felt by other investigations (Neyroud, 2001). The financial pressures facing police leaders regarding homicide investigation are unlikely to ease through any post-austerity climate or uplift in police officer numbers. Whilst the financial costs are huge, they may still appear insignificant when compared to the human consequences of homicide, involving wrecked lives, shattered families and stolen futures.

Detailed 'enquiry parameters' provide for the operational direction of a homicide investigation and largely frame the leadership intentions of the SIO.

Key policy areas around witness management, including the search for further witnesses, information and the means of gathering evidence/testimony are developed in the early stages of the investigation set-up. A number of witnesses may present themselves to the police at or immediately after the discovery of a homicide incident. Others, through fears of violence and/or witness intimidation or tensions in trust and confidence, may fail to assist the police. The SIO must respond positively and sensitively, supported by approaches that reassure individuals and the wider public. This includes reaching out and responding to the needs of diverse communities, their leaders and influencers and sharing the nature of enquiries to support appeals for witnesses and information. For ease of reference, witnesses to a homicide incident may be categorised as follows:

Significant Witnesses

- Those who may have been, or claim to have been an eye-witness or a witness to the immediate event in some other way;
- Those who stand in a particular relationship to the victim or have a central position in the enquiry;
- Vulnerable witnesses — as defined by section 16 Youth Justice and Criminal Evidence Act 1999 (some language reflects 1999 legal terminology);
- Child witnesses under the age of 17;
- Witnesses of any age whose quality of evidence is likely to be diminished because they:
  - Are suffering from a mental disorder (as defined by the Mental Health Act 1983).
  - Have a significant impairment of intelligence and social functioning (learning disability).
  - Have a physical disability or are suffering from a physical disorder.

Under the 1999 Act, vulnerable witnesses can be protected through a number of special measures that include the video or audio recording of their testimony with consent (as opposed to making a written record), and the playing back of the material as evidence-in-chief at court. This reduces some of the trauma of cross-examination and includes the facility to give evidence at court whilst shielded by a screen. The courts also have the facility for vulnerable witnesses to give evidence by live-link video.

Intimidated Witnesses — As Defined by Section 17 Youth Justice and Criminal Evidence Act 1999

Those witnesses whose evidence is likely to be diminished by reason of fear or distress. In determining whether a witness falls into this category, courts should take account of:

- The nature and alleged circumstances of the offence.
- The age of the witness.
- Where relevant, the social and cultural background and ethnic origins of the witness, the domestic and employment circumstances of the witness and any religious beliefs or political opinions of the witness.
- Any behaviour towards the witness by the accused, members of the accused's family or associates, or any other person who is likely to be either an accused person or witness in the proceedings.
- Complainants in cases of sexual assault.
- Witnesses to racially-motivated crime and elderly and frail witnesses, as well as families of homicide victims fall into the category of intimidated witnesses by virtue of further Home Office guidance (2002 and 2005). Intimidated witnesses, who may also be classified as vulnerable, can be similarly afforded special measures at court.

Source: *Murder Investigation Manual* (College of Policing, 2006).

'Intimidated' applies to being intimidated by the unfamiliar surroundings of court proceedings as well as suffering aggression from defendants and/or their supporters.

Hostile Witnesses

This category of witness may or may not also be classified as vulnerable and/or intimidated. They may be witnesses who were hostile to the police investigation from the outset or began as cooperative and helpful to the enquiry and became hostile at some later stage. Such witnesses can have complex needs and require careful and supportive handling. For example, they may be reluctant to appear at court, through a variety of reasons—not merely through fear or intimidation. For example, through work, travel or time-related matters, family reasons or religious beliefs. In extreme cases, the court can issue a witness summons with a power of arrest attached, in order to compel a person to attend court and give evidence. Such cases are rare and in any event can be counterproductive as hostile witnesses are not usually helpful to the court.

Within a trial context in court the term 'hostile witness' signifies someone who is deemed by the judge to be 'not desirous of telling the truth,' something which may become obvious by that witness starting to tell a different story in the witness box to one given earlier when interviewed by the police. Whilst there can be many reasons for this, genuine or otherwise (such as intimidation or threats) the effect in law is to render both the changed testimony in court worthless and earlier statements at the best unreliable and inadmissible hearsay. Hostile witness challenges are heard by the judge in the absence of the jury and any affected testimony 'ruled out' and not heard by the latter.

Conventional Witnesses

This category covers witnesses who are compliant and cooperative, are able to have their evidence testimony recorded in a written format and require no special measures or additional support. SIOs must record their reasons for the categorisation and treatment of witnesses within the policy document and be prepared to account for their decisions. Advances in forensics have created a much more scientific approach to homicide investigation, however the inherently human nature of the crime means that, professionally secured and supported, reliable eye-witness evidence remains both powerful and compelling.

Local enquiries relative to the geographical location of the crime scene(s) are essential components in tracing witnesses to advance an investigation. Those enquiries are also important in generating information and intelligence to expose further leads and signpost additional enquiries and evidential opportunities. Local geographic investigation can take a number of forms. For example, house-to-house enquiries made close to the scene(s) of the crime or at sites of relevant activity, including body disposal sites, suspect(s) escape routes or places where other evidential items have been recovered all have significant potential for further investigative opportunities. House-to-house enquiries can be seen as a traditional and well-established means of investigation, whereby the police literally 'knock doors' and speak to local residents, businesses and the general public about their recollections during the relevant time of the incident or relevant activity. In the early stages of an investigation, this methodology usually takes the form of fast-time 'witness trawls' and includes the hunt for CCTV. As the investigation progresses, however, the house-to-house and local surveys take on a more measured and structured form.

The SIO will formulate that structure, commonly under the management of an experienced detective. This is partly to ensure that all potential evidential opportunities are followed-up but also through the very real likelihood that further information, including CCTV will come to light. It also serves to maintain public interest and, with increased uniform patrols, can help to reassure communities. Furthermore, the SIO may arrange for 'anniversary visits.' These are follow-up police enquiries, made at significant post-event points. For example, the day after the incident, the week after, or even extending to monthly visits or longer. These are designed to trace people who may visit the area infrequently, or on given days of the week and could provide the police with key pieces of information.

Often, the SIO will formulate a questionnaire to direct officers on specific details when interviewing members of the public. In turn, questionnaires are commonly used in conjunction with 'Personal Descriptive Forms' (PDFs), onto which officers document individuals spoken to, including their personal details, appearance and clothing worn at the material time. The use of PDFs can be helpful in identifying persons who may resemble those seen by witnesses at relevant times and assist the police to trace, interview and eliminate 'persons of interest.'

In completing these tasks, investigators must constantly guard against witnesses', and their own, biases, assumptions and prejudices, including *epistemic imbalance*, noting the difference between rejecting someone's word for good reason and out of mere prejudice (Fricker, 2010). In addition, care must be taken not to advance the credibility of witness testimony and other evidence, through *confirmation bias*, i.e. searching for information that confirms prior beliefs and ignoring that which does not, motivated by several different characteristics (Ask, 2006).

Appealing for witnesses and information through mainstream and social media outlets is a significant role for the SIO and other members of the investigation's leadership team. All police forces have well-developed and skilled media relations staff. However, the SIO should exercise discretion when dealing with the media — including social media — to ensure accuracy, clarity and consistency. In relation to the mainstream media, including newsprint, television and radio, there is arguably a difference to be struck between local and national coverage. The local media, particularly local newspapers, are heavily reliant on the good faith of local police forces, in cooperating and facilitating general crime and community stories and pictures. They therefore tend to be more accurate in their representation of local police and community relationships and structures. It does not mean to say that sensationalism never emerges within local media coverage of homicide. Merely that the long-term business model for local media outlets places a higher emphasis on the preservation of positive relationships with local police forces. For the national media outlets, without the same local constraints, approaches can be very different. The SIO's media messages need to be precise and without ambiguity. Information released should be balanced with enough detail to inform, reassure and seek public assistance and support, with an understanding that the public have a fascination and desire to follow the details of major crimes.

The SIO, along with support from the force's media relations functions, must decide what information is appropriate to disclose to the public — always with the ultimate aim of appealing for witnesses and generating information and intelligence. Too much disclosure might assist the offender(s) in gaining information about the investigation and they may, as a result, evade justice. Whilst too little disclosure of information could lead to a loss of public interest and, more damagingly, unhelpful speculation on the part of the media and even less restrained discourse within social media circles involving the development of rumours and conspiracy theories. This can erode community trust and confidence, generate additional work for the enquiry team and make the police appear defensive and remote.

Within a typical homicide investigation, the police structures and processes, including job descriptions and role responsibilities of personnel, are highly defined and well-ordered. However, much about the task of the SIO within the operational practice of homicide investigation is about obtaining knowledge (Innes, 2003), through identifying and acquiring information. This can be a chaotic process (Williams, 2015), particularly at the beginning of an investigation;

there is a need to plot a path through that information, to interpret it, understand and hypothesise or form multiple hypotheses — to order and represent it. This must happen, to take a case through the courts (Grieve, 2015). Knowledge appears in a number of different forms and success lies in converting that knowledge into admissible evidence at court (Williams, 2015). Making sense of the differences between information, intelligence and evidence can be challenging for the families of victims and communities. The police must be able to explain these concepts in clear and appropriate terms and to allow for legal constraints that may prevent full disclosure. For example, information might be very relevant to an investigation but may have been provided anonymously or consist of intelligence gathered through covert policing methods. The provenance of intelligence sources might be sensitive and require substantial moral, ethical or legal protection. Often these areas aren't readily or easily converted into evidence admissible at court. The SIO's duty is to maintain accurate and accountable records, including entries within the policy document that rationalise decision-making. Where appropriate, an experienced SIO will also maintain a separate 'sensitive' document to cover policy areas of intelligence and information — for sharing with the CPS and that, following a successful application to the courts under public interest immunity rules, should not be disclosed to the accused's defence team.

The SIO also has some decision-making around how much information, about certain aspects of the investigation to share with the wider enquiry team. As discussed, there are certain areas, involving the dissemination of sensitive intelligence and information that are legally restricted or only disclosable on a strictly *need-to-know* basis. Historically, SIOs were routinely inclined to restrict information sharing within the enquiry team. Part of this approach was based on retaining some particulars that would be known only to the offender(s) and the SIO (and some other senior leaders). Thus, based on details admitted during interview, the SIO could be sure of the offender's culpability. This approach has become less common, with modern doctrine requiring a more open and ethical approach, through team meetings and briefing sessions. The tactical advantages being that if individual enquiry team members have greater detailed understanding of the investigation they are more likely to identify significant evidential opportunities when presented.

Within the policy document, it is wholly legitimate for the SIO to include any inferences and working hypotheses or hypothetical consideration of theories and events possible within an investigation. These are relevant so that the SIO can test received intelligence and information against the known facts of a case and thus determine its credibility. Care must be taken to ground any working hypothesis within the authentic structures of the investigation's parameters. Any later unproven theories around events are liable to attract criticism and challenge at court and could undermine the prosecution case—notwithstanding the duty of the police to seek, secure and preserve evidence that helps to prove or disprove the guilt of a suspect. The SIO should, of course, be open about any process gone through (Grieve, 2015) in outlining working hypotheses and converting knowledge into evidence. Decisions need to be balanced, consistent with the values of the organization (policing values), and defendable in a court of law (Adlam, 2003). Additionally, within the policy document, the SIO will regularly summarise the progress of the investigation, along with avenues for further enquiries, in the context of documenting a 'mature assessment.' This is also helpful, where the SIO requires some 'slow-time' or 'foot on the ball' moments (see earlier in this chapter), to consolidate understanding, develop thought processes and detail the outcomes of key policy decisions.

In a sense, the policy document provides the legacy of the SIO's leadership of a homicide investigation. It is subject to in-force scrutiny, including internal and, potentially external, review—and also through the coroner's, criminal and appeal courts. Given the evidence of a number of serious case reviews, the conduct of a homicide investigation extends to a lifetime of accountability for the SIO.

The Application of Forensic Science within Homicide Investigations

Forensic science refers to the application of various fields of science and technology to establish facts about a crime and secure evidence that is admissible in both civil and criminal law. The word 'forensic' originates from the Latin word *forensis* which translates as 'before the forum [in public]' (Forensic Science Service, 2013). Forensic science, as it relates to the investigation of crime, covers the study and interpretation of a broad range of scientific and technological disciplines including; fingerprint analysis, forensic pathology, entomology, linguistics, odontology, document examination and DNA (deoxyribonucleic acid) analysis. Developments in forensic science techniques and associated applications seem to be increasing exponentially. Not least through the principle of 'Moore's Law' in computer processing—the identification that approximate processing performance would double every two years (Shein, 2020). This has current and future consequences for the scale, speed and analysis of forensic and technical databases both nationally and internationally. Within the UK, for example, this includes the recording of millions of vehicle journeys, undertaken on motorways, many A roads and through city centres, by a national network of automatic number-plate recognition (ANPR) cameras. Furthermore, by 2011, the UK was assessed as having more than four million CCTV cameras and the largest DNA database in the world, said to have more than 4.25 million entries, covering one in every 14 inhabitants (Bingham, 2011).

DNA profiling and analysis arguably represents the most important scientific development in crime investigation since the implementation of fingerprint technology at the turn of the twentieth century. The DNA double-helix structure, identified through the 1962 Nobel Prize winning work of James Watson, Francis Crick and Maurice Wilkins, led on to significant advances in DNA profiling.

In 1984, Professor Alec Jeffreys discovered the variations in DNA, unique to each individual (University of Leicester, 2019). This breakthrough asserted these variations—meaning that even identical siblings do not share an identical DNA profile (though reliable 'familial DNA' can be traced across blood relatives). Furthermore, the FBI has estimated the odds of unrelated people sharing genetic (DNA) markers to be as remote as, 1 in 113 billion (Felch, 2008). The broad consensus being that DNA profiles are either unique, or the sharing of profiles so vanishingly small, it amounts to the same thing.

The sensitivity of DNA analysis further improved with the development of low copy number (LCN) DNA testing techniques. Since 1999, one billionth of a gram, equivalent to between 150 and 160 cells of DNA—has been the standard starting template for the purposes of obtaining a profile (Mansfield, 2010). This presents both opportunities and challenges for the police in the gathering of evidence at crime scenes. It includes the identification and prosecution of offenders from objects, suspects, witnesses and victims and the successful review of sometimes decades-old, unsolved cases. Received wisdom often implies that forensic evidence is viewed and presented as 'hard fact' (Brookman, 2005). However, the sensitivity of testing and the possibilities of the cross-contamination of samples, including through moveable objects, means that DNA evidence recovered from crime scenes could be linked to persons otherwise unconnected to the crime. Through Edmond Locard's longstanding 'principle of exchange' (circa 1912) — i.e. that material is physically exchanged between any surface that comes into contact with another — crime scene investigators and forensic scientists could inadvertently transfer DNA material between evidential items, or between scenes and during the recovery and packaging of items. Vulnerabilities also exist within laboratory conditions, during the examination and analysis of forensic items. DNA particles might be transferred to other surfaces, including central exhibits in the case (even though they may have been packaged), because a particle on the outside may end up on the inside (Mansfield, 2010). It is therefore essential that the SIO remains open-minded regarding the qualities of forensic science and takes on a questioning viewpoint, as forensic science often provides only moderately strong corroborative evidence and rarely presents absolute proof of guilt in isolation (College of Policing, 2006).

DNA is undoubtedly a remarkable discovery, but like any scientific advance, it should be treated with respect, and we should all be vigilant about its limitations (Mansfield, 2010). Alec Jeffreys (University of Leicester, 2019) makes a further point about DNA evidence. 'It does not solve crimes. It establishes whether sample X comes from person Y. It is then up to the court to interpret that — in the context of other evidence in a criminal case.' Therefore, forensic strategies developed and implemented by the SIO must effectively support and complement broader strategies and the investigation's overall direction. The success of DNA profiling technology and the sensitivity of forensic testing means that multiple items of evidence are available to investigation teams. Costs and budgetary constraints drive the simple reality that not every evidential exhibit seized during an investigation, and which might bear DNA or other forensic evidence, can be subjected to analysis. The SIO, working with forensic team partners must therefore prioritise, through proportionality and necessity, those exhibits that provide the best evidential opportunities. Any decision-making must be justifiable, not least in a court of law where defence advocates may argue their client's innocence on the basis that additional forensic testing would have revealed the true offender's identity.

Exponential advances in scientific techniques provide a large array of scientific support for the police — often applied under bespoke circumstances and subject to the needs of the investigation. Roles range across ligature and knot specialists (homicides involving hangings and bindings), ballistics experts (firearms and ammunition), blood pattern (and blood spatter) analysts, entomologists (study of insects and associations with body decomposition), botanists and criminological and psychological disciplines involving offending behaviours, offender profiling and geographical profiling. There are also more recent 'digital' forensic science roles, involving the rapidly expanding requirements of data and ICT-based analysis. SIOs must constantly manage their expectations about what forensic science can deliver in terms of quality, quantity and interpretation. Public opinion (and by distinction victims, witnesses and juries) is heavily influenced by crime fiction and broadcast documentaries where serious and complex homicide investigations, along with detailed forensic analysis, are rapidly bundled and neatly concluded. Queen's counsel, Michael Mansfield provides a salutary assessment of the application of forensic science:

> 'For a sizeable proportion of what passes as science depends upon the eye of the beholder and is highly subjective, and the perception of physical phenomena is highly susceptible, both consciously and unconsciously, to all sorts of personal beliefs and predilections. Without rigorous awareness and precautions, such a situation can have disastrous consequences, including, particularly in my area of the law, wrongful conviction and imprisonment.' (Mansfield, 2010)

Digital Forensics and Data Analytics — Future Technological Implications for Homicide Investigation

By 2022, the number of active smartphone users in the UK is projected to grow to 54 million individuals (O'Dea, 2019). The increasingly data rich environment and the way that people lead their lives, means that most crimes now contain a digital component. The future of tackling homicide — in common with general crime investigation — is one of increasing technological advancement and digital influences. Individual members of society will increasingly leave (digital) spores of identification and movements (McDermid, 2019). This provides investigators with an expanding list of standard evidential requirements involving mobile phone data and cell site analysis, computer technology, text and email messaging, social media, CCTV, ANPR and police body worn video cameras. All have causal links to the increasing complexity of homicide investigation, evidence gathering and the management of information. Whilst the sheer quantity of digitally-based information available to investigators provides clear benefits, there are also considerable operational and technical challenges. Initially these might involve accessing multiple platforms, often cloaked by encryption, with the further necessity of data washing to ensure relevance and compliance with rules of disclosure and other legal requirements concerning data handling and retention.

Through Moore's Law (above), the exponential expansion and speed of computer processing will increase the capacity of forensic data analysis. Nevertheless, information at scale will still require effective management, sifting and processing in order to make sense of the granular detail required for effective homicide investigation. An enduring feature of homicide investigation is the necessity for constant review — both formal and informal, so the performance of the enquiry can be evaluated and quality assured. Furthermore, it provides a mechanism for checking that no investigative opportunities have been missed (Innes, 2003). Additionally, the high levels of technical complexity relating to the conduct of various domains of enquiry means that to some extent errors have to be expected (Ibid). Although, policing agencies have invested in expanding IT systems for data collection, storage and retrieval, risks of public harm and damage to police organizational effectiveness remain, with the fear that important information may be lost within the system (Ibid). An important element of the investigative process is the ability to retrieve errors and to ensure that they do not completely undermine the integrity of an ongoing investigation (Ibid).

Predictive analysis and artificial intelligence systems are due to transform processing outputs and outcomes through the growing development and expansion of data analytics — framed by increasingly powerful algorithms. West Midlands Police provides an example of this approach. The force is developing its own data analytics programme, towards the management of offenders and the prevention of serious crime. Algorithms are set to interrogate a range of systems, involving millions of lines of data, held within West Midlands Police, in order to predict and support interventions to suppress future criminal behaviours, within a database of 200,000 offenders who are likely to transition from a state of low-to-high harm offending. The initiative includes £9.5 million of funding from the Home Office, which is hoping to make the algorithm available to all forces in England and Wales once it has been fully-tested (Malnick, 2020).

Data analytics will inevitably play a role in homicide prevention and suppression. The National Police Chiefs Council lead for Data Analytics, Detective Chief Superintendent Chris Todd, outlines that, 'the predictive tool under development is intended to identify those at the outset of criminal behaviour so that positive interventions can be put in place before they become most harmful' (Todd, 2019). The use of algorithms to inform professional policing practice is highly controversial and has profound implications for public policy, including the role of the private sector and overseas companies in developing appropriate technologies. The police use of data analytics and predictive analysis prompts the application of policing led interventions in people's lives — potentially from a young age. The predisposition to identify individuals and predict their criminal potential, based upon the machinations of an algorithm has serious implications for human rights and the nature of policing by consent. In addition, there is the already recognised nature of racial and demographic bias within data systems, creating dangers of analysis driving practice and the discrimination of minority groups, individuals and the disadvantaged within society. A great deal of the narrative has focussed on perceptions of bias in the data and therefore an assumption of bias in the application of the science it enables. Based on some early applications of data analytics, such assumptions are not unfounded (Todd, 2019).

To the credit of West Midlands Police, an independent ethics committee has been implemented that includes community activists, academics and lawyers, who regularly meet to address questions of legitimacy, inform future developments and scrutinise practice. Whilst machine-learning algorithms are currently being used for limited policing purposes, there is potential for the technology to do much more, and the lack of a regulatory and governance framework for its use is concerning (Babuta, 2018). The call for tighter regulation has also come from within the police service itself, with Cressida Dick, the Metropolitan Police Commissioner recently saying,

> 'We're now tiptoeing into a world of robotics, AI (artificial intelligence) and machine learning ... The next step might be predictive policing. People are starting to get worried about that ... particularly because of the potential for bias in the data or the algorithm [such as] live facial recognition software.' (Simpson, 2019)

She went on to prescribe that advances in facial recognition technology, artificial intelligence (AI) and robotics necessitated a new code of ethics and a strict legal framework (Ibid).

It is clear that these technologies are here to stay. There is little doubt that, in common with many other organizational and governmental approaches, algorithms will drive the analysis and interpretation of data in order to drive policy and practice. Digital forensics and data analytics have huge potential to increase the efficiency, effectiveness and economy of homicide investigation. Nevertheless, pressing questions remain around equality and the potential for bias within those data sets that underpin the application of the science. Unless these questions are satisfactorily resolved by legislators and professional practitioners and with full public consultation, there are substantial risks of undermining police legitimacy and community trust and confidence, particularly within minority groups.

Conclusion

At a pragmatic, instrumental level, in attempting to identify and catch killers, detectives are looking to collect information in order to establish how and why the victim died (Innes, 2003). The collection of information results in the acquisition of knowledge — the understanding of which allows the SIO to form a working hypothesis or multiple hypotheses regarding the details of the homicide incident. Knowledge must then be converted, through a rigorous, legally-compliant and ethical process of accreditation, where it can be represented through evidence in a court of law. The process of collecting information, knowledge conversion and the securing and preserving of evidence can be resource intensive and highly industrialised. Much depends on the complexity and nature of the homicide incident under investigation and effective investigation is always about making sense of granular detail.

Increasing professionalisation of homicide investigations owes much to reforms implemented through serious case reviews and previous *cause célèbres* like the Birmingham Six, Yorkshire Ripper murders and the murder of Stephen Lawrence. Police investigative structures and approaches, including the application of forensic science, matched with rigorous governance, quality assurance systems and review mechanisms have all been welcome features of best practice. Additionally, detective training and professional accreditation have been transformed, particularly since the MacPherson Enquiry into Stephen Lawrence's death. The SIO is the pivotal leader within homicide investigation with the cadre predominantly formed from those at inspector level, with training, experience and expertise overcoming the hegemony of the senior policing hierarchy. This partly signals work to change police culture where seniority and the police leader encapsulate ideals about both the heroism of the police *and* the heroism of leadership (Davis and Marisa, 2020).

This chapter has highlighted the issues of personal resilience and increases in the numbers of active homicide investigations allocated to individual SIOs. The recognition of stress and trauma in policing, together with a focus on the well-being of staff, represent a welcome shift in resisting dominant assumptions of the 'ideal' police officer (Ibid). It will take time for the present Government's ambition of an uplift in police numbers to work through to increased detective resilience, particularly within those specialist homicide investigation roles. In the meantime, risks remain of SIO 'burnout' and personal capacity that have potential for public harm.

Comment has also been made around emerging and future technologies, including data analytics, the use of algorithms and predictive analysis. These are all due to transform the daily lives of people and have a significant impact on the prevention and detection of crime, as well as on criminal behaviours. Ethical, legal and societal questions remain around the application of new technologies in policing. These must not contradict the reforms that have been made to improve the professionalisation and effectiveness of homicide investigation, over the past few decades. In common with policing generally, the journey has been one of ultimate progress, although the course has been far from smooth or predictable (Brain, 2010). There remains the certainty that policing, including the challenges of homicide investigation, will continue to dominate the future discourse around crime and criminal justice.

Questions to consider:
- What are the challenges of investigating more critical examples of homicide (a lack of an identifiable agent) within the context of the processes outlined in this chapter?
- In what ways does the investigative process differ from main-stream media accounts?
- What are some of the limitations of eye-witness testimony?
- In what way does the 'dark figure of crime' impact upon the recording of homicide statistics?

References

ACPO, Centrex (College of Policing) (2006), *Murder Investigation Manual*, Wyboston: National Centre for Policing Excellence.

Adlam, R and Villiers, P (2003), *Police Leadership in the Twenty-first Century*, Winchester: Waterside Press.

Ask, K (2006), *Criminal Investigation: Motivation, Emotion and Cognition in the Processing of Evidence*, Sweden: University of Gothenburg.

Babuta, A. O. (2018), *Machine Learning Algorithms and Police Decision-Making: Legal, Ethical and Regulatory Challenges*, September 21: http://www.rusi.org

Bingham, T (2011), *The Rule of Law*, London: Penguin.

Brain, T. (2010), *A History of Policing in England and Wales from 1974: A Turbulant Journey*, Oxford: Oxford University Press.

Brookman, F (2005), *Understanding Homicide*, London: Sage.

Centrex (2005), 'Major Incident Room Standardised Administrative Procedures,' *Major Incident Room Standardised Administrative Procedures*, Wyboston: Centrex.

College of Policing (2006), 'Murder Investigation Manual,' *Murder Investigation Manual* (Redacted edn.) — Authorised Professional Practice.

College of Policing (2014), 'Public Protection: Responding to a Sudden Death,' June, College of Policing — Approved Professional Practice.

College of Policing (2019), 'Family Liaison Officer (FLO),' https://profdev.college. police.uk/professional-profile/family-liaison-officer-flo/. Retrieved from College of Policing.

College of Policing (2019), 'Practice Advice: Dealing with Sudden Unexpected Death.'

CPS (2019), 'CPS: Murder and Manslaughter; Legal Guidance, Violent Crime,' March 3: https://www.cps.gov.uk/legal-guidance/homicide-murder-and-manslaughter

CPS (2019), 'Code for Crown Prosecutors,' March 18: www.cps.gov.uk/legal-guidance/ homicide-murder-and-manslaughter

Davis, C. and Marisa, S. (2020). *Critical Perspectives on Police Leadership,* Bristol: Policy Press.

Driscoll, C (2015), *In Pursuit of the Truth—A Life in the Met,* London: Ebury Press.

Elkin, M. (2019), *Homicide in England and Wales: Year Ending March 2018,* February 7: https://www.ons.gov.uk/peoplepopulationandcommunity/crimeandjustice/articles/ homicideinenglandandwales/yearendingmarch2018#toc

European Commission (2019), 'Peace, justice and strong institutions (statistical annex),' May: https://ec.europa.eu/eurostat/statistics-explained/index. php?title=SDG_16_-_Peace,_justice_and_strong_institutions_(statistical_ annex)#Death_rate_due_to_homicide

Felch, D. A. (2008), 'FBI Resists Scrutiny of "Matches",' July 20, *Los Angeles Times,* Los Angeles, CA.

Forensic Pathology Unit of the Home Office (2015), 'A Study into Decision Making at the Initial Scene of Unexpected Death,' January: https://assets.publishing.service. gov.uk/government/uploads/system/uploads/attachment_data/file/484298/Report_ into_the_2012_FSR_FP_Audit_Publication_copy_pdf.pdf

Fricker, M (2009), *Epistemic Injustice: Power & the Ethics of Knowing.* Oxford: Oxford University Press.

Forensic Science Service (2013), 'An Introduction to Forensic Science': fss.org.uk

Grieve, J. (2015), 'Recent Cold Case Reviews of the Jack the Ripper Case,' February 6, YouTube: https://www.youtube.com/watch?v=JBlbXCR2HCA&t=183s

Hannah, S. (2018), 'It's no mystery that crime is the biggest-selling genre in books,' April 12, *Guardian.*

Heeks, R. T. (2018), *The Economic and Social Costs of Crime,* London: Home Office.

Hines, W. (2019), @InspsWMFed—from Twitter, Birmingham, UK.

Innes, M. (2003), *Investigating Murder: Detective Work and the Police Response to Criminal Homicide,* Oxford: Oxford University Press.

Ministry of Justice (2007), 'Understanding the Corporate Manslaughter and Corporate Homicide Act 2007,' October: https://www.justice.gov.uk/downloads/legislation/bills-acts/manslaughter-homicide/manslaughter-homicide-act-2007.pdf

Malnick, E. (2020), 'Fears over police AI to identify future criminals,' February 23, *Sunday Times*, pp. 1–2.

Mansfield, M (2010), *Memoirs of a Radical Lawyer,* London: Bloomsbury.

McDermid, V. (2019), *David Wilson's Crime Files* (Interview), BBC Scotland.

Moore, G (1965), *Electronics Magazine*.

Neyroud, B. (2001). *Policing, Ethics and Human Rights,* Cullompton: Willan Publlishing.

O'Dea, S (2019), November 22, statista.com: https://www.statista.com/study/21666/smartphones-in-the-uk-statista-dossier/

Police and Criminal Evidence Act 1984, Section 24.

Rowe, M. (2014), *Introduction to Policing,* London: Sage.

Shein, E. (2020), 'Moore's Law turns 55: Is it still relevant?' April 17, Tech Republic: https://www.techrepublic.com/article/moores-law-turns-55-is-it-still-relevant/

Shepherd and Griffiths (2013), *Investigative Interviewing*, Oxford: Oxford University Press.

Simpson, J. C. (2019), 'Beware of Orwellian state, says Met chief Cressida Dick,' September 4, *Times*.

Todd, C. (2019), 'Putting ethics at the heart of data analytics,' April 30, Policing Insight: http://www.policinginsight.com

University of Leicester (2019), 'Genetic fingerprinting explained,' Department of Genetics and Genome Biology: https://www2.le.ac.uk/departments/genetics/jeffreys/explained

West Midlands Police (2014), Critical Incident Policy (Ops 23): https://foi.west-midlands.police.uk/wp-content/uploads/2014/05/Critical-Incidents.pdf

Williams, A (2014), *Forensic Criminology.* Abingdon and New York: Routledge.

CHAPTER 11

Conclusion

'Violence ends up defeating itself. It creates bitterness in the survivors and brutality in the destroyers'

Martin Luther King Jnr, Civil rights leader

Bringing this Textbook to a Close

As we draw this exploration into some of the worst atrocities committed by humanity to a close, let's briefly review and unpack some of the key themes identified. As with most social inquiries, the investigation may appear rather simple and straightforward at first, giving us a misguided perception that the answer(s) are just out-of-reach or out-of-frame. Despite this initial perception, though, it is apparent that even the process of defining homicide is deeply contentious and fraught with conceptual ambiguity.

When we began this project, we wanted to challenge the lack of nuance in predominantly media discussions around homicide and notions of what constitutes 'violence.' The book's opening chapters sought to explain, at times bluntly, the inadequacies of traditional frameworks and orthodoxies that have usually been used to investigate the subject area. As detailed within the opening, this textbook aims to draw upon — where relevant — critical strands of Criminology and Zemiology in order to move beyond traditional notions of criminality, homicide, violence, and harm. Within this therefore, the concluding chapter aims to consolidate these various discussions and provide some final remarks.

The first chapter to explore homicide critically examined concepts such as domestic, confrontational and revenge forms of homicide, noting the evident and — at times — more subtle differences between these criminal actions. So too, it explored historic and current trends in homicide rates in the UK, concluding that single homicide remains a relatively rare form of crime despite its recent statistical growth. It was also noted that single homicide, for the most part, is a male phenomenon both in terms of offending and victimisation. Plus that typologies are not exhaustive, nor necessarily fixed in nature, meaning that homicide can be divided in more ways than the ones discussed throughout both this particular chapter and the book more generally.

The most important message to take away from this book is that single forms of homicide are indeed rare events, despite what the mainstream media may present and perpetuate. *Chapter 3* explored the various theoretical explanations behind why someone may harm and kill another individual. Specifically, it was revealed that there is indeed no one explanation behind why someone would fatally harm another individual, and that we need to carefully consider a range of factors both within and external to the individual.

Chapter 4 was the first to introduce the concept of multiple homicide in the form of serial murder. One of the first factors discussed in relation to this form of homicide was the importance of definitions, and how those adopted by various law enforcement agencies either increased or decreased the perceived occurrence of serial murder. So too, that chapter also explored how there are currently two dominant schools of thought regarding theoretical explanations behind serial murder: the *medical-psychological tradition* and the *structural tradition*. These two traditions are indicative of wider debates in Criminology concerning whether we gain a deeper understanding into the actualities of such crimes by either exploring the internal mechanisms behind people who commit such crimes, or rather critically examining the wider social contexts in which they reside.

Chapter 5 continued this discussion pertaining to the notion of multiple homicide, and examined instances of mass and spree murder. In particular, it further explored the complexity of defining such forms of multiple homicide, along with the various similarities and differences between mass and spree murder characteristics. It also examined how acts of both mass and spree murder were generally a male phenomenon, and critically engaged with the contentious issue of the availability of firearms in certain countries.

Chapter 6 continued by examining mass murder and, specifically, acts of genocide committed by States. The chapter provided a case study of reserve police Battalion 101, and critically explored how 'ordinary men' could ultimately engage in such extreme acts of cruelty at the behest of those in power. It also explored the various stages of genocide, and how various configurations of structural and cultural violence can manifest themselves and set the stage for systematic mass murder of certain groups.

The theme of State sanctioned violence was further explored in *Chapter 7*, in which the death penalty and police killings were explored. Similar to the preceding chapter, it applied critical notions of violence beyond physical manifestations in order to demonstrate how particular individuals and groups are disproportionately subjected to such forms of State authorised violence. *Chapter 8* examined how, via the process of neo-liberalism and globalisation, private corporations motivated by the perpetual pursuit of profit can also inflict tremendous harm and even death. The chapter also presented some of the primary challenges and obstacles faced when attempting to prosecute and punish such forms of homicide, highlighting some of the key limitations of criminology in the process.

Chapter 9 provided an in-depth critical overview and examination into the consumption of murder and, specifically, serial murder. Specifically, this chapter discussed how, via a range of different media and products, society appears to be fixated with specific forms of murder that have now turned into a 'hot commodity.' Be it the numerous films and television shows, 'murder tours', 'death museums' and even serial killer 'action figures,' society appears to have positioned such criminals as celebrities within the modern mediascape.

Chapter 10 proceeded to provide an in-depth overview of the process involved in homicide investigations, with particular attention towards such factors as the categorisation of homicides, along with the various steps that need to be followed by investigators and prosecutors.

To summarise, these various chapters present an in-depth and multi-faceted overview of the complex nature of homicide and what constitutes violence, along with the various challenges in attempting to address and punish such actions.

Homicide: Conceptual Disarray?

One of the central questions asked throughout this book has been: why do people only recognise and understand particular forms of violence that results in death? While we emphasise the importance of understanding more conventional notions of murder and other forms of homicide that are a result of direct acts of violence, it is also important—as criminologists—for us to see past this rather myopic conceptualisation. Similar to how this book started, we return to society's fascination with the act of serial murder, perhaps the most well-known and popularised form of direct violence, in order to understand this fixation with this very specific form of homicide. According to Seltzer (1997), the rare crime of serial murder, and society's supposed fascination with such a phenomenon, is best understood and conceptualised within the notion of 'wound culture.' Seltzer suggests that such a culture is defined as a collective that is addicted to violence, 'not merely [as] a collective spectacle but one of the crucial sites where private desire and public space cross' (Ibid, p. 2). In exploring this mass addiction to the spectacle of violence, Seltzer denotes:

> 'The convening of the public around scenes of violence—the rushing to the scene of the accident, the milling around the point of impact—has come to make up a wound culture: the public fascination with torn and opened bodies and torn and opened persons, a collective gathering around shock, trauma, and the wound.' (Seltzer, 1997, p. 3)

Taking the above quote into consideration, Seltzer suggests that society consists of a pathological public sphere, which is underpinned by a fusion of the public space and an individual's private fantasy—ultimately blurring the lines between what is public and what is private. As a consequence, the public have become obsessive in sympathising and gathering around the spectacle of others' suffering. Furthermore, the pathological public sphere is, according to Seltzer, everywhere and crossed by the vague and shifting 'lines between the singularity or privacy of the subject, on the one side, and collective forms of representation, exhibition, and witnessing, on the other' (Ibid, p. 4). Seltzer's primary aim is to define and articulate contemporary culture as an immense and multi-faceted system, designed by philosophies and concepts that often splinter into intolerable antagonisms and exasperating obscurities. In attempting to illustrate and contextualise this argument, he refers to his perceived personification of society's 'wound culture': the serial killer. According to Seltzer, serial killers and the act of serial killing 'has its place in a culture in which addictive violence has become a collective spectacle, one of the crucial sites where private desire and public fantasy cross' (1998, p. 253).

While we agree with this notion put forth by Seltzer, it is important to acknowledge that this is predicated on the rather restrictive definition of violence that consists only of those acts with an identifiable agent. Given the extreme difficulties many face in attempting to identify and articulate other forms of violence (such as the structural and cultural forms defined and alluded to throughout this book) (Treadwell et al, 2013), it makes sense that we, as a collective, hold such rigid views towards violence and the subsequent harms and deaths that they may cause. Even by just adopting this narrow definition of violence, it is clear that there is still a myriad of issues that obfuscate the reality of homicide. For instance, we have explored the very complex process of separating the various conceptualisations of manslaughter (voluntary and involuntary) from those actions deemed to be murder. As we have covered earlier, the definition used to determine an act of murder is also contentious, with significant emphasis being placed on the importance of *mens rea*. As a result of this, we tend to ignore or neglect other configurations that can result in the death of one or many individuals. For instance, with the current advancements in technology and changing nature of the work place, harms are continually shifting and may, in certain instances, result in the death of an individual who was not victim to direct forms of violence. So too, it has become evident that—as criminologists—we tend to focus on those actions already codified in criminal law and, as such, we fail to recognise and fully understand the range of harms that exist beyond those recognised in law.

Homicide, Violence and the Mediascape

For us to have a more comprehensive and nuanced understanding of homicide beyond simply definitions generated by criminal law, we need to recognise the importance of how cultural representations of violence also shape society's understandings. Specifically, as we move beyond the arguments and concepts presented in this book, it is important to continually question and critique why certain forms of violence (and by extension homicides) are continually presented to us via a multitude of media platforms (films, television, mainstream media news coverage), while other forms are barely mentioned or ignored entirely. We are in an age where the serial killer and mass shooter dominate our homicide 'lexicon', yet we rarely consider the devastating impact of corporate killings nor the role of the State in some of history's most tragic moments. For instance, at the time of writing this conclusion, research conducted at University College London on the impact of austerity reported that an estimated 120,000 deaths could be linked to health and social care cuts (Watkins et al, 2017). While it is understandable that people tend to focus on those extreme acts of violence that disrupt normality (such as serial killers, knife crime and acts of terrorism) due to their perceived news value, we should also consider those acts of violence inherent within normality itself. Despite this need to re-orientate this discussion, we continually fail to properly identify, articulate, and critically discuss these normalised forms of violence (and subsequent deaths) — why is this the case?

The ever-increasing popularity of mainstream media accounts of serial murder and associated violence within popular culture serve as a distraction from the objective violence that has proliferated and eventually culminated in the incessant stream of violent reactions within contemporary society. Whilst the consumer gazes at the screen reliving dulcet accounts of 'familiar monsters' such as Ed Kemper and Ted Bundy (and their fictional equivalents in the form of Hannibal Lecter and Dexter), there has been a fundamental shift in Seltzer's wound culture. No longer are these familiar monsters the existential threat they were once perceived to be, nor were they ever. In the increasingly destabilised west they are a both a comfort zone for the viewer to access the familiar violence whilst disavowing the realities of subjective (direct) violence. Such 'evil' caricatures of the most extreme and unconscionable human actions presented within a space the viewer perceives as tangible allows such a retreat from the realities of both symbolic and ontic violence. In an age where mass shootings are commonplace (Gun Violence Archive, 2019), Daesh have spawned as a by-product of the invasion of Iraq (Anderson, 2017) and African-Americans are still routinely murdered during routine policing duties (Cazenave, 2018), the subjective violence has perhaps never been greater. Meanwhile objective violence is routinely displayed within the nation, most notably in recent years through the Flint Water Crisis (Clark, 2019) the Black Lives Matter movement (Lowery, 2017) and the detainment of minors deemed to be within the country illegally (BBC News, 2019). All of this before we account for the catastrophic effects of climate change yet to come which loom over every nation and society on the planet.

If we too combine the onset of developed technologies as previously mentioned, with the prevalence of websites such as WorldStarHipHop or the notorious 'Bum Fights' we can see that the western world does not have a fascination with torn and open bodies *per se*, but a need to acknowledge violence as a part of their lived reality and digest this within a safe and palpable manner which enables the fetishist disavowal of the wider harms they are bound into through society's current structures.

Other forms of violent media can be utilised to demonstrate this aside from those focusing on serial murder. For instance, we see an increase in 'palatable violence' within consumer culture, such as the exponential rise in popularity of mixed martial arts in recent years. Within this particular modicum the Ultimate Fighting Championship (UFC) is the prime example with a meteoritic rise over the previous decade which resulted in some particular fights being as high-grossing as top-level boxing. So too, especially in the UK we have seen a rise in bare knuckle boxing of late. Such sports which were previously marginalised are now regularly televised. Within this notion we can begin to draw historical comparisons. Indeed within the Roman Empire it was commonplace for emperors to utilise the amphitheatre and associated inter-personal violence as a public spectacle to distract the population from the reality of the politics of the time (Kohne and Ewigleben, 2000).

The torn and open wound (i.e. the serial murderer, knife crime and acts of mass murder) is a familiar monster which we the audience can brush upon and against. This offers the opportunity to recognise that society is increasingly violent, despite the claims of academics such as Pinker (2011), but to fetishistically disavow the realities of the violence which proliferates in contemporary society. Much of the violence in not tangible, physical nor visual in a way which enables the general public to ascertain and make sense of it. Violence is much more than just a physical act of interpersonal devastation and to grasp onto the notion that it is as simplistic as the 'psychopath' who wreaks destruction on a community before being apprehended is somewhat comforting. The confrontation between the individual and the actuality that violence is perhaps infinite and out of their control is at best uncomfortable. With the acknowledgement that violence is not dispensed in a finite, clear cut and easily recognisable way almost impossible.

To put this more simply, we generally fail to scrutinise those who operate within the upper echelons of society—those individuals or institutions with much economic and cultural capital. Such individuals and institutions have significant influence in how certain behaviours are codified in law, and how the said behaviours are represented in the mainstream media. Yet, as this book has demonstrated in the chapters that explored death at the hands of the State and corporate killings, we need to take a much closer look at how the actions of those with tremendous amounts of capital can cause far more harm than other forms of homicide that dominate headlines. In essence, while it is indeed important to acknowledge and address orthodox accounts of violence that can result in death, we need to also pay careful attention to those forms of systemic violence that due to their very nature tend to go unnoticed.

Closing Comments

When it comes to the concept of 'crime' and more specifically 'homicide', almost without exception, serial killers are at the front and centre of students' awareness and, for some, one of the reasons why they enrolled on a Criminology degree course. Also prominent are notions of policing, popular understandings of prisons, and a great many tabloid inspired 'usual suspects' that come to over-saturate popular discussions around crime. Of course, the term crime and the spheres of crime and criminal justice are much broader, and yet, all too frequently we have found that a tendency to see crime in a rather narrow way is the hallmark of the contemporary moment.

In the face of growing disparity between the rich and poor, unimaginable environmental devastation, increasing far right sentiments and, with the advent of social media, the notion a 'social bulimia' (Young, 2007) in which more and more people feel alienated, now is the time to move beyond sensationalism and well-worn tropes and towards a more meaningful form of academic/public dialogue. This is only further compounded when we consider that we are witnessing the rise of 'fake news.' As a result, crime has become a commodity which is packaged and sold to an audience who have become primed to alter their views and perceptions to fit whatever is the next 'horrific' and 'shocking' 'newsworthy' story they are presented with. The potency of this statement is only strengthened when we consider a tweet of billionaire reality television personality and 45th President of the USA Donald J Trump:

'It is my opinion that many of the leaks coming out of the White House are fabricated lies made up by the #FakeNews media.' (@realDonaldTrump, 28 May 2017)

Certain hot topics can be effortlessly instrumentalised: the fear of alienation, the abuse of power, and questions of war and peace are all at risk. Academics, students and members of the public need to be able to look beyond the next sensationalised news headline or tweet in order to gain a more insightful and holistic understanding of crime, violence, and harm. So too, as an academic discipline, it is of the upmost importance that Criminology continues to question and critically scrutinise the intellectual 'toolkits' available to us, and whether or not they have utility in elucidating the challenges posed in contemporary society.

It is within this academic mission to remain critical and in tune with modern challenges that this textbook attempts to re-orientate and re-engage with these orthodox accounts of homicide in a more nuanced and meaningful way, whilst also shedding some much needed light on other lesser known forms of violence that can result in death.

We argue that, alongside the sciences, including Astronomy, Physics and Biology, Criminology is of the utmost importance with regard to informing the public of the complexities, nuances and challenges we all face in an effort to create a more peaceful, safe, and fair society.

References

Anderson, S. (2017), *Fractured Lands: How the Arab World Came Apart*, London: Anchor Books.

BBC News (2019), 'Child refugees "still being held" at Dungavel Centre,' 1 June: https://www.bbc.co.uk/news/uk-scotland-48479102

Cazenave, N. A. (2018), *Killing African Americans: Police and Vigilante Violence as a Racial Control*, New York: Routledge.

Clark, A. (2019), *The Poisoned City: Flint's Water and the American Urban Tragedy*, London: Picador.

Gun Violence Archive (2019): https://www.gunviolencearchive.org/

Kohne, E. and Ewigleben, C. (2000), *Gladiators and Caesars: The Power of Spectacle in Ancient Rome*, California: California University Press.

Pinker, S. (2011), *The Better Angels of Our Nature*, London: Penguin Books.

Seltzer, S. (1997), '"Wound Culture": Trauma in the Pathological Public Sphere,' MIT Press, Vol. 80, pp. 3–26.

Treadwell, J; Briggs, D, Winlow, S and Hall, S. (2013), 'Shopocalypse Now: Consumer Culture and the English Riots of 2011,' *British Journal of Criminology*, Volume 53(1), pp. 1–17.

Watkins, J., Wulaningsih, W., Da Zhou C., Marshall, D. C., Sylianteng, G. D. C., Rosa, P. G. D., Miguel, V. A., Raine, R., King, L. P. and Maruthappu, M. (2017), 'Effects of Health and Social Care Spending Constraints on Mortality in England: A Time Trend Analysis,' *BMJ Open*, doi: 10.1136/bmjopen-2017-017722

Index

www.ingramcontent.com/pod-product-compliance
Lightning Source LLC
Chambersburg PA
CBHW060030030426
42334CB00019B/2258